TRAIL
POSTS

TRAIL POSTS

A LITERARY EXPLORATION OF CALIFORNIA'S STATE PARKS

EDITED BY
MALCOLM MARGOLIN AND MARIKO CONNER

WITH SELECTION INTRODUCTIONS
BY SYLVIA LINSTEADT

FOREWORD BY
ELIZABETH GOLDSTEIN,
CALIFORNIA STATE PARKS FOUNDATION

Heyday, Berkeley, California
California State Parks Foundation, San Francisco, California

Library of Congress Cataloging-in-Publication Data
Trail posts : a literary exploration of California's State Parks /
edited by Malcolm Margolin and Mariko Conner ; with selection introductions by Sylvia Linsteadt ; foreword by Elizabeth
Goldstein.
    pages cm
  ISBN 978-1-59714-272-4 (pbk. : alk. paper)
  1. Parks--California--Literary collections. 2. California--Liter-
ary collections. I. Margolin, Malcolm, editor of compilation.
II. Conner, Mariko, editor of compilation.
  PN6071.P293T73 2014
  808.8'032794--dc23
                    2014005781

Cover Photo and Design: Ashley Ingram
Interior Design/Typesetting: Ashley Ingram
Printing and Binding: United Graphics, Mattoon, IL
Map: Ben Pease, Pease Press Cartography

Orders, inquiries, and correspondence should be addressed to:
    Heyday
    P.O. Box 9145, Berkeley, CA 94709
    (510) 549-3564, Fax (510) 549-1889
    www.heydaybooks.com

10 9 8 7 6 5 4 3 2 1

CONTENTS

FOREWORD

California state parks provide access to some of our most cherished landscapes and deeply felt historical events. In 2014 the California state park system turns 150 years old, and from its beginnings in Yosemite Valley, it has grown and flourished to encompass a vast array of wilderness areas, urban parks, recreation areas, and historical sites. Geographically the parks include landscapes as distinct as the humid redwood forests in the north and the dry expanses of southern deserts. They include westernmost coasts, inland mountains, and eastern borders. They interpret our state's early history, from Native California through the Mission and Mexican eras to the American takeover and the transformative gold rush. They reveal diverse communities and personal histories, including an African American utopian settlement founded by a former slave, an immigration station for newly arrived Asians, a paean to the citrus industry, the mansions of governors and newspaper moguls, and a nineteenth-century Russian fort, to name just a few.

California's state parks have been much in the news these past few years for threats of park closures, reduced budgets, and other crises. Now more than ever we must emphasize the assets our parks are to California. They display the state's inimitable natural beauty, they give visitors opportunities to experience history where it happened, and they are a space dedicated to play. It is through our personal connections to our state parks that we can learn to speak up, defend, and work toward sustainable solutions to keep our parks accessible—and in the news for *good* reasons.

One way to connect to state parks is to simply go visit them. Explore. Sleep out under the stars. Hike, run, or bike until you can't go any farther. Sit quietly beneath a towering redwood. Catch that elusive perfect wave you'd been waiting for while floating on your board, bobbing like a sea otter just offshore.

And what better way to add depth and dimension to your experience than to read stories about them—eyewitness accounts, crafted poetry and fiction, thought-provoking essays?

The editors of *Trail Posts* have paired more than forty of our state parks with literary excerpts that illuminate their space in the human imagination. These voices are sure to show you a new side of your favorite parks, and they might even introduce you to parks you've never heard of, ones that might become favorites as well. How many people have driven on Interstate 5 unaware that John Muir praised the grasslands just a few miles away as a "bed of honey-bloom, so marvelously rich that…your foot would press about a hundred flowers at every step"? The pieces contained in this volume have the potential to change the way you look at even the least "natural" of your surroundings.

Conversely, the parks can lead you to the literature. Perhaps you've heard of, or even visited, Fort Ross, on the Mendocino coast. In these pages, find a spooky story set there by Gertrude Atherton, a California-born author whose bright career has been all but forgotten, and who herself found much inspiration in tales from the local Indian tribes. This collection gives a sense of the historic sweep and natural treasures of the Golden State, while it also illustrates the depth of its literary heritage.

As we have been doing for over four decades, CSPF encourages new generations of Californians to go out and explore state parks from as many perspectives and angles as possible. We hope seasoned park aficionados and newcomers alike will enjoy the words and images (many of the latter gleaned from our free monthly photo contests) in *Trail Posts*, and that in doing so feel the spark of either a renewed dedication to, or a new passion for, our amazing state parks.

Elizabeth Goldstein, President
California State Parks Foundation

ACKNOWLEDGMENTS

We are grateful to the California State Parks Foundation for its support of this book and for the welcome sense of partnership that made this project such a joy. We especially thank Elizabeth Goldstein, President, and Jerry Emory, Director of Communications, for their vision and cooperation.

We would like to thank Christopher O'Sullivan and Heyday intern Emmerich Anklam for their help with researching and collecting material. Anne Helen Petersen deserves special thanks for her advice.

Finally, we are grateful to David Kipen, whose extraordinary and encyclopedic knowledge of California literature shaped *Trail Posts* in its earliest stages of life.—*MM and MC*

TRAIL POSTS

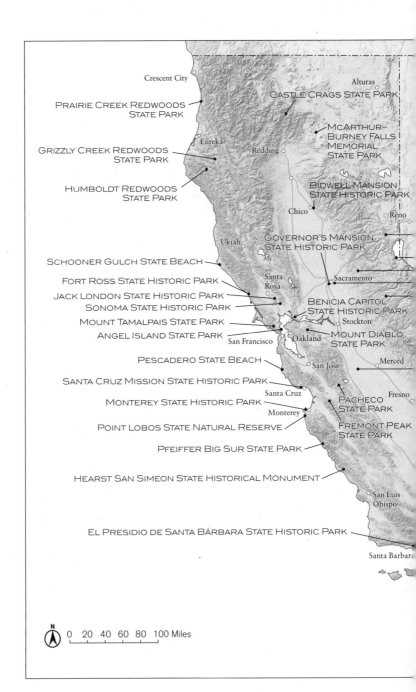

Crescent City

Alturas

CASTLE CRAGS STATE PARK

PRAIRIE CREEK REDWOODS
STATE PARK

McARTHUR–
BURNEY FALLS
MEMORIAL
STATE PARK

Eureka

Redding

GRIZZLY CREEK REDWOODS
STATE PARK

BIDWELL MANSION
STATE HISTORIC PARK

HUMBOLDT REDWOODS
STATE PARK

Chico

Reno

Ukiah

GOVERNOR'S MANSION
STATE HISTORIC PARK

SCHOONER GULCH STATE BEACH

Santa
Rosa

Sacramento

FORT ROSS STATE HISTORIC PARK

JACK LONDON STATE HISTORIC PARK
SONOMA STATE HISTORIC PARK

BENICIA CAPITOL
STATE HISTORIC PARK

Stockton

MOUNT TAMALPAIS STATE PARK

ANGEL ISLAND STATE PARK

San Francisco

Oakland

MOUNT DIABLO
STATE PARK

Merced

PESCADERO STATE BEACH

San Jose

SANTA CRUZ MISSION STATE HISTORIC PARK

Santa Cruz

Fresno

MONTEREY STATE HISTORIC PARK

Monterey

PACHECO
STATE PARK

POINT LOBOS STATE NATURAL RESERVE

FREMONT PEAK
STATE PARK

PFEIFFER BIG SUR STATE PARK

HEARST SAN SIMEON STATE HISTORICAL MONUMENT

San Luis
Obispo

EL PRESIDIO DE SANTA BÁRBARA STATE HISTORIC PARK

Santa Barbara

N

0 20 40 60 80 100 Miles

FEATURED PARKS

- Donner Memorial State Park

- Emerald Bay State Park
- Marshall Gold Discovery State Historic Park
- Sutter's Fort State Historic Park
- Indian Grinding Rock State Historic Park

- Mono Lake Tufa State Natural Reserve

- Great Valley Grasslands State Park
- Millerton Lake State Recreation Area

- Colonel Allensworth State Historic Park

Bakersfield

Arthur B. Ripley Desert Woodland State Park

Antelope Valley California Poppy Reserve

Lancaster

Los Angeles State Historic Park

Los Angeles

Riverside   Palm Springs

California Citrus State Historic Park

Long Beach   Bolsa Chica
State Beach   Salton Sea State Recreation Area

Anza-Borrego Desert State Park

Old Town San Diego State Historic Park

San Diego

PRAIRIE CREEK REDWOODS STATE PARK

In the late 1980s, Stephen Sillett and Marwood Harris, then students at Reed College, recklessly and without ropes climbed to the top of one of the ancient giants in Prairie Creek Redwoods State Park. What they discovered three hundred feet above the forest floor would give birth to a new field of study. Soil in the fissures of the bark, moistened by rain and fog, had nourished a profusion of plants (huckleberry bushes, small trees, ferns, and other flora), and these in turn provided a rich habitat for a number of animals. Sillett would go on to teach in the Department of Forestry and Wildlife Resources at Humboldt State University and is considered a pioneer in what eventually came to be known as "canopy studies."

Renowned for its forests of old-growth redwoods, Douglas firs, western hemlocks, and other trees, the 14,187-acre Prairie Creek Redwoods State Park offers camping, interpretive materials, seventy-five miles of trails, and abundant wildlife that includes Roosevelt elk, black bears, and mountain lions.

The author of the following excerpt, Richard Preston, is a well-known science writer and novelist who lists among his interests and accomplishments "recreational tree climber."

RICHARD PRESTON
from *THE WILD TREES*

Hiking fast, leading the way along the trail through the redwoods that day in Northern California, Steve Sillett came to
the banks of a west-running creek. He stopped and looked
around. There was a grove of big trees there, near the creek. He
wanted to see them more clearly. He went off the trail and began
bushwhacking through undergrowth. Marwood went into the
thickets after him.

Scott hurried along, and found that Steve was leading them
into a tunnel of greenery that arched over the creek. The tunnel
ended abruptly, opening out into a stand of big coast redwoods.
Steve and Marwood took off their backpacks and explored the
area, and eventually they ended up standing at the base of a
large redwood, looking into its crown.

"What's your opinion, Tree Badger?" Marwood said to Steve
in a low voice.

"I'm lusting for this tree."

Scott asked them what they intended to do. They didn't
really answer him. They began walking in circles around the
base of the redwood, staring up into it. The redwood was about
three hundred feet tall—thirty stories tall—with a diameter of
about fifteen feet near its base. The trunk was an enormous,
furrowed cylinder, with no branches on its lower reaches. Far
above the ground, a few whiffs of small branches popped out
of the trunk, and then, higher up, a tangle of limbs emerged
and wandered out of sight, buried in clouds of foliage. They
couldn't see the top. It is doubtful that anyone had ever paid
much attention to the tree, at least not since Europeans had
come into the country. The land around Prairie Creek was originally inhabited by the Yurok people. As far as I know, the Yurok
didn't give names to individual redwoods, although surely they
were familiar with the giants. This nameless tree was a redwood
giant.

"There's no way," Marwood said thoughtfully, gazing up
the trunk.

"I see a way," Steve said.

Scott was standing next to them. "You guys aren't going to try to climb this tree, are you?" he said.

No answer. Steve took a few steps backward and then made a running leap at a small redwood standing next to Nameless. He grabbed a branch on that small tree that was eight feet above the ground, and suddenly he was standing on top of the branch—he had managed to swing himself up to it in a fluid movement. Then he began climbing from branch to branch, laddering his way up the little redwood. Marwood glanced at Scott with a distracted look on his face, dusted his hands together, and leaped up and began following Steve. The two Reed students were free-climbing the tree—climbing it without ropes or safety equipment.

"Hey. You guys? I really think this is not very smart," Scott called up after them. "You know what, we need to keep going. Are you listening? Steve? Marty? Steve?"

• • • • •

In less than ten minutes, Steve Sillett had gotten close to the top of the small tree. The topmost portion of a tree is called its leader. The leader is a kind of finger that the tree uses to probe its way toward the sun.

Steve started climbing up along the leader, moving carefully and slowly over delicate branches. It narrowed to a pole that was thinner than his wrist, and it began swaying under his weight. Eventually he found himself standing seventy feet above the ground, balancing on a branch and holding the leader with one hand, having climbed as far as he could go, looking across at Nameless, the giant redwood.

A spray of branches frizzed out of a monstrous trunk across from him. The trunk was about twelve feet in diameter at this point, and it looked like a curving wall. A little branch stuck out of the wall, directly in front of him. He wanted to grab that branch. He edged closer to it, and the leader of the smaller tree began to bend under his weight.

There was a gap of empty space between the branches of the little redwood and Nameless. Marwood and Steve hadn't noticed the gap when they looked up from the ground. They had thought that the little tree's branches touched the big tree's branches, so they could walk across.

Steve studied the situation. If he could just reach out far enough he might be able to grab the little branch on Nameless. This is going to be a big extension, he thought. Keeping one hand wrapped around the leader, he reached his other hand out as far as possible. He ended up standing spread-eagled. He threw his weight outward. The little tree started bending closer to Nameless, but the target branch was still out of reach.

He was in a crux.

Marwood Harris clung to the branches below Steve Sillett, staring up at him through his gold-rimmed spectacles.

Steve paused. He looked up into the crown of Nameless. It was deep, explosive, mysterious. He looked seventy feet down.

Steve Sillett suffered from acrophobia, a fear of heights. It was a compulsive, uncontrollable fear of heights, which most people have to some degree and some people have to an extreme degree. His acrophobia wasn't overwhelming, but it could come on suddenly. Up in a high place, he would begin to feel dizzy and a sense of panic would creep into his soul, and his mind would fill with a horror of the void below. He would start whispering to himself, saying, Oh...oh, and he would begin to get a sensation of weightless acceleration, until he could actually feel his body falling down through space to death.

A distance of fifty feet above the ground is known to climbers as the redline. They hold it as a rule of thumb that if you fall fifty feet to hard ground you will very likely die. Indeed, an adult human can easily die after falling ten feet, if he lands on his head.

A person who is dropping in free fall through space often turns upside down and falls headfirst. This happens because, with most people, the upper half of the body is heavier than the lower half, and so the person tips over and plunges head-downward, like an arrow with a weighted point. In a headfirst landing after a fifty-foot fall, the shock crushes the skull and breaks the neck, destroying the brain and shearing the spinal cord off at the base of the skull. Instant death. No matter which way the victim lands, the impact normally breaks the victim's back, leaving him paralyzed (if he survives). If the person happens to land feetfirst, a shockwave travels up the legs, breaking them in many places, shattering the lower spine, and cutting the spinal cord. The lungs can collapse from the force of the impact, or they can be punctured by broken ribs, and the flattened or torn lungs can fill up with blood, causing the victim to drown in his blood. Major internal organs, including the liver, the kidneys, the spleen, and the bladder, as well as the aorta, can burst during the impact. If they split apart, they flood the body cavity with blood—catastrophic internal hemorrhage.

Steve Sillett was at about the height of the big top in a circus. He began to feel a bad sensation in his stomach, as if he were about to let it all go in his pants. Not good, since he was standing above Marwood. He tried to focus his mind on the problem. The gap was really not very large, he thought. He would have to let go of the small redwood and make a leap into the big tree, and catch a branch with his hands, like catching the bar of a trapeze. He had to jump high, or his body wouldn't clear the branches of the little redwood and he'd get tangled and would fall. If I was standing on the ground and I had to make this jump, I could do it, he thought. So if it's physically doable on the ground, why can't I do it up here? He tried to force his hand to just let go of the tree. Just let go.

• • • • •

Down on the ground, Scott Sillett saw that his brother was getting ready to jump. "Oh, my God," he whispered. "Steve!" he cried out. "What the hell are you doing? Are you crazy, Steve?"

No reply.

"Listen to me! *If you fall, you will die.* Do you understand that concept?" Scott screamed. He tried to get Marwood's attention.

"Marty, talk to him! Tell him not to do it!...You fucking idiots, we're miles from help! If you guys fall, I'm going to have to squeegee your corpses off the forest floor! I'm going to have to drag your shattered bodies out of here...."

Marwood Harris wasn't really listening. This is just one of those hairy things, he said to himself.

"Goddammit!" Scott screamed at his brother. "Listen to me!" The branch on the big redwood looked delicate. Steve couldn't really tell if it was strong enough to support his weight.

The lowest branches on the trunk of a redwood are called epicormic branches. Epicormic branches occur on many kinds of trees. They often arise out of scars left from broken branches, and they often come out in fan-shaped sprays called epi sprays. In redwoods, these branches are not solidly attached to the trunk, and can easily break or fall off the tree.

Steve Sillett didn't know what an epicormic branch was.

There was another problem, although Steve and Marwood didn't realize it. Hanging from the branch was a yellow jackets' nest the size of a cannonball; it wasn't visible from the small redwood.

"I can't watch you die, Steve!" Scott shouted. "I'm getting out of here! I'm going to look for birds."

Scott swept into the undergrowth. He was furious with his younger brother. He started hiking down along the creek, heading for the sea. He didn't go very far. How could he abandon Steve? He couldn't, so he waited by the creek in silence, feeling incredibly angry. The only thing he could hear was the sound of running water. He dreaded hearing a scream followed by a meaty thud.

In the top of the young redwood tree, Steve Sillett let go, and jumped into redwood space.

• • • • •

As Steve Sillett leaped out of the small tree, its top sprang upward. He felt gravity go to zero, and everything seemed to slow down. Feeling alert and calm, he watched the branch of the large redwood approach with drawn-out and perceivable slowness. The branch came into his hands. He closed his fingers around it.

There was a jerk. He found himself hanging from the branch by both hands, bouncing, with his feet kicking around in the air. He immediately began to travel along the branch, going hand over hand as he hung from it, trying to get himself over to the trunk. It wasn't a difficult move, it was just a monkey hang. Any kid could do it on a jungle gym. He didn't dare look down. He got himself over to the trunk, then he snapped his body upward and got one foot on the branch, and in one fluid movement he stood up on the branch, grabbed another branch above him and swung up to it, and stood balancing, motionless.

"It's doable," he said to Marwood. He was surprised at what had just happened, and his thoughts went: we're primates, and those opposable thumbs are awesome.

Marwood climbed into position and got ready. He thought, Well, if Steve can do it...He actually felt fairly confident that he could pull off the move. It was just that there was no safety rope to stop his fall if he made an error. Blow the move and lose your life. He got himself into focus and jumped.

• • • • •

The next thing Steve knew, Marwood was hanging by his hands from the lowest branch of Nameless and screaming. The branch was shaking, and Marwood was writhing under it. He looked as if he were getting electric shocks. "Shit, there's bees!" he screamed. He was surrounded by darting yellow jacket wasps.

Marwood traveled hand over hand in a monkey hang, while the wasps stung him on the neck and hands.

For one bad moment, Steve thought that Marwood might get stung in the eyes, and would let go of the branch and fall to his death. But Marwood wasn't about to let go, no matter what. He got over to the trunk, got his feet planted in the bark, and hauled himself up onto the branch and stood on it, swearing loudly. Holding on to the bark with one hand, balancing himself on the branch, he swatted the yellow jackets off his neck and face, and then, still cursing, he began to climb upward at remarkable speed.

The approach of Marwood Harris in a swarm of wasps encouraged Steve Sillett to keep climbing higher. He went from branch to branch. Marwood followed below him. The yellow jackets faded away.

Farther up the trunk, Steve arrived at a blank zone, where there were no branches. He couldn't see any way to climb higher. Above him, extending twelve feet, was an empty, grooved surface of bark. At the top of the stretch of empty trunk there was a strong-looking branch.

He looked down. Mistake. He was ninety feet up. The fear of heights came over him in a sickening wave, worse than before. What am I doing here? he thought. I'm going to die. He began to climb upward along the surface of the bark, Spider-Man style, jamming his hands and feet into cracks in the bark. This climbing tactic is known to rock climbers as crack jamming, or crack climbing. To perform a crack-climbing move, you jam a hand or a foot into a crack, get it stuck there, and then put your weight on the stuck part of your body and lunge upward with one hand, jamming it into a crack that's higher up.

With a series of crack-climbing moves, Steve climbed up the twelve feet of sheer redwood bark. He managed to get to the next branch, and he grabbed it, swung himself up onto that branch, and stood on it. He was somewhere in the lower tiers of Nameless, in the patchy zone of epicormic branches, where sprays of epi branches grow like fuzz on a redwood's trunk. He badgered Marwood, telling him it was easy, dude, and that he should have no problem getting up twelve feet of bare bark.

They both ended up standing on a big branch, at around 120 feet above the ground. They had arrived at the base of the crown of Nameless.

CASTLE CRAGS STATE PARK

From a distance, the granite spires and domes of Castle Crags, namesake of the 3,904-acre Castle Crags State Park, really do look like the spindly towers, buttresses, and ramparts of some time-weathered fort, rising out of dark pine and fir forest. Scrubbed into these shapes by glaciers and millennia of wind and rain, Castle Crags is over 6,500 feet tall and towers above the northern Sacramento River Valley. From the top of the Crags Trail—a 5.5-mile-round-trip hike with a 2,200-foot elevation gain—the views of the Crags, and of Mount Shasta to the north, are magnificent.

Although today the park is a peaceful retreat for fishing, swimming, hiking, and camping, Castle Crags certainly has borne witness to its fair share of conflict. It looks down on the old Siskiyou Trail (now Interstate 5), a trade and travel route running from California to Oregon that was used first by Native peoples and then later by European and American trappers, explorers, and gold seekers. Conflict was inevitable along this route, and the 1855 Battle of Castle Crags is among the most notable of the many clashes that occurred in the area. Poet and adventurer Joaquin Miller, who lived for a time among the Wintu and Modoc peoples, was wounded in this battle. He describes the experience in the following excerpt from "The Battle of Castle Crags," a pamphlet issued in 1894 as an advertisement for a nearby summer resort.

JOAQUIN MILLER
from "THE BATTLE OF CASTLE CRAGS"

It is equitable to set Mountain Joe down as the first earnest and permanent proprietor of all this region round about here, for he tilled the soil, built some houses, and kept a sort of hotel, and guided people to the top of Mount Shasta, to say nothing of his ugly battles with the Indians for his home.

I first saw this strange man at his own campfire when a school-lad at home in Oregon, where he had camped near our place with his pack-train. He told us he was in the habit of going to Mexico for half-wild horses, driving them up to Oregon, and then packing them back to California, by which time they were tamed and ready for sale. He told my brother and me most wondrous tales about his Soda Springs, Mount Shasta, the Lost Cabin, and a secret mine of gold. He talked to us of Fremont till the night was far spent, and father, with the schoolteacher, had to come out after us. But what won my heart entirely was the ease with which he reached his left hand, and taking "Di Bella Galica" from my father, divided "Gaul in three parts" in the ashes of the campfire as he read and translated the mighty Roman by the roaring Oregon. He was a learned foreigner, of noble birth, it was said, certainly of noble nature. I could not forget Mountain Joe and his red men, and his Mexicans and mules and horses; and so, in the fall of 1854, I ran away from school and joined him at Soda Springs, now Castle Crag Tavern.

He was my ideal, my hero. You will find him in one character or another, for he had many characters, in nearly all my work. I cannot say certainly as to his hidden treasures, though he always seemed to have pots of gold to draw on in those days; but I can frankly confess that I have drawn on him and his marvelous stories, making them my own, of course, for all these years,—a veritable mine, indeed, to me.

I found him fortressed in the old Hastings barracks, before mentioned, though the place had been nearly destroyed by fire in his absence. We guided a few parties here and there, taking the first party to the top of the mountain that ever reached that point with ladies, I believe, and then returned to Yreka for the winter, going back to Lower Soda over the spring snowbanks with a tremendous rush of miners that Mountain Joe had worked up by his stories of the Lost Cabin and mysterious gold mines.

Thousands on thousands of men! The little valley of Soda Creek back of Castle Crag Tavern was a white sea of tents. Every bar on the Sacramento was the scene of excitement. The world was literally turned upside down. The rivers ran dark and sullen with sand and slime. The fishes turned on their sides and died. But the enraged miners found almost nothing. Mountain Joe disappeared. Men talked of hanging "Mountain Joe's boy." The game disappeared before the avalanche of angry and hungry men. The Indians had vanished at their first approach, and were starving in the mountains.

The tide went out as it came in—suddenly, savagely. Deeds of cruelty to Mexicans and half-tamed Indians who tried to be friendly and take fish in the muddied waters were not rare, as the disgusted miners retired from the country either up or down the river, leaving trails of dead animals, camp *debris* and cast-iron oaths behind. As they went Joe came, and the Indians came, furious! We treated them well, tried to make friends of them once more, but they would have none of it.

By the end of June, 1855, the last miner had left our section; and soon the last Indian left us to go on the warpath. Mountain Joe and I were now utterly alone, with not even a Mexican to take care of the pack-train and do the cooking. But we kept on. We had quite a garden, but it was needing water; so Joe and I took our guns each day, leaving the store or trading-post to care for itself, and went up the creek to work on a ditch.

Meantime, ugly stories were afloat; and ugly sullen Indians came by now and then—Modocs on their way across to the Trinity Indians, by the pass up little Castle Creek. They would not sit down, nor eat, nor talk. They shook their heads when we talked, and assumed to not know either the Shasta or Chinook dialect. The Trinity Indians were in open revolt beyond Castle Crags, and Captain Crook from Fort Jones, near Yreka, the famous General Crook, was in the field there. He drove them up Trinity River to Castle Crags, but had no decisive battle.

One hot morning, while we were at work on the ditch, Joe suddenly dropped his pick and caught up his gun. A horse went plunging up the valley past us with an arrow quivering in his shoulder; and smoke began to curl above the pines from the burning trading-post. We hastened down, but did not see a single Indian, nor did we see another horse or mule. All had silently disappeared in the half hour we had held our faces to the earth in the ditch.

Blotches of flour from torn sacks here and there made a white trail up over the red foothills on the brown, sweet-smelling pine-quills, and, without a word, Joe led cautiously on, I at his heels. The savages divided soon, the party with the horses going to the right, toward the Modoc country, the party with the stores, leaving a trail of flour, to the left, toward Castle Crags. This latter Joe followed, crossing the river at a ford, and going up the left bank of little Castle Creek. The canyon shuts in very close after a time. In a narrow pass the spilt flour was suspiciously plentiful and Joe led across the spurs of the mountain toward what is now Sisson. It was called Strawberry Valley then, and was kept by two brothers by the name of Gordon. We were desperately worn and hungry, and they treated us well.

As said before, there were and had for some time been rumors of coming trouble. Joe and I turned back from Sisson to give the alarm and get help along the river. Portuguese Flat, which it took us two days to reach through the mountains, as we dared not take the trail, was the nearest post. Dog Creek, the ghost of which may be dimly seen in Delta now, was then a prosperous camp, and full of men. Judge Gibson, then the only magistrate in the country, had married an influential chief's daughter, and, by a wise and just course, had gained great authority, and had kept this tribe, the Shastas, from taking part in the great uprising which finally spread all over the Coast. The Indians had determined on a war of extermination. It ended in the utter extinction of many tribes in Oregon and some in California.

Courage was not lacking in those days, but coolness and experience in Indian warfare were wanting. Gibson had all these. So had Mountain Joe; but Joe had lost an eye by an arrow, and the other eye was not good. So he deferred to Gibson.

Major Dribelbies, then sheriff, and Ike Hare, each took active part in trying to keep down the uprising of savages, and also in getting up an expedition against those in revolt, while Joe and I went back, and, with such friends as we could gather, waited at the base of Castle Crags for Gibson and his men.

Amazing as it may seem, he brought but about fifty, all told, Indians and white; and yet he was the only man who could have done as well. The miners were already more than disgusted with the country; and Indians rarely fight Indians in a general uprising like this. Mountain Joe could raise but ten men of his own.

Gibson led straight up Big Castle Creek, as if avoiding Castle Crags and the savages entrenched there. He kept himself almost entirely with his Indians, and hard things were said of him by the worn and discouraged white volunteers. They suspected that he was afraid to make the fight, and was trying to join the regulars under Crook in the Trinity Mountains.

At last, when our shoes and moccasins, as well as patience, were worn out, he turned sharply to the right, making the entire circuit of the Castle. We rested by a deep, dark lake which the Indians call the abode of their devil, Ku-ku-pa-rick, and they refused to approach its grassy, wooded shores.

Here Gibson, leaving his Indians for the first time, passed from man to man as they crouched under the trees. He told them that there was to be a fight, and a fight to a finish; that the hostiles were not an hour distant, and that no one could turn back and live, for if we did not kill them they would kill us. He told us that they had come down out of the Castle to kill deer, and so their arrows were not poisoned, and that we could swim.

He broke us up in parties, putting good and bad together, with Indians at the head of each. He told me to go with Joe, whom he sent to make a show of attack on the side next to Soda Springs. When near the hostiles Joe put me behind a tree on the edge of a small open place, and told me to stay there. Then he went on, creeping through the dense brush, to place the other men. I put some bullets into my mouth so as to have them handy, but I do not know what I did with them. I fired a few shots after Joe opened the fight, but hit only brush and rocks I reckon. And now pandemonium! Indians do not often yell in battle; but on both sides of us now the yelling was simply fiendish. They yelled from the top of the Castle to the bottom, it seemed to me.

We had taken the enemy entirely unawares, asleep, most of them, after the morning's chase, and our first shots brought down their dozing sentinels on the rocks. Finally there was some parleying, and the yelling, the whiz of arrows and the crack of rifles stopped. Then some Indian women came out and across the little gorge to Joe and his men, and I, thinking they had all surrendered, walked out into the open. Gibson called from the rocks ahead of me and to my right: "Boys, the fight now begins, and we've got to git them or they git us. Come on! Who will go in with me?" I answered that I would go, for it was all a picnic so far as I had yet seen, and I ran around to him. But there was blood on his hands and blood on his face, blood on all of his Indians, and most of the white were bloody and hot.

The enemy used arrows entirely. They could tell where we were, but we knew where they were only when we felt their sting. Gibson led, or rather crept, hastily on, his head below the chaparral. No one dared speak. But when we got in position, right in the thick of it, our men opened. Then the arrows, then the yelling, as never before! The women and children prisoners down with Joe set up the death song, as if it was not already dismal enough. The savages bantered us and bullied us, saying we were all going to be killed before the sun went down; that we were already covered with blood, and that they had not lost a man. I had not yet fired a shot since joining Gibson, and, rising up to look for a target, he told an Indian to "pull the fool down by the hair," which he promptly did.

The battle had lasted for hours. The men were choking, and the sun was near going down. We must kill or be killed, and that soon. We must do our work before dark. The white man has little show with an Indian in battle at night.

Gibson gathered all who could or would go, and took still another place by storm. Then Lane fell, mortally hurt by an arrow in the eye. I saw Gibson's gun fall from his hand from the very deluge of arrows; then all was blank, and I knew no more of that battle.

The fight was over when I came to my senses, and it was dark. A young man by the name of Jameson was trying to drag me through the brush; and it has always seemed to me that a good many people walked over me and trod on me. I could hear, but could not see. An arrow had struck the left side of my face, knocked out two teeth, and had forced its point through at the back of my neck. I could hear, and I knew the voices of Gibson and Joe. They cut off the point of the arrow, and pulled it out of my face by the feather end. Then I could see. I suffered no pain, but was benumbed and cold as we lay under the pines. Joe held my head all night expecting that I would die. Gibson had the squaw prisoners carry his wounded down to the pack-trail on the banks of the Sacramento. They laid us down under some pines and pretty juniper trees on the west side of the swift, sweet river. And how tender and how kind these heroic men were! I was as a brother to them now,—their boy hero. Only the day before I had been merely "Mountain Joe's boy."

Gibson's loss in killed was considerable for so small a number engaged,—several Indians, though only one white man. Indians never give their loss, because of encouragement to the enemy; and Mountain Joe and Gibson, for a like reason, always kept their list of killed and wounded as low as possible, and spoke of the battle of Castle Crags as a trifling affair. Yet General Crook, in his letter to Captain Gibson, marveled that he ever got out with a single man.

I had promised to mark the grave of Ike Hare with a fragment of granite from Castle Crags, so that those who pass up and down the pleasant walks around Castle Crag Tavern might look with respect on the resting-place of a brave man and an honest legislator of two States. But my little tablet would seem so pitiful in the mighty presence of Mount Shasta.

MCARTHUR-BURNEY FALLS MEMORIAL STATE PARK

The native Pit River Tribe of the region between Mount Lassen and Mount Shasta considered the twin McArthur-Burney Falls a "power spot." Darryl Babe Wilson (Achuma-We/Atsuge-We) recalls a childhood in which the oaks and lakes and rivers of the area were haunted by spirits called *Elam'ji* that his mother and grandmother could speak to in their native tongue. At night their presence might be mistaken for the sound of Canada geese passing in the dark toward nearby Lake Britton. Wilson is now a Pit River elder and a writer of profound beauty. He has authored numerous essays, short stories, and the memoir *The Morning the Sun Went Down*.

A visit to the 910-acre McArthur-Burney Falls Memorial State Park, located on the Pit River near Redding, is a reminder of the strong and ancient forces of nature—including pounding waterfalls 129 feet high, porous basalt rock from long-ago volcanic events, and the smells of incense cedar and ponderosa pine—that have shaped the culture and spirituality of Native people in the region for thousands of years.

DARRYL BABE WILSON
"ELAM'JI"

Our old barn this evening somehow took on a mean, confused look. Maybe it was the position of the moon, or the stringy clouds over the mountains, or the owl hooting from the oak forest nearby. We wondered. A strange, heavy thickness permeated the evening as darkness wrapped all around us. It seemed hard to breathe.

Three grown-ups, old friends of the family, were visiting overnight. The adults would go deer hunting before dawn. The adults were smoking and talking, making small plans for the morning. My brothers and sisters and the dogs milled around, and I listened to the adult conversation, thinking that maybe I would be invited to go hunting, too.

We were all outside in the heavy evening, cloaked in hesitation or expectation. The velvet shadows of the trees made me feel like a powder-shadow. I could see my hand move in the darkness, but I could not tell for sure whose hand it was. If I blinked hard, I couldn't see anything for a few seconds after I opened my eyes, except a rainbow pattern that changed and moved, then vanished.

There was a hush. The adults stopped smoking. I could feel all of the eyes studying the darkness.

Then from the old barn, about fifty yards from where we were all standing, a thicker, darker shadow ran down the old barn road that curved below the house and forked out into the meadow beyond. Cold fear streaked up and down my spine, tingling.

The running shadow made no noise. We could barely see its form, and the broken shadows of the oak forest kept blurring it out of existence. Sometimes it disappeared among the darkest shadows. Then the shadow somehow reappeared again, running heavily toward the meadow.

My eyes have always tricked me in the dark. If I looked behind or in front of the fleeing form, I could see it. But if looked directly at it, I could not. I heard a limb break, but everyone else said they only heard silence. Must have been my imagination.

I could "feel" that spirit as it ran. Why was the spirit running where we could see it? Perhaps it wanted to be seen, to deliver a message. My mother's mom always talked about the mysterious presence of the *Elam'ji*—"the unknowable," "spirit." She was always seeing *Elam'ji* in the blackest part of night. She talked to these spirits in the old language. It seemed that they were present only when she was around. But she was far, far away tonight, clear in Alturas.

An intense chill flashed through me, and I instantly got ghost goosebumps. The hair all over my body stood erect. My knees seemed to lock together. If that spirit ran toward me, I would not be able to move. Maybe I could jump like a kangaroo rat. My body seemed very light. When I tried to move, nothing worked! I was holding my breath and could not breathe. I peered into the darkness, but could see nothing but thick blobs of shadows. Everyone was silent. Listening. Staring.

Finally somebody moved. The grass rustled. A dry oak limb snapped underfoot. There was life! I began breathing again, but it was hard labor, like somebody had tied a rope tightly around my chest.

We were all merely enjoying the summer evening—or were we? Maybe we were secretly commanded by this spirit to be outside so it could let us know that it was alive. Maybe there would be an invasion of these shadowy spirits. My child's imagination raced in so many directions. What if more shadows came? What if they took over? What if they began a war? What if they took us away in the dark?

The old ones say there is a Rock Man roving the land at night. He listens for crying children. He can tell when a child is crying because it is hungry, or because it is wet and needs attention, or because it is brokenhearted or lonely and neglected. It is the brokenhearted and neglected that he takes in the night. In the morning the baby is not there with its mother and father. It is far away.

They say there is another tribe that has "gone on ahead." They are around us all of the time, but we can't see them because they are in another world, the world of Rock Man and other spirits. We can look right through them, we can even run right through them, but we don't know they are there. The spirit-tribe does not allow other people into their world. They speak our language and not foreign languages. They are very smart, that spirit-tribe.

This *Elam'ji* seemed to be heavy, ambling like a massive man, but not making any sound. In my imagination I could see his eyes, blue with moving clouds, like the sky. They must be able to see both in the night and in the light because they *looked*. I had felt that "look" in the forest—that Rock Man look, that spirit-tribe look. It is true, what the old ones say— we are never alone.

Our friends said they too felt something or saw a spirit running down the road below the house. They held their breath, convinced there was "something." We knew we were not imagining this whole episode. In the darkness we stumbled down to the old barn road. I did not want to go along, but I was sure not going to be left alone in the suffocating black silence with an invisible spirit. It was terribly quiet. Only our breathing and our confused visions scraped the darkness.

Somebody lit a match. Flickering orange light. We studied the ground, straining to find a broken limb or bent grass. Maybe freshly turned leaves. Nothing. Another match. Soon there were several matches going. Nothing. All of our senses alert, we listened to the darkness all around us.

We breathed deeply. I wanted to go home and crawl under the bed. That was the safest place in the world, especially if you had a puppy with you. Mine was soft and warm. He liked me. I called him "Boy."

The spirit-thing was gone. Sometimes Grams went out at night and whispered in the old language. She spoke softly, and we could not hear. She did not want us to hear. I believe she was speaking with the spirit-beings.

Somehow I began breathing normally again. Yet every sound in the darkness startled me: a rustling leaf, a breaking twig, the call of the owls. When a breeze moved the oak forest, a shiver ran through my body. I leaned on Mom and stayed close to Dad, trembling. Like a herd of blind deer in the darkness we moved toward the house. I fell over tree limbs and each time I was sure the others would leave me there in the dark, and something would get me.

We stopped. We tensed.

In the blackness above the forest there came a threatening, whooshing sound. It moved slowly across the sky. I knew it was a war battalion of spirits flying in to get us all. I froze. We all did. My knees were locked together. Neither could I blink. My feet seemed to be nailed to the ground.

The whooshing was overhead now, coming from the east. The east, where many bad spirits originate. The east, beyond the salt waters where the legends say bad spirits dwell.

Then we heard the unmistakable bugle call of the Canadian goose. "Honkers" we called them. Dad's great-aunt Effie called them *hongas*. A tribe of geese was feathering down to land on Lake Britton in the dark. They made a wide pattern like an airplane circling before coming in for a landing. In my mind's eye I could see them. A huge V formation, floating softly down, circling, their black necks and heads slowly moving from side to side as their soft brown eyes studied the waters, the forest, the landscape through the darkness. Their immense wings out and curved, their black feet trailing behind. The wind whooshing their huge bodies forward. So beautiful. Not like the spirit that scared us all—at least, me.

When we arrived at our very dark house, two adults went inside first. I squeezed somewhere in the middle of the frightened tribe. I could feel the darkness in the house with my fingers, like soot. After striking a match, Daddy located a kerosene lamp and lit it. That was better. Light. Warmth. Hope. Maybe the Rock Man spirit-people did not like lamplight. Maybe now they would stay away.

Orange-black shadows danced around the room as the flame from the lamp moved with our every breath. Shadows crept across the windows. In the deep corners, enough dark defied the flickering light to hide a spirit! I did not look into the corners or under the table. I moved closer to Mom and Dad. It was somehow safer next to Daddy. That spirit-being might get me, but Daddy would get the spirit back.

I did not close my eyes all that night. Just stared. Shadows formulated in the total darkness of our bedroom. They oozed across the ceiling like smoke-snakes; they floated and swam around, changing shapes and sizes. And they all "looked" right at me.

• • • • •

"*Loqme*," Old Uncle would say, meaning how beautiful the approaching day promised to be. The silver of first light danced off the forest upon the mountains to the east, a sterling silver, a shiny promise. I made it through the night without a spirit getting me. Boy, *loqme*, for sure!

The thick black of our bedroom slowly changed to dark gray, then heavy shadows took form. The ceiling, the door, the chair began to take shape. Soon lots of light poured in. I knew in the light the spirits could not steal me without somebody seeing them, and the spirits knew it.

Slowly, like a just-waking porcupine, I got out of bed, my head heavy without rest. My eyes, open all night, burned dry. My arms and legs ached, since I had been tense and twisted, waiting for a spirit to grab me. My stomach was like a knot in a rope that the horses used to pull a plow. My teeth ached, I had clenched them so hard. I could have bitten a ten-penny nail in half.

The other kids were sleeping, as were the puppies. I shuffled outside to look at the silver sun streaming through the forest. I saw that Mom and Dad and the others had already gone hunting; the hunting knife with the leather handle was gone from its place just beside the door.

I slowly, deliberately worked my way around the house to look down the hill toward the place where the spirit ran the night before. I peeked around the corner, knowing the spirit could not tell if I was there because I was so quiet and small.

As my right eye searched the oak-forest shade more carefully than a whisper, my heart stopped. The ghost goosebumps—ready all the time—jumped up.

There, leaning against an oak tree, "looking" at me, was a soft, silvery, shadowy outline. *Elam'ji!*

I tried to die in order to keep the spirit from getting me. My skin nearly crawled off my body like the snake's does. I was fear-frozen in a staring match with the spirit. He kept looking at me. I was shaking and my knees were locked together again. I could not run.

Then the spirit vanished into the oak tree, like magic. It did not come out the other side. That amazed me as much as it frightened me. Yet my body shivered. My spirit trembled.

Then a calm moved across my world. Like the Elders say, that made me imagine: blue sky was in his eyes and summer clouds there too, clear past the mountains. It was like looking into tomorrow and into the next day.

Why was I trembling? The spirit-beings would not get me. I was not neglected. Mom and Dad loved me. A sweetness moved in and softened the look from the spirit-being.

Maybe it was Great-Grandpa, whom I had never met. He never met me either. Perhaps this spirit was a messenger. The old ones always said the spirits bring messages, if you can understand them. This must be a good spirit.

I soon realized that the spirit was friendly. For some reason I trusted it just a little. I grew. And grew bolder.

$$\bullet \ \bullet \ \bullet \ \bullet \ \bullet$$

Later that morning the adults came from the direction of Lake Britton. The men had taken turns carrying the deer. Mom and Reitha were trailing behind, carrying the rifles and talking and laughing softly. Soon we would eat *wa'hach* (bread slowly cooked on a griddle without grease) strong enough to wrap around chunks of *dose me'suts* (venison), along with potatoes fried in bacon grease, eggs over easy, and fresh, cool water.

Hunger made me forget about the spirit. Then I remembered him again. I wondered why I simply could not forget. Laughter occasionally erupted as the men cut the meat, the women peeled potatoes, and the kids got wood for the fire. Even the dogs were happy. Let the owls hoot in the daytime. We were going to live!

See, I knew the spirit was bringing good luck and not bringing bad warnings. I was confident about life again. But still I wondered why the hair on my neck kept crawling like a lazy caterpillar.

GRIZZLY CREEK REDWOODS
STATE PARK

The range of coast redwood trees *(Sequoia sempervirens)*—the tallest trees in the world—is confined to the narrow belt along the Pacific Coast from Monterey County to the very southern edge of Oregon. Nowhere else is the combination of fog drip, heavy rain, and moderate temperatures just right to nourish these trees, whose lineage stretches back to when dinosaurs roamed a much moister earth. When standing in the presence of three-hundred-foot-tall old-growth redwoods, it is not hard to imagine that ancient world of colossal beasts.

Nor is it hard to understand the overwhelming awe and emotion that gripped legendary activist Julia Butterfly Hill upon her first visit to Grizzly Creek Redwoods State Park in Humboldt County. The trees of this 429-acre state park, off the beaten track from the well-known Avenue of the Giants, were Hill's introduction to the giant species that would become her home from 1997 through 1999. For 738 days, Hill lived 180 feet up a redwood tree on two small platforms, in protest against the Pacific Lumber Company, which was clear-cutting a grove of redwoods near Stafford, also in Humboldt County. (The two parties eventually came to an agreement.)

In Grizzly Creek Redwoods State Park, the Van Duzen River converges with Grizzly Creek, offering an ideal viewing spot for watching salmon run in the winter. The old-growth forest is dense and quiet, with massive thickets of sword ferns, rich arrays of damp-loving mushrooms, and the sweet aroma of redwood duff. It is home to mountain lion, river otter, black-tailed deer, and spotted owl alike. The park offers overnight camping as well as day-use activities like hiking, swimming, and barbecuing.

JULIA BUTTERFLY HILL

from *THE LEGACY OF LUNA*

I suppose if I look back (or down, as the case may be), my being here isn't all that accidental. I can see now that the way I was raised and what I was raised to believe probably prepared me for where I am now, high in this tree, with few possessions and plenty of convictions. I couldn't be here without some deep faith that we all are called to do something with our lives—a belief I know comes directly from my parents, Dale and Kathy—even if that path leads us in a different direction from others.

Even when I was a child, we hardly lived what people would call a normal life. Many of my early memories are full of religion. My father was an itinerant preacher who traveled the country's heartland preaching from town to town and church to church. My parents, my two brothers, Michael and Daniel, and I called a camping trailer home (excellent preparation for living on a tiny platform), and we went wherever my father preached. My parents really lived what they believed; for them, lives of true joy came from putting Jesus first, others second, and your own concerns last.

Not surprisingly, we were very poor, and my parents taught us how to save money and be thrifty. Growing up this way also taught us to appreciate the simple things in life. We paid our own way as much as possible; I got my first job when I was about five years old, helping my brothers with lawn work. We'd make only a buck or so, but to us that was a lot. I had my share of fun, but I definitely grew up knowing what *responsible* meant. My folks taught me that it was not just taking care of myself but helping others, too. At times, like right now, I have lived hand to mouth. But I knew that sometimes the work of conveying the power of the spirit, the truth as I understood it, was as important as making money. I've always felt that as long as I was able, I was supposed to give all I've got to ensure a healthy and loving legacy for those still to come, and especially for those with no voice. That is what I've done in this tree.

By the time I was in high school in Arkansas, life settled down for us, and I lived the life of an average teenager, working hard and playing hard. I knew how to have fun, and I enjoyed myself and the time I spent with my friends. I was a bit aimless, volunteering for a teen hot line here, modeling a bit there, saving money to move out on my own. I suppose I had the regular dreams of a regular person.

All that changed forever, though, that night in August 1996 when the Honda hatchback I was driving was rear-ended by a Ford Bronco. The impact folded the little car like an accordion, shoving the back end of the car almost into the back of my seat. The force was so great that the stereo burst out of its console and bent the stick shift. Though I was wearing a seat belt, which prevented me from being thrown through the windshield, my head snapped back into the seat, then slammed forward onto the steering wheel, jamming my right eye into my skull. The next morning when I woke up, everything hurt. "I feel like I've been hit by a truck," I said out loud, and then I started to laugh. "Wait a minute, I *was* hit by a truck!"

Although the symptoms didn't surface immediately, it turned out that I had suffered some brain damage. It took almost a year of intensive therapy—much of it alternative—for the information tunnels in my brain to be retrained and rerouted and for my short-term memory and motor skills to return. For a time it was uncertain whether I was ever going to be able to function normally again.

When your life is threatened, nothing is ever the same. I suddenly saw everything in a new light. All the time and space I had taken for granted became precious. I realized that I had always been looking ahead and planning instead of making sure that every moment counted for something. I also saw that had I not come through the way I did, I would have been very disappointed with my empty life. Perhaps because I had injured the left, analytical side of my brain, the right, a more creative side, began to take over, and my perspective shifted. It became clear to me that our value as people is not in our stock portfolios and bank accounts but in the legacies we leave behind.

My parents' legacy began to take hold. I guess I really am the daughter of a preacher through and through after all. Having survived such a horrible accident, I resolved to change my life, and I wanted to follow a more spiritual path. If I was again to become whole—and that meant body, mind, and spirit—I was going to have to find out where I was meant to be and what I needed to do. Lying in bed, still under many doctors' care, I decided that when I was well enough I would go on a journey around the world. I would visit the places that had deep spiritual roots. In those roots, in that common thread of spirituality, I felt, I would find my sense of purpose. The insurance settlement from the accident would help provide the funds. But I couldn't leave the country until the lawsuit I had filed after my accident had been settled. And, of course, I couldn't go anywhere until I got well.

Ten months later, I was finally released from my last doctor's care. I was ready to go. But where? In just two weeks, adventure presented itself. My next-door neighbors, Jori and Jason, whom I had known for years, along with a friend of theirs named Barry, announced that they were setting out on a trip to the West Coast.

"Our fourth backed out, and we really need someone else to help pay for gas," they told me. "You want to go with us?"

I couldn't have been happier. It wasn't the world, but it was a start. We set off in June. Our group was eager to see Washington's Olympic rain forests, but our travel plans were loose. We met a stranger in passing who told us that if we were heading west, we had to stop in Humboldt County and see the Lost Coast and the redwoods, one of the largest undeveloped coastlines left in this country. I was convinced. We changed course and followed his advice.

After stopping at the magnificent shore, we entered Grizzly Creek State Park to see the California redwood giants. When Jason and Jori learned that their dog would not be allowed on the trail, they decided to walk the road that circles the campground and admire the redwoods from there.

That wasn't enough for me.

"There's something about these trees," I said. "I have to get away from all the tourists and the cars and really get out in this forest."

"Well, Julia, we're only gonna stay for a few minutes, maybe fifteen minutes tops," they countered.

"No problem," I answered. "If I'm not back when you're ready to go, just leave my stuff at the ranger's station and tell them I'll be glad to pay however much it costs to store it there. But I'm going out."

As I crossed the highway, I felt something calling to me. Upon entering the forest, I started walking faster and faster, and then, feeling this exhilarating energy, I broke into a run, leaping over logs as I plunged in deeper.

After about a half mile, the beauty of my surroundings started to hit me. I slowed down for a better look. The farther I walked, the larger the ferns grew, until they were so big that three people with outstretched arms couldn't have encircled them. Lichen, moss, and fungus sprouted everywhere. Around each bend in the path, mushrooms of every shape and size imaginable burst forth in vivid hues of the rainbow. The trees, too, became bigger and bigger. At first they seemed like normal trees, but as I leaned my head back as far as I could, I looked far up into the air. I couldn't even see their crowns. Hundreds of feet high, they were taller than fifteen-, eighteen-, even twenty-story buildings. Their trunks were so large that ten individuals holding hands would barely wrap around them. Some of the trees were hollow, scorched away by lightning strikes, yet they still stood. These trees' ancestors witnessed the dinosaur days. Wrapped in the fog and the moisture they need to grow, these ancient giants stood primordial, eternal. My feet sank into rich earth with each step. I knew I was walking on years upon years of compounded history.

As I headed farther into the forest, I could no longer hear the sounds of cars or smell their fumes. I breathed in the pure, wonderful air. It tasted sweet on my tongue. Everywhere I turned, there was life whether I could see, smell, hear, taste, or touch it or not. For the first time, I really felt what it was like to be alive, to feel the connection of all life and its inherent truth—not the truth that is taught to us by so-called scientists or politicians or other human beings, but the truth that exists within Creation.

The energy hit me in a wave. Gripped by the spirit of the forest, I dropped to my knees and began to sob. I sank my fingers into the layer of duff, which smelled so sweet and so rich and so full of layers of life, then lay my face down and breathed it in. Surrounded by these huge, ancient giants, I felt the film covering my senses from the imbalance of our fast-paced, technologically dependent society melt away. I could feel my whole being bursting forth into new life in this majestic cathedral. I sat and cried for a long time. Finally, the tears turned into joy and the joy turned to mirth, and I sat and laughed at the beauty of it all.

HUMBOLDT REDWOODS
STATE PARK

In Humboldt Redwoods State Park, the Northern spotted owl makes its home in the oldest and biggest trees in the world: the coast redwoods. William Leon Dawson, famed ornithologist and bird photographer who authored the massive *Birds of California* in 1923, likens this small owl to "some patriarchal gnome," a description that brings a suitable air of mystery and intrigue to this rare yet humble bird.

Like so many things about the endangered Northern spotted owl, its specific reasons for nesting almost exclusively in old-growth fir and redwood forests are something of an enigma. Whatever the case, this owl is about as rare as the colossal trees themselves, which only grow in their natural range, from Monterey County to southern Oregon. At their true old-growth size they flourish mainly on the Northern California coast, especially along the Avenue of the Giants, a central attraction of Humboldt Redwoods State Park. Some 17,000 acres of the 51,650-acre park are old-growth forest, and any and all wanders on the one hundred miles of trails will afford breathtaking views of the towering trees, in whose swaying boughs roost the handsome owls Dawson so eagerly praised.

For those not so avian-inclined, the park is also host to a variety of activities, from camping to swimming to horseback riding.

WILLIAM LEON DAWSON

"SPOTTED OWL"

Even the sight of a Spotted Owl is counted a bit of a rarity in these parts; and specimens taken are still dutifully reported in the columns of the "Condor," or elsewhere. Yet when the great day comes, the bird of mystery is likely to prove as obliging as a well-bred hen or shall we say as a sleepy rooster? It may be his favorite roost that we have blundered upon, all in a shady dell, unfrequented of men. There is no need for anxiety.

The bird is mildly curious himself, and not in the least alarmed. His aspect is anything but ferocious—benevolent, rather—and he looks for all the world like some patriarchal gnome disturbed at his slumbers, yet not resentful. We vote him handsome at the first breath, and admiration grows as we dwell upon the sleekness, the mellow rotundity, and the exquisite harmony of the figure, and especially of the costume before us. Spotting suggests the conspicuous, and this bird is spotted with white from head to foot, on a background the deepest of wood-browns; and yet the pattern blends in so perfectly, is so essential a part of the checkered sunlight falling upon branch and leaf beside him, that we say, "Why, of course. How could he be any different?" Whereas an object merely brown or merely white would stand out here like a sore thumb, this camouflaged stat-uette almost disappears under the searching eye. We must circle about him to coax an inclination of the head, or a tell-tale movement of the foot. Now and again the benignant creature winks prodigiously, and the ladies with us shriek with laughter. Silly things! The bird is not winking at *them*. He was up late last night and the sun hurts his eyes, that's all.

There is no clear-cut account of the notes, and especially of the mating "song," of the Spotted Owl. Clay enjoyed a mid-night serenade wherein the birds produced a "ghostly racket," preceded by a long-drawn-out whining, which gradually increased to a grating sound. In this performance two birds, attracted, no doubt, by the light, ventured upon a limb within three feet of the inquisitive student. Peyton likens the call of the male to the distant baying of a hound, and Dickeys confirms this estimate.

Little is known, either, of the food habits of this rare owl. Dickey found rather scanty remains of mice and brush rats at the owl's nest, and saw feathers of crested jays which he attributed to a Strigine banquet. Curiously, however, two instances are on record where remains of Pygmy Owls, *Glaucidium gnoma,* have been found in the stomachs of recently killed Spotted Owls. Evidently there is scant courtesy among brigands.

BIDWELL MANSION
STATE HISTORIC PARK

Racing against hunger and the elements, twenty-two-year-old John Bidwell crossed the Rockies and the Sierra in 1841 with the first party to use the California Trail to reach the future Golden State. By the age of thirty, Bidwell had worked as the business manager for gold rush entrepreneur John Sutter, fought in the Mexican-American War, and served on the California Senate; he would go on to run for president as the Prohibition Party candidate in 1892. Also among Bidwell's many accomplishments was the 1860 founding of the city of Chico, in the Sacramento Valley.

In 1868, John Bidwell and his wife, Annie, married and moved into the three-story Italianate mansion he had been working on for three years. Their home became the social hub of the Sacramento Valley, replete with gas lighting, modern plumbing, and a total of twenty-six rooms. Some of the distinguished guests included William Tecumseh Sherman, John Muir, Susan B. Anthony, and President Rutherford B. Hayes. The Bidwell Mansion State Historic Park is located in downtown Chico at 525 Esplanade, and its many ornate rooms are open for public viewing on daily guided tours.

In the following excerpt, Bidwell describes his epic trip across the Sierra into California.

JOHN BIDWELL

from *ECHOES OF THE PAST*

We were now in what is at present Nevada, and probably within forty miles of the present boundary of California. We ascended the mountain on the north side of Walker River to the summit, and then struck a stream running west which proved to be the extreme source of the Stanislaus River. We followed it down for several days and finally came to where a branch ran into it, each forming a cañon. The main river flowed in a precipitous gorge, in places apparently a mile deep, and the gorge that came into it was but little less formidable. At night we found ourselves on the extreme point of the promontory between the two, very tired, and with neither grass nor water. We had to stay there that night. Early the next morning two men went down to see if it would be possible to get down through the smaller cañon. I was one of them, Jimmy Johns was the other. Benjamin Kelsey, who had shown himself expert in finding the way, was now, without any election, still recognized as leader, as he had been during the absence of Bartleson. A party also went back to see how far we should have to go around before we could pass over the tributary cañon. The understanding was that when we went down the cañon if it was practicable to get through we were to fire a gun so that all could follow; but if not, we were not to fire, even if we saw game. When Jimmy and I got down about three-quarters of a mile I came to the conclusion that it was impossible to get through and said to him, "Jimmy, we might as well go back; we can't go here." "Yes, we can," said he, and insisting that we could, he pulled out a pistol and fired.

It was an old dragoon pistol, and reverberated like a cannon. I hurried back to tell the company not to come down, but before I reached them the captain and his party had started. I explained, and warned them that they could not get down; but they went on as far as they could go and then were obliged to stay all day and all night to rest the animals, and had to go among the rocks and pick a little grass for them, and go down to the stream through a terrible place in the cañon to bring water up in cups and camp kettles, and some of the men in their boots, to pour down the animals' throats in order to keep them from perishing. Finally, four of them pulling and four pushing a mule, they managed to get them up one by one, and then carried all the things up again on their backs—not an easy job for exhausted men.

In some way, nobody knows how, Jimmy got through that cañon and into the Sacramento Valley. He had a horse with him—an Indian horse that was bought in the Rocky Mountains, and which could come as near climbing a tree as any horse I ever knew. Jimmy was a character. Of all men I have ever known I think he was the most fearless; he had the bravery of a bulldog. He was not seen for two months—until he was found at Sutter's, afterwards known as Sutter's Fort, now Sacramento City.

We went on, traveling as near west as we could. When we killed our last ox we shot and ate crows or anything we could kill, and one man shot a wildcat. We could eat anything. One day in the morning I went ahead, on foot of course, to see if I could kill something, it being understood that the company would keep on as near west as possible and find a practicable road. I followed an Indian trail down into the cañon, meeting many Indians on the way up. They did not molest me, but I did not quite like their looks. I went about ten miles down the cañon, and then began to think it time to strike north to intersect the trail of the company going west. A most difficult time I had scaling the precipice. Once I threw my gun ahead of me, being unable to hold it and climb, and then was in despair lest I could not get up where it was, but finally I did barely manage to do so, and make my way north. As the darkness came on I was obliged to look down and feel with my feet, lest I should pass over the trail of the party without seeing it. Just at dark I came to an immense fallen tree and tried to go around the top, but the place was too brushy, so I went around the butt, which seemed to me to be about twenty or twenty-five feet above my head. This I suppose to have been one of the fallen trees in the Calaveras Grove of *Sequoia gigantea* or mammoth trees, as I have since been there, and to my own satisfaction identified the lay of the land and the tree. Hence I concluded that I must have been the first white man who ever saw *Sequoia gigantea*, of which I told Frémont when he came to California in

1845. Of course sleep was impossible, for I had neither blanket nor coat, and burned or froze alternately as I turned from one side to the other before the small fire which I had built, until morning, when I started eastward to intersect the trail, thinking the company had turned north. But I traveled until noon and found no trail; then striking south, I came to the camp which I had left the previous morning.

The party had gone, but not where they said they would go; for they had taken the same trail I followed into the cañon, and had gone up the south side, which they had found so steep that many of the poor animals could not climb it and had to be left. When I arrived, the Indians were there cutting the horses to pieces and carrying off the meat. My situation, alone among strange Indians killing our poor horses, was by no means comfortable. Afterwards we found that these Indians were always at war with the Californians. They were known as the Horse Thief Indians, and lived chiefly on horse flesh; they had been in the habit of raiding the ranches even to the very coast, driving away horses by the hundreds into the mountains to eat. That night I overtook the party in camp.

A day or two later we came to a place where there was a great quantity of horse bones, and we did not know what it meant; we thought that an army must have perished there. They were, of course, horses that the Indians had driven in and slaughtered. A few nights later, fearing depredations, we concluded to stand guard—all but one man, who would not. So we let his two horses roam where they pleased. In the morning they could not be found. A few miles away we came to a village; the Indians had fled, but we found the horses killed and some of the meat roasting on a fire.

We were now on the edge of the San Joaquin Valley, but we did not even know that we were in California. We could see a range of mountains lying to the west—the Coast Range— but we could see no valley. The evening of the day we started down into the valley we were very tired, and when night came our party was strung along for three or four miles, and every man slept where darkness overtook him. He would take off his saddle for a pillow and turn his horse or mule loose, if he had one. His animal would be too poor to walk away, and in the morning he would find him, usually within fifty feet. The jaded horses nearly perished with hunger and fatigue. When we overtook the foremost of the party the next morning we found they had come to a pond of water, and one of them had killed a fat coyote. When I came up it was all eaten except the lights and the windpipe, on which I made my breakfast.

From that camp we saw timber to the north of us, evidently bordering a stream running west. It turned out to be the stream that we had followed down in the mountains—the Stanislaus River. As soon as we came in sight of the bottom land of the stream we saw an abundance of antelopes and sandhill cranes. We killed two of each the first evening. Wild grapes also abounded. The next day we killed fifteen deer and antelopes, jerked the meat, and got ready to go on, all except the captain's mess of seven or eight, who decided to stay there and lay in meat enough to last them into California. We were really almost down to tidewater, and did not know it. Some thought it was five hundred miles yet to California. But all thought we had to cross at least that range of mountains in sight to the west before entering the Promised Land, and how many beyond no man could tell. Nearly all thought it best to press on lest snows might overtake us in the mountains before us, as they had already nearly done on the mountains behind us (the Sierra Nevadas). It was now about the first of November. Our party set forth bearing northwest, aiming for a seeming gap north of a high mountain in the chain to the west of us. That mountain we found to be Mount Diablo. At night the Indians attacked the captain's camp and stole all their animals, which were the best in the company, and the next day the men had to overtake us with just what they could carry in their hands.

The next day, judging from the timber we saw, we concluded there was a river to the west. So two men went ahead to see if they could find a trail or a crossing. The timber proved to be along what is now known as the San Joaquin River. We sent two men on ahead to spy out the country. At night one of them returned, saying they came across an Indian on horseback without a saddle, who wore a cloth jacket but no other clothing. From what they could understand the Indian knew Mr. Marsh and had offered to guide them to his place. He plainly said "Marsh," and of course we supposed it was the Dr. Marsh before referred to who had written the letter to a friend in Jackson County, Missouri, and so it proved. One man went with the Indian to Marsh's ranch and the other came back to tell us what he had done, with the suggestion that we should go and cross the river (San Joaquin) at the place to which the trail was leading. In that way we found ourselves two days later at Dr. Marsh's ranch, and there we learned that we were really in California and our journey at an end. After six months we had now arrived at the first settlement in California, November 4, 1841.

DONNER MEMORIAL STATE PARK

The words "Donner Party" inescapably evoke the horrors of starvation, cannibalism, snowed-in Sierra passes, and the hardest of hardships of early pioneer life in California. Rarely, however, is the fate of the eighty-one party members who were stuck at Donner Lake and nearby Alder Creek in the winter of 1846 so compassionately portrayed as in James D. Houston's novel *Snow Mountain Passage*. Told in the honest tones of banished party member James Frazier Reed and, as in the following passage, the young Patty Reed—whose doll is still exhibited at Sutter's Fort—Houston breathes humanity into the Donner Party's struggle for survival.

Today, the chilling events of that ill-fated expedition are honored at Donner Memorial State Park, located on Donner Lake in Truckee. The 3,293-acre park is thick with Jeffrey pines and white firs and glaciated boulders and rock formations. In addition to boating, fishing, hiking, and camping, the park features opportunities to learn about, and reflect on, the Donner Party. The Emigrant Trail Museum details the story of the group as well as other, less notorious human histories of the area, including overviews of the area's native peoples and of the construction of the transcontinental railroad. Outside the museum, Pioneer Monument commemorates the Donner Party, standing twenty-two feet tall to mark the height of the snowfall that brutal winter of '46.

JAMES D. HOUSTON

from *SNOW MOUNTAIN PASSAGE*

Some people say the darkest hour comes just before the dawn.
Old sayings like that are easy to quote years later when you've
had some time to think back over your life. You don't quote
them when you're in the middle of that darkest hour and
cannot see a flicker of dawn peeping through in any direction.
Nobody was quoting it at the lake camp around about the
middle of February, when every one of us was wasting away,
some seeing things, others going blind. Keseberg's baby boy
had died, and William Eddy's wife, Eleanor. In our family all
that stood between us and starvation was three hides mama
had conserved, and one morning Mrs. Graves showed up
saying those hides belonged to her.

She was claiming them, she said, until mama could settle
her debt. She had worked herself into a fit. This time mama
was not to be outshouted. They stood in the snow screaming at
each other, pulling those smelly cattle hides this way and that.
Mama finally tore two of them loose. Elizabeth still held on to
one. She had brought along her seventeen-year-old son, who
was as skinny as a stick, like the rest of us, but mama didn't
have enough strength left to go after Elizabeth and her son too.
They dragged that one hide back to their cabin, and mama set
to work scraping at the two we had left.

After that I remember sitting still a lot. My mind would
simply go away. I don't know how many days went by. It was
about the time our last square of hide was boiled up that
we heard a voice from somewhere far off, a voice we didn't
recognize. We were down inside the Breens' cabin, with just
the fireplace light. A little streak of late afternoon was leaking
down the stairwell. I didn't say anything. I had been seeing
angels in the darkness and hearing them sing beautiful songs.
Sometimes they would call to me, and in my mind I would
answer. I listened for this voice to come again. And it did.

"Hallooww!" it called.

This time mama said, "Did you hear that?"

I looked around. I knew then everyone had heard it. Mama and Peggy Breen went scrambling for the ice stairs. I was right behind them. We came up into the light and saw men spread through the trees between us and the lake, big-bundled shaggy men, still calling, "Halloww! Hallooww!" When they saw us they stopped and stared at what must have been a horrifying sight, witches and scarecrows rising out of the snow.

Mama's voice was just a scratchy quaver. "Are you...?" She could hardly speak. "Are you men from California?"

"Yes, ma'am," one fellow shouted.

She fell onto her knees, weeping and laughing. "Thank the Lord," she said. "You've come at last."

Others were climbing out of the cabins now, my baby brothers, and Phillipine, the whole Breen clan. Patrick's prayers had been answered, it seemed, and Virginia's too. In our eyes these men were saints. Maybe they were the angels I'd been hearing in the dark, their voices floating toward me from beyond the mountains to the west. Maybe one of them was papa. I scanned their frosted eyes and craggy faces. He wasn't there. He wasn't there. I said, "Where's papa?" my voice so tiny in the hubbub of sobs and hallelujahs mama didn't hear me.

Once they slung down their loads, it didn't matter who they were or how they got there. They had packed in biscuits and jerked beef. We groveled and wept and gobbled up the morsels passed around to us, and begged for more, but they knew better than we did what can happen when you try to fill a shrunken belly.

The leader was a fellow named Glover. He had come across the plains and had camped with our party a time or two along the Platte. Mama remembered him. That night he slept with us, while the other men divided up among the cabins. We didn't know it at the time, but they were almost as bad off as we were. Our pitiful shelters were the first warm spots they'd seen in three weeks of being wet and cold and worn down with the climbing.

Since that time I've heard it said that these men in the rescue party did it for the money. It's true that they were earning wages they couldn't have made any other way. This was two years before the Gold Rush. You could buy a pound of butchered beef for two cents and a whole chicken for fifty cents. Five dollars a day was a huge amount. But something else was driving them. It wasn't family. None of them had relatives to rescue. Maybe it was some sense of kinship for the big trek we would later call the Great Migration. They had all come across to California in the past six months. I happen to think it was more than that. From time to time in this life people actually do courageous things. In my view now, looking back, it was nothing but valiant, and I cannot fault any of them for what happened next.

Those seven men needed a lot more rest. They also knew the sooner we started out, the better. They'd come through two bad storms to reach us. Now the skies were clear. The big question was, Who to take? Counting our camp and Donner's camp there were over fifty still alive. Mr. Glover made promises. Rescue teams would be going back and forth, he said, until everyone was on the other side. Some folks were too weak to walk, or too sick. Uncle George Donner, for instance. The hand he cut trying to plane a new axle had festered and the infection had spread all through him. He couldn't travel, and his wife, Tamsen, she wouldn't leave without him. They sent two of their little girls and two of Jacob Donner's children. Lewis Keseberg was bedridden, but Phillipine was still healthy and not quite so loyal. She could hike out, she said, with their little girl, Ada. The Breens sent their two oldest boys, while the rest of the family stayed put a while longer, since they had some meat in reserve. As for us, mama had nothing left, not even a scrap of hide, so we all ended up among the two dozen who set out from the lake camp behind the rescue team.

Just before we left, Keseberg emerged from the hole leading down to his buried lean-to. No one had seen him for weeks. With his son dead and his wife and daughter leaving, he didn't want to live alone. He was hobbling down to widow Murphy's. He had cut a forked branch into a homemade crutch. His tangled beard was so greasy it looked gray instead of blond. The weeks of pain had lined his face. The way his tortured eyes blinked and squinted against the light, he was like a convict released from a dungeon. He didn't look at us. He just hobbled across the snow, wincing with each tiny step. I have to confess, I hoped then I would never see him again. What a relief it was to leave that man behind, to leave those dreadful cabins behind at last, the lice, the stink, the smoky darkness. I felt that I too had been imprisoned and was finally set free.

Up ahead, someone led the way in a pair of snowshoes. The rest of us were supposed to follow along, stepping where he stepped. If you had short legs like Tommy and me, it wasn't easy. We had to climb in and out of each deep step. Tommy was four, going on five. In the whole party he was the youngest one walking, and the smallest. I called back to him a few times, "C'mon, Tommy. Papa's gonna be here pretty soon." Then my breath gave out. I couldn't do both, call to him and climb in and out of those holes everyone ahead of us made deeper and mushier.

Mama urged us on, lifting us from time to time, but we fell farther behind with each step. The party had hiked about two miles, stretched out along the side of Truckee Lake, with me and Tommy right at the end, when Mr. Glover came back and told mama we were slowing everyone else down. If we couldn't make better time we'd have to go back to the cabins.

"I'm sorry, Mrs. Reed. I got to think about the welfare of the whole party and make it across while we got the weather on our side."

Mama said if we went back she'd go with us. The whole family would go back together and wait for another rescue team. Mr. Glover, he got real stern, said he couldn't let her do that. "Every person able to walk has to walk out of here. You go back with your children, you'll only eat the others' food. Everyone that goes helps them that stays behind."

Virginia and James Junior had started to cry. Mama begged Mr. Glover not to leave us. She said it wasn't fair, it wasn't right. He said he could tell by looking at us we were too weak to walk and we were too much to carry. Two of his men were already carrying infants, and there was still the summit trail to climb.

Mama couldn't stand what he was telling her to do. She looked around at the four of us, and what I saw then was the most terrible look I've ever seen on any face before or since. It was the wild, stark near-madness that comes into the eyes when you have eaten almost nothing for weeks and your flesh wastes away and leaves the bones and sockets showing. And it was something else. It was the mother's bottomless terror. She had already climbed the summit trail. She knew what awaited us up there. She now had to face the fact that Tommy and I would both perish if we kept on going the way we'd been going, spindly as we were, and down to nothing, with no meat on our bones. She also knew returning to the cabins was no better, maybe even worse.

When Mr. Glover saw she could not speak, he said he would come back for us. Mama turned her anguished and accusing eyes on him. She made him promise that he himself would do this, and he said he would. When they got to Bear Valley, he told her, if no other rescue team had started in, he would turn right around and come back for the two of us.

Mama dropped to her knees in the snow and pulled Tommy close and told him to stay right with me, and she would be seeing us again in a few days. Poor Tommy was so numb and cold and hungry you couldn't tell if he had any idea what was being asked of him.

She hugged me close and looked into my eyes. "Never forget that I love you, Patty. And papa loves you too."

I still do not know what possessed me to say what I said just then. Something in me had shifted. I know enough now to give words to what it was. The little girl inside me went away, as surely as if a path had opened up through the trees. She just stepped out of my body and walked down that path and into the Sierra Nevada forest, never to return. I had already seen more than you ought to see by the time you are that age. I had seen my father stab another man in the chest and watched that man bleed to death. I had heard wounded animals screaming for water in the desert night, and heard the widow Murphy crying out from her cabin like a lone wolf howling in the woods. I had watched people starving and watched my own brothers shrivel up till there was nearly nothing left and watched my mother walk away from me, out across the snow and disappear. As she prepared to do this yet again I was able for the first time to imagine my own death and to imagine that I would not see her anymore. At moments like this you are supposed to cry. I wasn't able to cry. She was the one who cried. I was the one who stood there giving motherly advice. I know now my words cut through her as surely as if a sword of ice had dropped off one of the limbs above us and speared her heart. It makes me weep to think of it. Yes, seventy-five years later my own tears come dripping down to match those she wept that day.

"Well, mother," I said, "if you never see me again, you do the best you can."

Is that too hard-hearted for an eight-year-old? Somehow I was prepared for my death and for hers too. I told as much to Mr. Glover after we turned and started back. It disturbed him, I know. In my eyes then he seemed to be an executioner. Later I would see that he was a very decent man, though rough and rugged in his looks, red-eyed from the cold and from his monumental efforts.

"Don't you talk like that," he said to me. "I give your mama my word, and I mean to keep it."

[...]

It was like the first time mama left, but harder because Tommy didn't move much. Sometimes I had to hold a mirror to his lips to make sure he was breathing. Sometimes his eyes would open, and he would almost seem to speak. I would warm our slivers of meat and fry up some flour; then chew Tommy's portion to soften it and try to make him eat.

I don't know who was worse off then—him, because he had no idea of what was going on around us, or me, because I did. I remember hearing Patrick and Peggy say things I didn't understand. Years later I came to see that they already knew what was happening at the other cabin, where someone had gone out and uncovered Milt's body, buried in the snow, and started cutting away parts of him for food. Whether it was the widow started it, or Keseberg, no one would ever be able to say for sure.

My heart went out to widow Murphy, and still does. She was called "widow" because her husband had died on her. The fact is, she wasn't much older than mama, not yet forty. You have to give her credit for trying something most single women wouldn't have dared in that day and age. She had started west on her own, with seven children. Two of her daughters had married young and had brought their children. For a while it had been quite a clan, three wagonloads. William Foster was her son-in-law. So was William Pike, the fellow Foster shot in the back. She'd lost a boy at the lake camp. Five more of her children had already hiked out, leaving her with one small son, a boy about my age. Little by little she'd been losing her eyesight and losing her mind. By the time Keseberg moved in, she'd probably forgotten who he was. In her sad hunger she'd probably forgotten who Milt was.

I thank the Lord I had lost the will to walk more than fifty feet at a time. After Mr. Glover left I never wandered far enough in her direction to see any sign of what was going on— though I think I must have known. Deep down I must have. I must have chosen not to understand the words Patrick and Peggy whispered on the other side of the blanket.

As I think back upon those weeks it seems as if the mountains themselves had revealed an appetite, as if somewhere among the snowy crevices and windblown granite slopes there were ancient and empty places that had to be filled, laying claim to what little energy and life force remained for us. It had a pull, and it had a voice, and you couldn't resist it. When the angels came to visit I could not tell if they were heavenly angels or mountain angels, and it didn't make much difference which, their music was so sweet. They would visit me at all times of the day and night, and before long I stopped hearing much of anything but their voices. They would come from far away like the flute notes of distant birds approaching, single notes I would hear before I saw the wings. Then they'd be all around, white-winged angels singing in a forest filled with silver light. Sometimes they wouldn't sing. They would float and beckon, and start to drift away, and I would call out, "Don't go! Don't go!" And back they'd come, as if they'd just been teasing me, flirting and teasing.

[...]

One day I felt compelled to get outside. Something was calling me up into the light, whether angels with wings or the white-robed visitor again, I did not know. Something was out there. I had to know what it was.

It took a lot of effort, climbing the snow stairs. I listened for the flute notes, the tender voices coming from the lake. I remember the sky was very blue when I stepped out onto the snow. The air was quiet. The figure coming toward me through the trees this time was dark and large. No wings. No furry robes. The arms were pumping, as if punching at the air, like someone running but in slow motion, fighting through the snow. And then a call came toward me.

"Patty!"

I knew this voice. It wasn't Salvador. It wasn't Mr. Glover. My heart stopped. I had been seeing so many things, hearing so many things, I closed my eyes. Again the voice called, "Patty?" like a question.

He was closer, his huge pack thrown down behind him, and his hat thrown down. I could see his face, his beard, as he lunged toward me, calling, "Patty! Patty! Is it you?"

I tried to run, sure he would disappear before I reached him. I tried to call out, "Papa!" My voice stuck in my throat. The snow had been melting. It was soft. I couldn't lift my legs high enough to run. I fell forward. Then he was over me, lifting me. I looked into his eyes. As he held me his face filled with fear at what he saw, and that made me afraid. I threw my arms around his neck. He hugged me close against his coat, against his chest.

"It's okay, darlin'," he said, "we're okay now," his voice soothing away my confusion, his voice sweeter than all those others I'd been hearing.

I still couldn't talk. With my face pushed into the thick, scratchy wool of his coat I sobbed and sobbed. He held me until I got my breath and found my voice.

"I'm so hungry, papa. I've never been so hungry."

"I know, darlin'. I have something for you that we baked last night."

He set me down and fetched his pack, where he had a little cloth bag. He brought out a tiny biscuit about the size of a thimble. I'd never seen anything so beautiful. "Here ya go, darlin'. Just bite off a little bit. Eat it real slow."

I ate that and he gave me another one. I could see the bag was full of these biscuit morsels. My heart swelled with new love for him.

"I knew you'd come back, papa."

"You knew I wouldn't leave my little girl behind."

"Did you see James Junior and Virginia?"

"Yes, we did. By now they're safe and sound in California."

"Have you been to California, papa?"

"I sure have, darlin'."

"Is it far away?"

"Hardly any ways at all. Where's Tommy now?"

"He's down below, papa. He's sleeping. He sleeps most all the time. I tried to feed him whenever I could. But after a while..." I started to cry again. "After a while there wasn't any more..."

The days and weeks of tears I hadn't been able to feel came gushing forth. Again he picked me up and held me close and I felt his body shaking next to mine, like the day by the Humboldt when we cut away his hair. Then he put me down and gave me another biscuit and told me to sit still while he went below.

I sat there nibbling, each crumb a precious gift, until papa climbed back up the stairs carrying Tommy, so small against his coat he looked like a doll. Papa had been crying again, and he was trying not to. He didn't have time to cry.

Patrick had followed him and stood at the top of the stairs. I don't know what had passed between them in the darkness. Maybe nothing. They watched each other for quite a while.

Papa said, "I thank you, Patrick, for giving shelter to my children."

"It hasn't been easy here."

"I can see that."

"We've got our own."

"I saw your boys up past the summit. They'll be all right. Glover's a good man."

"They're good boys too."

And there they stood, meeting again, two men from Ireland who never cared much for each other in the best of days. For the first time in all these months I felt sorry for Patrick. He looked so shrunken next to papa, who'd left the company in disgrace and had now returned, weary from the climbing but in good health and vigorous after five months of constant motion, while Patrick had been mostly waiting, stiff from sitting and from nursing his kidney stones. In his eyes there was a look I now understand. His fear was that he'd be left behind, that papa bore some grudge and would rescue us but no one else. Knowing Patrick, the way his mind worked in those days, this is probably what he himself would have done, if supplies were short and there were weaker ones to contend with. The night Milt Elliott starved to death, Patrick still had meat in his cabin. Maybe he was afraid papa would find out about that.

At last papa said, "Get your family ready. We're starting back right away, with everyone who can walk."

EMERALD BAY STATE PARK

Any visitors to the enormous alpine shores of Lake Tahoe who have wandered breathing deep through the pines, who have placed their feet in that snowmelt water, will understand why Mark Twain calls a visit to Tahoe as healing as any doctor's prescription. Twain asserts, in his usual jaunty tone, that "three months of camp life on Lake Tahoe would restore an Egyptian mummy to his pristine vigor." In the selection that follows, Twain recounts four splendid days he and a friend spent at Tahoe, subsisting on the cache of food left behind by friends from a boarding house whom they called the Irish Brigade, or the Brigade Boys. They also made good use of their boat, drifting blissfully atop the clear deeps of the lake.

The surface of Lake Tahoe rests at some 6,225 feet above sea level, and it is 1,645 feet deep, making it the largest alpine lake in North America and the second deepest in the United States. Its outstanding beauty has made Tahoe and the surrounding mountains a major destination year round. On the California side, several state parks and recreation areas include parts of the lake, including the 1,533-acre Emerald Bay State Park, home to a stunning panorama of the lake and the fabled Vikingsholm mansion. A visit to any vista of this two-million-year-old lake, dark blue and seemingly bottomless, will make your breath deeper and your step lighter.

MARK TWAIN

from *ROUGHING IT*

It was the end of August, and the skies were cloudless and the weather superb. In two or three weeks I had grown wonderfully fascinated with the curious new country, and concluded to put off my return to "the States" a while. I had grown well accustomed to wearing a damaged slouch hat, blue woolen shirt, and pants crammed into boot-tops, and gloried in the absence of coat, vest and braces. I felt rowdyish and "bully" (as the historian Josephus phrases it, in his fine chapter upon the destruction of the Temple). It seemed to me that nothing could be so fine and so romantic. I had become an officer of the government, but that was for mere sublimity. The office was an unique sinecure. I had nothing to do and no salary. I was private secretary to his majesty the Secretary and there was not yet writing enough for two of us. So Johnny K—— and I devoted our time to amusement. He was the young son of an Ohio nabob and was out there for recreation. He got it. We had heard a world of talk about the marvelous beauty of Lake Tahoe, and finally curiosity drove us thither to see it. Three or four members of the Brigade had been there and located some timber lands on its shores and stored up a quantity of provisions in their camp. We strapped a couple of blankets on our shoulders and took an axe apiece and started—for we intended to take up a wood ranch or so ourselves and become wealthy. We were on foot. The reader will find it advantageous to go horseback. We were told that the distance was eleven miles. We tramped a long time on level ground, and then toiled laboriously up a mountain about a thousand miles high and looked over. No lake there. We descended on the other side, crossed the valley and toiled up another mountain three or four thousand miles high, apparently, and looked over again. No lake yet. We sat down tired and perspiring, and hired a couple of Chinamen to curse those people who had beguiled us. Thus refreshed, we presently resumed the march with renewed vigor and determination. We plodded on, two or three hours longer, and at last the Lake burst upon us—a noble sheet of blue water lifted six thousand three hundred feet above the level of the sea, and walled in by a rim of snow-clad mountain peaks that towered aloft full three thousand feet higher still! It was a vast oval, and one would have to use up eighty or a hundred good miles in traveling around it. As it lay there with the shadows of the mountains brilliantly photographed upon its still surface I thought it must surely be the fairest picture the whole earth affords.

We found the small skiff belonging to the Brigade boys, and without loss of time set out across a deep bend of the lake toward the landmarks that signified the locality of the camp. I got Johnny to row—not because I mind exertion myself, but because it makes me sick to ride backwards when I am at work. But I steered. A three-mile pull brought us to the camp just as the night fell, and we stepped ashore very tired and wolfishly hungry. In a "cache" among the rocks we found the provisions and the cooking utensils, and then, all fatigued as I was, I sat down on a boulder and superintended while Johnny gathered wood and cooked supper. Many a man who had gone through what I had, would have wanted to rest.

It was a delicious supper—hot bread, fried bacon, and black coffee. It was a delicious solitude we were in, too. Three miles away was a saw-mill and some workmen, but there were not fifteen other human beings throughout the wide circumference of the lake. As the darkness closed down and the stars came out and spangled the great mirror with jewels, we smoked meditatively in the solemn hush and forgot our troubles and our pains. In due time we spread our blankets in the warm sand between two large boulders and soon fell asleep, careless of the procession of ants that passed in through rents in our clothing and explored our persons. Nothing could disturb the sleep that fettered us, for it had been fairly earned, and if our consciences had any sins on them they had to adjourn court for that night, anyway. The wind rose just as we were losing consciousness, and we were lulled to sleep by the beating of the surf upon the shore.

It is always very cold on that lake shore in the night, but we had plenty of blankets and were warm enough. We never moved a muscle all night, but waked at early dawn in the original positions, and got up at once, thoroughly refreshed, free from soreness, and brim full of friskiness. There is no end of wholesome medicine in such an experience. That morning we could have whipped ten such people as we were the day before—sick ones at any rate. But the world is slow, and people will go to "water cures" and "movement cures" and to foreign lands for health. Three months of camp life on Lake Tahoe would restore an Egyptian mummy to his pristine vigor, and give him an appetite like an alligator. I do not mean the oldest and driest mummies, of course, but the fresher ones. The air up there in the clouds is very pure and fine, bracing and delicious. And why shouldn't it be?—it is the same the angels breathe. I think that hardly any amount of fatigue can be gathered together that a man cannot sleep off in one night on the sand by its side. Not under a roof, but under the sky; it seldom or never rains there in the summer time. I know a man who went there to die. But he made a failure of it. He was a skeleton when he came, and could barely stand. He had no appetite, and did nothing but read tracts and reflect on the future. Three months later he was sleeping out of doors regularly, eating all he could hold, three times a day, and chasing game over mountains three thousand feet high for recreation. And he was a skeleton no longer, but weighed part of a ton. This is no fancy sketch, but the truth. His disease was consumption. I confidently commend his experience to other skeletons.

I superintended again, and as soon as we had eaten breakfast we got in the boat and skirted along the lake shore about three miles and disembarked. We liked the appearance of the place, and so we claimed some three hundred acres of it and stuck our "notices" on a tree. It was yellow pine timber land—a dense forest of trees a hundred feet high and from one to five feet through at the butt. It was necessary to fence our property or we could not hold it. That is to say, it was necessary to cut down trees here and there and make them fall in such a way as to form a sort of enclosure (with pretty wide gaps in it). We cut down three trees apiece, and found it such heart-breaking work that we decided to "rest our case" on those; if they held the property, well and good; if they didn't, let the property spill out through the gaps and go; it was no use to work ourselves to death merely to save a few acres of land. Next day we came back to build a house—for a house was also necessary, in order to hold the property. We decided to build a substantial log-house and excite the envy of the Brigade boys; but by the time we had cut and trimmed the first log it seemed unnecessary to be so elaborate, and so we concluded to build it of saplings. However, two saplings, duly cut and trimmed, compelled recognition of the fact that a still modester architecture would satisfy the law, and so we concluded to build a "brush" house. We devoted the next day to this work, but we did so much "sitting around" and discussing, that by the middle of the afternoon we had achieved only a half-way sort of affair which one of us had to watch while the other cut brush, lest if both turned our backs we might not be able to find it again, it had such a strong family resemblance to the surrounding vegetation. But we were satisfied with it.

We were land owners now, duly seized and possessed, and within the protection of the law. Therefore we decided to take up our residence on our own domain and enjoy that large sense of independence which only such an experience can bring. Late the next afternoon, after a good long rest, we sailed away from the Brigade camp with all the provisions and cooking utensils we could carry off—borrow is the more accurate word—and just as the night was falling we beached the boat at our own landing.

• • • • •

If there is any life that is happier than the life we led on our timber ranch for the next two or three weeks, it must be a sort of life which I have not read of in books or experienced in person. We did not see a human being but ourselves during the time, or hear any sounds but those that were made by the wind and the waves, the sighing of the pines, and now and then the far-off thunder of an avalanche. The forest about us was dense and cool, the sky above us was cloudless and brilliant with sunshine, the broad lake before us was glassy and clear, or rippled and breezy, or black and storm-tossed, according to Nature's mood; and its circling border of mountain domes, clothed with forests, scarred with land-slides, cloven by canyons and valleys, and helmeted with glittering snow, fitly framed and finished the noble picture. The view was always fascinating, bewitching, entrancing. The eye was never tired of gazing, night or day, in calm or storm; it suffered but one grief, and that was that it could not look always, but must close sometimes in sleep.

We slept in the sand close to the water's edge, between two protecting boulders, which took care of the stormy night-winds for us. We never took any paregoric to make us sleep. At the first break of dawn we were always up and running footraces to tone down excess of physical vigor and exuberance of spirits. That is, Johnny was—but I held his hat. While smoking the pipe of peace after breakfast we watched the sentinel peaks put on the glory of the sun, and followed the conquering light as it swept down among the shadows, and set the captive crags and forests free. We watched the tinted pictures grow and brighten upon the water till every little detail of forest, precipice and pinnacle was wrought in and finished, and the miracle of the enchanter complete. Then to "business."

That is, drifting around in the boat. We were on the north shore. There, the rocks on the bottom are sometimes gray, sometimes white. This gives the marvelous transparency of the water a fuller advantage than it has elsewhere on the lake. We usually pushed out a hundred yards or so from shore, and then lay down on the thwarts, in the sun, and let the boat drift by the hour whither it would. We seldom talked. It interrupted the Sabbath stillness, and marred the dreams the luxurious rest and indolence brought. The shore all along was indented with deep, curved bays and coves, bordered by narrow sand-beaches; and where the sand ended, the steep mountain sides rose right up aloft into space—rose up like a vast wall a little out of the perpendicular, and thickly wooded with tall pines.

So singularly clear was the water, that where it was only twenty or thirty feet deep the bottom was so perfectly distinct that the boat seemed floating in the air! Yes, where it was even *eighty* feet deep. Every little pebble was distinct, every speckled trout, every hand's-breadth of sand. Often, as we lay on our faces, a granite boulder, as large as a village church, would start out of the bottom apparently, and seem climbing up rapidly to the surface, till presently it threatened to touch our faces, and we could not resist the impulse to seize an oar and avert the danger. But the boat would float on, and the boulder descend again, and then we could see that when we had been exactly above it, it must still have been twenty or thirty feet below the surface. Down through the transparency of these great depths, the water was not *merely* transparent, but dazzlingly, brilliantly so. All objects seen through it had a bright, strong vividness, not only of outline, but of every minute detail, which they would not have had when seen simply through the same depth of atmosphere. So empty and airy did all spaces seem below us, and so strong was the sense of floating high aloft in mid-nothingness, that we called these boat-excursions "balloon-voyages."

We fished a good deal, but we did not average one fish a week. We could see trout by the thousand winging about in the emptiness under us, or sleeping in shoals on the bottom, but they would not bite—they could see the line too plainly, perhaps. We frequently selected the trout we wanted, and rested the bait patiently and persistently on the end of his nose at a depth of eighty feet, but he would only shake it off with an annoyed manner, and shift his position.

We bathed occasionally, but the water was rather chilly, for all it looked so sunny. Sometimes we rowed out to the "blue water," a mile or two from shore. It was as dead blue as indigo there, because of the immense depth. By official measurement the lake in its centre is one thousand five hundred and twenty-five feet deep!

Sometimes, on lazy afternoons, we lolled on the sand in camp, and smoked pipes and read some old well-worn novels. At night, by the camp-fire, we played euchre and seven-up to strengthen the mind—and played them with cards so greasy and defaced that only a whole summer's acquaintance with them could enable the student to tell the ace of clubs from the jack of diamonds.

We never slept in our "house." It never occurred to us, for one thing; and besides, it was built to hold the ground, and that was enough. We did not wish to strain it.

By and by our provisions began to run short, and we went back to the old camp and laid in a new supply. We were gone all day, and reached home again about nightfall, pretty tired and hungry. While Johnny was carrying the main bulk of the provisions up to our "house" for future use, I took the loaf of bread, some slices of bacon, and the coffee-pot, ashore, set them down by a tree, lit a fire, and went back to the boat to get the frying-pan. While I was at this, I heard a shout from Johnny, and looking up I saw that my fire was galloping all over the premises!

Johnny was on the other side of it. He had to run through the flames to get to the lake shore, and then we stood helpless and watched the devastation.

The ground was deeply carpeted with dry pine-needles, and the fire touched them off as if they were gunpowder. It was wonderful to see with what fierce speed the tall sheet of flame traveled! My coffee-pot was gone, and everything with it. In a minute and a half the fire seized upon a dense growth of dry manzanita chapparal six or eight feet high, and then the roaring and popping and crackling was something terrific. We were driven to the boat by the intense heat, and there we remained, spell-bound.

Within half an hour all before us was a tossing, blinding tempest of flame! It went surging up adjacent ridges— surmounted them and disappeared in the canyons beyond— burst into view upon higher and farther ridges, presently—shed a grander illumination abroad, and dove again—flamed out again, directly, higher and still higher up the mountain side— threw out skirmishing parties of fire here and there, and sent them trailing their crimson spirals away among remote ramparts and ribs and gorges, till as far as the eye could reach the lofty mountain-fronts were webbed as it were with a tangled net-work of red lava streams. Away across the water the crags and domes were lit with a ruddy glare, and the firmament above was a reflected hell!

Every feature of the spectacle was repeated in the glowing mirror of the lake! Both pictures were sublime, both were beautiful; but that in the lake had a bewildering richness about it that enchanted the eye and held it with the stronger fascination.

We sat absorbed and motionless through four long hours. We never thought of supper, and never felt fatigue. But at eleven o'clock the conflagration had traveled beyond our range of vision, and then darkness stole down upon the landscape again.

Hunger asserted itself now, but there was nothing to eat. The provisions were all cooked, no doubt, but we did not go to see. We were homeless wanderers again, without any property. Our fence was gone, our house burned down; no insurance. Our pine forest was well scorched, the dead trees all burned up, and our broad acres of manzanita swept away. Our blankets were on our usual sand-bed, however, and so we lay down and went to sleep. The next morning we started back to the old camp, but while out a long way from shore, so great a storm came up that we dared not try to land. So I baled out the seas we shipped, and Johnny pulled heavily through the billows till we had reached a point three or four miles beyond the camp. The storm was increasing, and it became evident that it was better to take the hazard of beaching the boat than go down in a hundred fathoms of water; so we ran in, with tall whitecaps following, and I sat down in the stern-sheets and pointed her head-on to the shore. The instant the bow struck, a wave came over the stern that washed crew and cargo ashore, and saved a deal of trouble. We shivered in the lee of a boulder all the rest of the day, and froze all the night through. In the morning the tempest had gone down, and we paddled down to the camp without any unnecessary delay. We were so starved that we ate up the rest of the Brigade's provisions, and then set out to Carson to tell them about it and ask their forgiveness. It was accorded, upon payment of damages.

We made many trips to the lake after that, and had many a hair-breadth escape and blood-curdling adventure which will never be recorded in any history.

SCHOONER GULCH
STATE BEACH

Among the many shorebirds seen skittering and pecking at the water's edge on stilt-long legs, their beaks like pencils sketching at the sand, is the elegant sanderling. Found up and down the California coast, the sanderling was perhaps best described by Bradford Torrey, a Southern California ornithologist who spent many a long afternoon observing these exuberant waterbirds from a comfortable vantage on the shore.

At Schooner Gulch State Beach in Mendocino County, sanderlings congregate in darting, white-feathered flocks through the winter, chasing the tideline on skinny legs for the little morsels hidden just under the surface of the sand. Here, the waves are wild and cold, the cliffs steep down to the water, and the beach perfect for picnicking and watching the shorebirds with the same glee as did Bradford Torrey himself.

BRADFORD TORREY

from *FIELD-DAYS IN CALIFORNIA*

Here, for instance, is a flock of sanderlings, a score, perhaps, or, not unlikely, a hundred. The tide is falling; they have had a long rest, sitting in a close bunch on the dry sand while the beach has been flooded; and now see how busy they are! Every time a wave recedes, down they run in its wake to seize any bit of edible life that it may have left behind. Till the last moment they stay, pecking hastily right and left in the suds, not to lose a morsel; and then, as the next breaker comes rolling in, back they scamper up the beach as fast as their legs will bear them. If they get their toes wet, it is no killing matter; but they keep a sharp lookout against anything worse than that. The most timorous of screaming human surf-bathers could not be more insistent upon that score.

If you do not enjoy this animated scene, then it is hard to think what you are made of. All their movements are so quick, so eager, and so graceful! And the birds themselves are so pretty, snowy white, with black, or black and brown, markings.

But they are even more engaging if you catch them at their bath. This they sometimes take in the uppermost reaches of the surf, a hurried and none too comfortable operation, as it looks, since they must retreat every time another wave comes in. They much prefer, I think, the edges of some still tide-pool, where they can dip and splash at their leisure.

About the bathing itself, as far as I have observed, there is nothing peculiar; but after it I once saw them practising what was to me a trick as novel as it was pleasing. Standing on the sand, they sprang straight into the air again and again to a height of six or eight inches, shaking themselves vigorously while so doing, evidently for the purpose of drying their feathers. At the first instant I thought they might be catching low-flying insects such as swarm here and there about patches of seaweed or on the edge of shallow still water. "Bravo!" said I, when I discovered my mistake; "you have shown me some-thing new."

On the same occasion I noticed, what I had often noticed before, their strong propensity for standing and running (hopping, I ought to say, I suppose, lest some youthful critic, shocked at my ignorance, should esteem it his duty to set me right) on one leg. Sometimes half the flock will be thus engaged. And the wonder is that they get over the ground almost or quite as quickly on one leg as on two. At any rate, they keep up with the procession,—which is the principal aim of most of us,—no matter how fast it is moving.

Just why sanderlings, or any other birds, should habitually balance themselves thus in sleep or when at rest, is more than I have ever seen explained or been able myself to divine. A swan, say, with its big body and long neck, or a tall heron, born to go on stilts, or a caged canary—how have they come to find this unnatural-looking, awkward-looking, difficult-looking, Simeon-Stylites-like attitude the acme of comfort?

Fancy yourself trying it to-night instead of getting between the sheets. What long hours of peaceful slumber you would enjoy! Sleeping or waking, even if you are a trained athlete, I would not give you any great length of time in which to maintain the attitude, to say nothing of finding it conducive to repose.

As for *running* on one leg, that, so far as I know, is a trick peculiar to sanderlings. As well as I can recall, I have never found any other kind of bird attempting it; except of course, disabled individuals, which show plainly enough by their awkwardness that their one-legged performances, such as they are, are matters of painful necessity.

Whether sanderlings have the happiness to feel a comfortable touch of pride in this singularity of theirs is a question to be left for such as possess a better, more instinctive, knowledge than I am favored with as to what goes on inside of fur and feathers.

MARSHALL GOLD DISCOVERY STATE HISTORIC PARK

When carpenter James Marshall first found "something shining in the bottom of the ditch" and lifted it up into the cold morning sun shining down on the American River, he could not have fathomed the gold mania that would change San Francisco and the Sierra foothills forever. In fact, on that fated day in 1848, he could barely believe the luminous lump was gold at all, which was why he took it to be thoroughly appraised by an expert. From that point, despite his best efforts—and the best efforts of his boss, John Sutter—it didn't take long before word was out and thousands of people were arriving to the area with shovels, pans, and picks ready to seek their fortunes.

The 575-acre Marshall Gold Discovery State Historic Park, located in El Dorado County near the small gold rush town of Coloma, is a walk back through time. Preserved historical buildings from the forty-niner era include Marshall Cabin and a Chinese general store called the Wah Hop Store, and the park also boasts a replica of Sutter's original mill as well as a museum featuring mining exhibitions. Hikers can take the loop made by the Monroe Ridge Trail and the Monument Trail past an old spring house, historic fruit orchards, and the river itself, where a statue of Marshall points to the precise place where he first sifted gold from the water and created a new California.

JAMES W. MARSHALL

"MARSHALL'S OWN ACCOUNT OF THE GOLD DISCOVERY"

In May, 1847, with my rifle, blanket, and a few crackers to eat with the venison (for the deer then were awful plenty), I ascended the American River, according to Mr. Sutter's wish, as he wanted to find a good site for a saw-mill, where we could have plenty of timber, and where wagons would be able to ascend and descend the river hills. Many fellows had been out before me, but they could not find any place to suit; so when I left I told Mr. Sutter I would go along the river to its very head and find the place, if such a place existed anywhere upon the river or any of its forks. I traveled along the river the whole way. Many places would suit very well for the erection of the mill, with plenty of timber everywhere, but then nothing but a mule could climb the hills; and when I would find a spot where the hills were not steep, there was no timber to be had; and so it was until I had been out several days and reached this place, which, after first sight, looked like the exact spot we were hunting.

You may be sure Mr. Sutter was pleased when I reported my success. We entered into partnership; I was to build the mill, and he was to find provisions, teams, tools, and to pay a portion of the men wages. I believe I was at that time the only millwright in the whole country. In August, everything being ready, we freighted two wagons with tools and provisions, and accompanied by six men I left the fort, and after a good deal of difficulty reached this place one beautiful afternoon and formed our camp on yon little rise of ground right above the town.

Our first business was to put up log houses, as we intended remaining here all winter. This was done in less than no time, for my men were great with the ax. We then cut timber, and fell to work hewing it for the framework of the mill. The Indians gathered about us in great numbers. I employed about forty of them to assist us with the dam, which we put up in a kind of way in about four weeks....I left for the fort [after] giving orders to Mr. Weimar to have a ditch cut through the bar in the rear of the mill, and after quitting work in the evening to raise the gate and let the water run all night, as it would assist us very much in deepening and widening the tail-race.

I returned in a few days, and found everything favorable, all the men being at work in the ditch. When the channel was opened it was my custom every evening to raise the gate and let the water wash out as much sand and gravel through the night as possible; and in the morning, while the men were getting breakfast, I would walk down, and, shutting off the water, look along the race and see what was to be done, so that I might tell Mr. Weimar, who had charge of the Indians, at what particular point to set them to work for the day. As I was the only millwright present, all of my time was employed upon the framework and machinery.

One morning in January—it was a clear, cold morning; I shall never forget that morning—as I was taking my usual walk along the race after shutting off the water, my eye was caught with the glimpse of something shining in the bottom of the ditch. There was about a foot of water running then. I reached my hand down and picked it up; it made my heart thump, for I was certain it was gold. The piece was about half the size and of the shape of a pea. Then I saw another piece in the water. After taking it out I sat down and began to think right hard. I thought it was gold, and yet it did not seem to be of the right color: all the gold coin I had seen was of a reddish tinge; this looked more like brass. I recalled to mind all the metals I had ever seen or heard of, but I could find none that resembled this.

Suddenly the idea flashed across my mind that it might be iron pyrites. I trembled to think of it! This question could soon be determined. Putting one of the pieces on a hard river stone, I took another and commenced hammering it. It was soft, and didn't break: it therefore must be gold, but largely mixed with some other metal, very likely silver; for pure gold, I thought, would certainly have a brighter color.

When I returned to our cabin for breakfast I showed the two pieces to my men. They were all a good deal excited, and had they not thought that the gold only existed in small quantities they would have abandoned everything and left me to finish my job alone. However, to satisfy them, I told them that as soon as we had the mill finished we would devote a week or two to gold hunting and see what we could make out of it.

While we were working in the race after this discovery we always kept a sharp lookout, and in the course of three or four days we had picked up about three ounces—our work still progressing as lively as ever, for none of us imagined at that time that the whole country was sowed with gold.

In about a week's time after the discovery I had to take another trip to the fort; and, to gain what information I could respecting the real value of the metal, took all that we had collected with me and showed it to Mr. Sutter, who at once declared it was gold, but thought with me that it was greatly mixed with some other metal. It puzzled us a good deal to hit upon the means of telling the exact quantity of gold contained in the alloy; however, we at last stumbled on an old American encyclopedia, where we saw the specific gravity of all the metals, and rules given to find the quantity of each in a given bulk.

After hunting over the whole fort and borrowing from some of the men, we got three dollars and a half in silver, and with a small pair of scales we soon ciphered it out that there was no silver nor copper in the gold, but that it was entirely pure.

This fact being ascertained, we thought it our best policy to keep it as quiet as possible till we should have finished our mill. But there was a great number of disbanded Mormon soldiers in and about the fort, and when they came to hear of it, why it just spread like wildfire, and soon the whole country was in a bustle. I had scarcely arrived at the mill again till several persons appeared with pans, shovels, and hoes, and those that had not iron picks had wooden ones, all anxious to fall to work and dig up our mill; but this we would not permit. As fast as one party disappeared another would arrive, and sometimes I had the greatest kind of trouble to get rid of them. I sent them all off in different directions, telling them about such and such places, where I was certain there was plenty of gold if they would only take the trouble of looking for it. At that time I never imagined that the gold was so abundant. I told them to go to such and such places, because it appeared that they would dig nowhere but in such places as I pointed out, and I believe such was their confidence in me that they would have dug on the very top of yon mountain if I had told them to do so.

The second place where gold was discovered was in a gulch near the Mountaineer House, on the road to Sacramento. The third place was on a bar on the South Fork of the American River a little above the junction of the Middle and South forks. The diggings at Hangtown [now Placerville] were discovered next by myself, for we all went out for a while as soon as our job was finished. The Indians next discovered the diggings at Kelsey's and thus in a very short time we discovered that the whole country was but one bed of gold. So there, stranger, is the entire history of the gold discovery in California—a discovery that hasn't as yet been of much benefit to me.

GOVERNOR'S MANSION STATE HISTORIC PARK

The elaborate Governor's Mansion, set back on the corner of 16th and H Streets in Sacramento, was originally built in 1877 for a hardware merchant named Albert Gallatin. After being occupied by first the Gallatins and then the Steffens family (including the famous muckraker Lincoln Steffens), the thirty-room house was sold in 1903 to the State of California to be used as the governor's official abode. The mansion housed thirteen of California's governors, until Ronald Reagan, who vacated for more modern quarters after just a few months. It has been unoccupied ever since.

Visitors today can wander the ornate rooms and take in the opulence of the six Italian marble fireplaces and elaborate moulding and paneling, as well as see the Steinway piano of Governor Pardee and the Persian rugs of Mrs. Earl Warren. As eminent writer Joan Didion put forth in her biting and beautiful essay "Many Mansions": "The old Governor's Mansion does have stairs and waste space, which is precisely why it remains the kind of house in which sixty adolescent girls might gather and never interrupt the real life of the household. The bedrooms are big and private and high-ceilinged and they do not open on the swimming pool and one can imagine reading in one of them, or writing a book, or closing the door and crying until dinner."

JOAN DIDION
"MANY MANSIONS"

The new official residence for governors of California, unland-
scaped, unfurnished, and unoccupied since the day construction
stopped in 1975, stands on eleven acres of oaks and olives on a
bluff overlooking the American River outside Sacramento. This
is the twelve-thousand-square-foot house that Ronald and Nancy
Reagan built. This is the sixteen-room house in which Jerry
Brown declined to live. This is the vacant house which cost the
State of California one-million-four, not including the property,
which was purchased in 1969 and donated to the state by such
friends of the Reagans as Leonard K. Firestone of Firestone
Tire and Rubber and Taft Schreiber of the Music Corporation
of America and Holmes Tuttle, the Los Angeles Ford dealer. All
day at this empty house three maintenance men try to keep the
bulletproof windows clean and the cobwebs swept and the wild
grass green and the rattlesnakes down by the river and away
from the thirty-five exterior wood and glass doors. All night
at this empty house the lights stay on behind the eight-foot
chainlink fence and the guard dogs lie at bay and the telephone,
when it rings, startles by the fact that it works. "Governor's
Residence," the guards answer, their voices laconic, matter-of-
fact, quite as if there were some phantom governor to connect.
Wild grass grows where the tennis court was to have been. Wild
grass grows where the pool and sauna were to have been. The
American is the river in which gold was discovered in 1848, and
it once ran fast and full past here, but lately there have been
upstream dams and dry years. Much of the bed is exposed. The
far bank has been dredged and graded. That the river is running
low is of no real account, however, since one of the many peculiarities of the new Governor's Residence is that it is so situated
as to have no clear view of the river.

It is an altogether curious structure, this one-story one-
million-four dream house of Ronald and Nancy Reagan's. Were
the house on the market (which it will probably not be, since,
at the time it was costing a million-four, local real estate agents
seemed to agree on $300,000 as the top price ever paid for a

house in Sacramento County), the words used to describe it would be "open" and "contemporary," although technically it is neither. "Flow" is a word that crops up quite a bit when one is walking through the place, and so is "resemble." The walls "resemble" local adobe, but they are not: they are the same concrete blocks, plastered and painted a rather stale yellowed cream, used in so many supermarkets and housing projects and Coca-Cola bottling plants. The door frames and the exposed beams "resemble" native redwood, but they are not: they are construction-grade lumber of indeterminate quality, stained brown. If anyone ever moves in, the concrete floors will be carpeted, wall to wall. If anyone ever moves in, the thirty-five exterior wood and glass doors, possibly the single distinctive feature in the house, will be, according to plan, "draped." The bathrooms are small and standard. The family bedrooms open directly onto the nonexistent swimming pool, with all its potential for noise and distraction. To one side of the fireplace in the formal living room there is what is known in the trade as a "wet bar," a cabinet for bottles and glasses with a sink and a long vinyl-topped counter. (This vinyl "resembles" slate.) In the entire house there are only enough bookshelves for a set of the World Book and some Books of the Month, plus maybe three Royal Doulton figurines and a back file of *Connoisseur,* but there is $90,000 worth of other teak cabinetry, including the "refreshment center" in the "recreation room." There is that most ubiquitous of all "luxury features," a bidet in the master bathroom. There is one of those kitchens which seem designed exclusively for defrosting by microwave and compacting trash. It is a house built for a family of snackers.

And yet, appliances notwithstanding, it is hard to see where the million-four went. The place has been called, by Jerry Brown, a "Taj Mahal." It has been called a "white elephant," a "resort," a "monument to the colossal ego of our former governor." It is not exactly any of these things. It is simply and rather astonishingly an enlarged version of a very common kind of California tract house, a monument not to colossal ego but to a weird absence of ego, a case study in the architecture of limited possibilities, insistently and malevolently "democratic," flattened out, mediocre and "open" and as devoid of privacy or personal eccentricity as the lobby area in a Ramada Inn. It is the architecture of "background music," decorators, "good taste." I recall once interviewing Nancy Reagan, at a time when her husband was governor and the construction on this house had not yet begun. We drove down to the State Capitol Building that day, and Mrs. Reagan showed me how she had lightened and brightened offices there by replacing the old burnished leather on the walls with the kind of beige burlap then favored in new office buildings. I mention this because it was on my mind as I walked through the empty house on the American River outside Sacramento.

· · · · ·

From 1903 until Ronald Reagan, who lived in a rented house in Sacramento while he was governor ($1,200 a month, payable by the state to a group of Reagan's friends), the governors of California lived in a large white Victorian Gothic house at 16th and H Streets in Sacramento. This extremely individual house, three stories and a cupola and the face of Columbia the Gem of the Ocean worked into the molding over every door, was built in 1877 by a Sacramento hardware merchant named Albert Gallatin. The state paid $32,500 for it in 1903 and my father was born in a house a block away in 1908. This part of town has since run to seed and small business, the kind of place where both Squeaky Fromme and Patricia Hearst could and probably did go about their business unnoticed, but the Governor's Mansion, unoccupied and open to the public as State Historical Landmark Number 823, remains Sacramento's premier example of eccentric domestic architecture.

As it happens I used to go there once in a while, when Earl Warren was governor and his daughter Nina was a year ahead of me at C. K. McClatchy Senior High School. Nina was always called "Honey Bear" in the papers and in *Life* magazine but she was called "Nina" at C. K. McClatchy Senior High

School and she was called "Nina" (or sometimes "Warren") at weekly meetings of the Mañana Club, a local institution to which we both belonged. I recall being initiated into the Mañana Club one night at the old Governor's Mansion, in a ceremony which involved being blindfolded and standing around Nina's bedroom in a state of high apprehension about secret rites which never materialized. It was the custom for the members to hurl mild insults at the initiates, and I remember being dumbfounded to hear Nina, by my fourteen-year-old lights the most glamorous and unapproachable fifteen-year-old in America, characterize me as "stuck on herself." There in the Governor's Mansion that night I learned for the first time that my face to the world was not necessarily the face in my mirror. "No smoking on the third floor," everyone kept saying. "Mrs. Warren *said*. No smoking on the third floor *or else.*"

Firetrap or not, the old Governor's Mansion was at that time my favorite house in the world, and probably still is. The morning after I was shown the new "Residence" I visited the old "Mansion," took the public tour with a group of perhaps twenty people, none of whom seemed to find it as ideal as I did. "All those stairs," they murmured, as if stairs could no longer be tolerated by human physiology. "All those stairs," and "all that waste space." The old Governor's Mansion does have stairs and waste space, which is precisely why it remains the kind of house in which sixty adolescent girls might gather and never interrupt the real life of the household. The bedrooms are big and private and high-ceilinged and they do not open on the swimming pool and one can imagine reading in one of them, or writing a book, or closing the door and crying until dinner. The bathrooms are big and airy and they do not have bidets but they do have room for hampers, and dressing tables, and chairs on which to sit and read a story to a child in the bathtub. There are hallways wide and narrow, stairs front and back, sewing rooms, ironing rooms, secret rooms. On the gilt mirror in the library there is worked a bust of Shakespeare, a pretty fancy for a hardware merchant in a California farm town in 1877. In the kitchen there is no trash compactor and there is no "island" with the appliances built in but there are two pantries, and a nice old table with a marble top for rolling out pastry and making divinity fudge and chocolate leaves. The morning I took the tour our guide asked if anyone could think why the old table had a marble top. There were a dozen or so other women in the group, each of an age to have cooked unnumbered meals, but not one of them could think of a single use for a slab of marble in the kitchen. It occurred to me that we had finally evolved a society in which knowledge of a pastry marble, like a taste for stairs and closed doors, could be construed as "elitist," and as I left the Governor's Mansion I felt very like the heroine of Mary McCarthy's *Birds of America,* the one who located America's moral decline in the disappearance of the first course.

• • • • •

A guard sleeps at night in the old mansion, which has been condemned as a dwelling by the state fire marshal. It costs about $85,000 a year to keep guards at the new official residence. Meanwhile the current governor of California, Edmund G. Brown, Jr., sleeps on a mattress on the floor in the famous apartment for which he pays $275 a month out of his own $49,100 annual salary. This has considerable and potent symbolic value, as do the two empty houses themselves, most particularly the house the Reagans built on the river. It is a great point around the Capitol these days to have "never seen" the house on the river. The governor himself has "never seen" it. The governor's press secretary, Elisabeth Coleman, has "never seen" it. The governor's chief of staff, Gray Davis, admits to having seen it, but only once, when "Mary McGrory wanted to see it." This unseen house on the river is, Jerry Brown has said, "not my style."

As a matter of fact this is precisely the point about the house on the river—the house is not Jerry Brown's style, not Mary McGrory's style, *not our style*—and it is a point which presents a certain problem, since the house so clearly is the style not only of Jerry Brown's predecessor but of millions of Jerry

Brown's constituents. Words are chosen carefully. Reasonable objections are framed. One hears about how the house is too far from the Capitol, too far from the Legislature. One hears about the folly of running such a lavish establishment for an unmarried governor and one hears about the governor's temperamental austerity. One hears every possible reason for not living in the house except the one that counts: it is the kind of house that has a wet bar in the living room. It is the kind of house that has a refreshment center. It is the kind of house in which one does not live, but there is no way to say this without getting into touchy and evanescent and finally inadmissible questions of taste, and ultimately of class. I have seldom seen a house so evocative of the unspeakable.

SUTTER'S FORT
STATE HISTORIC PARK

Originally named New Helvetia by John Sutter in honor of his Swiss roots, Sutter's Fort began as an agricultural colony and trading outpost in 1839. It was the first non-Native settlement in the Central Valley, and it boasted a thriving wheat crop, sawmill, and numerous living compounds. Today, the historic fort still stands in the heart of Midtown Sacramento and offers a window back into early pioneer California, complete with exhibitions, gold rush–era reenactments, and demonstrations of trades ranging from blacksmithing to carpentry to weaving.

The Swiss-born French writer Frédéric-Louis Sauser—a.k.a. Blaise Cendrars—was best known for his modernist poetry and his collaborations with avant-garde artists and filmmakers when he published his first novel, *Gold: The Marvellous History of General John Augustus Sutter*, in 1925. In the following selection, Sutter's New Helvetia takes shape amidst the political instability and violence of California's colonial period. Despite the fraught circumstances surrounding its formation, the settlement's agricultural bounty brings enormous wealth and even a sense of tranquility to Sutter—just before gold is discovered on his property and everything changes.

BLAISE CENDRARS
(Translated by Nina Rootes)
from *GOLD: THE MARVELLOUS HISTORY OF GENERAL JOHN AUGUSTUS SUTTER*

His first expedition on horseback has brought Sutter into the
Sacramento Valley. The incredible fertility of the soil and the
luxuriant vegetation decide for him: he will settle here. Returning from this reconnaissance, he learns that the first convoy of
Kanakas has just landed. There are 150 of them and they are
housed in the hamlet of Yerba Buena, at the far end of the Bay
of San Francisco. His partners in Honolulu have engaged nine-
teen whites to come over with them; they are tough, cheerful
men, hard-bitten and ready for anything. Sutter reviews them.
They are armed to the teeth.

Immediately, Sutter makes the overland journey to Monterey.
He does it at a single stretch, riding night and day.

John Augustus Sutter presents himself to Governor Alvarado.
He announces his intention of setting up in the country. His
Kanakas will clear the land. His small armed band will form
a vigilant cordon to prevent incursions by the totally hostile
tribes to the north. He intends to reassemble the Indians from
the former Missions, distribute land to them and set them to
work under his direction.

"More and more ships," he says, "will be coming from
Honolulu, where I have formed a substantial company. New
convoys of Kanakas will be landing in the bay which I have
chosen and further teams of white men will arrive with them,
men in my pay. Give me a free hand, and I will get the country
back on its feet."

"And what do you propose to call your ranch?"

"*New Helvetia.*"

"Why?"

"Because I am Swiss and a Republican."

"Good. Do what you want. I will grant you a concession for
ten years, in the first instance."

• • • • •

Sutter and his troop travel up the Sacramento Valley.

At the head sail three ex-whalers, still decked out for sea and with a small cannon aboard. Then come the 150 Kanakas dressed in horizontally-striped shirts that reach down to their knees. They have made themselves odd little pointed hats from the leaves of tulip-trees. Following them along the banks and through the swamps are thirty wagons loaded with provisions, seeds and munitions, as well as some fifty horses, seventy-five mules, five bulls, two hundred cows and five flocks of sheep. The rearguard, some on horseback, some in canoes, with rifles slung across their backs and leather caps tilted over one ear, are keeping close ranks and driving everyone forward when the going gets rough.

• • • • •

Six weeks later, the valley presents a ghostly spectacle. Fire has swept this way, a fire that smouldered under the low-hanging, acrid smoke of the bracken and the shrubby trees before flaring up like a torch, high, straight, implacable, in a single blaze. On all sides now, they see smoking stumps, twisted bark, splintered branches. The great solitary trees are still standing, but riven, scorched by the flames.

There is work to be done!

The oxen plod to and fro. The mules pull the plough. Seed is scattered. There is not even time to root out the blackened stumps, so the furrows skirt round them. The cattle are already wallowing in the marshy prairies, the sheep are on the hills and the horses are grazing in a paddock surrounded by thorn-bushes. At the confluence of two rivers, they are throwing up earthworks and building the ranch-house. Roughly-hewn tree-trunks and planks six inches thick are used in its construction. Everything is solid, large, massive, conceived for the future. The buildings are laid out in a line: barns, storehouses and granaries. The workshops are on the banks of the river, the Kanaka village in a ravine.

Sutter keeps an eye on everything, directs everything, super-vises the execution of the work down to the last detail; he is at every work-site at once and does not hesitate to put his hand to the task personally when one or other of the work-gangs is a man short. Bridges are built, tracks cleared, swamps drained, a well sunk, ponds, drinking-troughs and irrigation channels dug. A first palisade already protects the farm, a small fort is planned. Emissaries scour the Indian villages, and 250 of the Indians formerly protected by the Missions are brought in, together with their wives and children, to work on the various projects. Every three months, new convoys of Kanakas arrive and the lands under cultivation now stretch as far as the eye can see. Thirty-odd whites, men who have been settlers in this country for some time, come to offer their services. They are Mormons. Sutter pays them three dollars a day.

And prosperity is not long in coming.

4,000 oxen, 1,200 cows, 1,500 horses and mules and 12,000 sheep are dispersed around New Helvetia, covering an area that takes several days to walk round. The harvests yield 530 per cent and the granaries are full to bursting.

As early as the end of the second year, Sutter is able to buy some fine farms along the coast, near Fort Bodega. They belong to the Russians, who are pulling out. He pays 40,000 dollars cash for them. He plans to go in for stock-breeding on the grand scale there and, more particularly, to improve the bovine strain.

· · · · ·

In colonizations of this kind, it is sometimes possible to overcome the difficulties of a purely material nature, that arise day by day, with relative ease; a will of iron and strenuous labour, backed up by suitable equipment, may succeed in imposing a new order on the secular laws of nature, and even in transforming the aspect of a virgin land and the climatology of a region forever, but the human element is not so easily mastered.

From this point of view, John Augustus Sutter's position was absolutely typical.

At the moment of his arrival, California was on the brink of a revolution. In Mexico itself, the Compañia Cosmopolitana had just been formed with the avowed aim of pillaging what was left of that unhappy country once occupied by the Mission settlements. Powerful political groups had just embarked a force of two hundred adventurers to be unleashed on this so-recently-prosperous land. While these men were at sea, General Santa Anna overthrew President Farias and immediately sent a courier, via Sonora, to Governor Alvarado giving him strict orders to oppose the landing of these roughnecks by force. The band was broken up just off San Diego, between the Pacific and the bay, and those of its members who managed to escape infested the country, giving themselves up to banditry. Two gangs were formed and the partisans put the country to fire and blood. Sutter was wise enough not to interfere, and skillful enough to come to terms with both factions. However, hunters, trappers and fur-traders, all of American nationality, had infiltrated into the very heart of the region, and they formed a small but very active nucleus who wanted California to join the Union. Here again, Sutter was able to manoeuvre without compromising himself, for, while the Americans benefited from his secret support (every six months he sent a courier over the mountains to carry his reports to St Louis; one of his messengers even presented himself in Washington, to submit a plan of conquest: Sutter demanded personal command of the troops and exacted one-half of the territories conquered as his reward), in the eyes of the Mexicans, his heroic conduct on the frontier, where he energetically repelled the constant incursions of savage tribes, made him appear as such a faithful ally of the government that they gave him the title Guardian of the Northern Frontier, with the rank of captain. And, to recompense him for his services, Alvarado made him a grant of eleven square leagues of land, an area as vast as the little canton of Basle, his homeland.

The Indians were Sutter's biggest headache.

The savage tribes of the Upper Sacramento looked askance upon his settlement. These ploughed lands, these farms with their flocks and herds, these buildings that sprang up everywhere, were encroaching on their hunting grounds. They had taken up arms and, by night, set fire to barns and haystacks while, in broad daylight, they murdered the lonely shepherds and raided the cattle. There were frequent armed clashes, shots were exchanged and never a day passed but a dead man was carried back to the farmhouse: the scalped corpse of a wood-cutter, a hideously-mutilated planter or a militiaman struck down from behind. Never had Sutter had such good reason to congratulate himself on his brainwave of importing a Kanaka work-force as during these first two years of incessant skirmishes. Without them, he could never have achieved his goal.

There were six villages full of these islanders.

. . . . .

In spite of the struggles, the battles, the political complications, the ever-present threat of revolution, in spite of murders and fire-raising, John Augustus Sutter was proceeding methodically with his plan.

New Helvetia was taking shape.

The dwelling-houses, the ranch-house, the principal buildings, the granaries and warehouses were now surrounded by a wall five feet thick and twelve feet high. At each corner stood a rectangular bastion, armed with three cannon. Six other guns defended the main entrance. There was a permanent garrison of one hundred men. Further, all the year round, the immense domain was guarded by watchmen and patrols. The militiamen, recruited in the bars of Honolulu, had married Californian wives who accompanied them wherever they were posted, carrying the baggage, grinding corn and making bullets and cartridges. In times of danger, all these people fell back upon the small fort and helped to reinforce the garrison there. Two small boats, armed with cannon, were anchored in front of the fort, ready to sail up either the American River or the Sacramento.

The men who ran the sawmills (where the giant trees of the locality were sawn up) and the innumerable workshops were mostly ships' carpenters, helmsmen or boatswains who, while in port on the coast, had been persuaded to desert their sailing-ships for a wage of five dollars a day.

It was not unusual to see white men coming to the ranch-house to apply for work, attracted by the renown and the prosperity of the settlement. They were poor colonists who had not been successful on their own, mostly Russians, Irishmen and Germans. Sutter parcelled out land to them, or employed them according to their various skills.

Horses, hides, talc, wheat, flour, maize, dried meat, cheese, butter, planks and smoked salmon were embarked daily. Sutter sent his produce to Vancouver, Sitka, the Sandwich Islands and to all the ports of Mexico and South America, but, first and foremost, he provisioned the numerous ships that now came to drop anchor in the bay.

It was in this state of bustling prosperity that Captain Frémont found New Helvetia when he came down from the mountains after his memorable crossing of the Sierra Nevada.

Sutter had gone out to meet him with an escort of twenty-five splendidly-accoutred men. The horses were stallions. The riders' uniforms were made of a dark green cloth relieved by yellow braid. With their caps tipped over one ear, the lads had a martial look about them. They were all young, strong and well-disciplined.

Countless flocks of prime beasts were grazing in the lush prairies. The orchards were glutted with fruit. In the kitchen-gardens, vegetables from the Old World grew side by side with those from tropical countries. There were springs and canals everywhere. The Kanaka villages were neat and clean. Every man was at his appointed task. A most pleasing order reigned everywhere. Avenues of magnolia, palm-trees, bananas, camphor-trees, oranges, lemons and pepper-plants traversed the vast cultivated tracts to converge on the ranch-house. The walls of the *hacienda* were smothered in bougainvillaea, rambler roses and fleshy geraniums. A curtain of jasmine hung down before the master's door.

Sutter kept a splendid table. Hors-d'oeuvres; trout and salmon from the local rivers; baked ham *à l'Ecossaise*; wood-pigeon, haunch of venison, bear's paw; smoked tongue; sucking-pig stuffed *à la rissole* and dredged with tapioca flour; green vegetables, cabbage-palm, okra salad; fruit of every kind, fresh and preserved; mountains of *pâtisserie*. Rhine wines and several bottles of fine old wines from France, which had been so carefully handled that they had travelled round the world without being spoiled. The food was served by young women from the Islands and young Indian half-breed women who brought in the dishes wrapped in napkins of a pristine whiteness. They came and went with an imperturbably serious air, while a Hawaiian orchestra played outlandish airs, the *Marche de Berne,* with thumb-beats on the backs of the guitars, the *Marseillaise* with the sonorities of the bugle in the strings. The heavy antique tableware was made of Castilian silver-plate and struck with the royal arms.

Sutter presided, surrounded by his associates. Amongst the guests was Governor Alvarado.

· · · · ·

Sutter was accredited with the most important banking-houses in both the United States and Great Britain. He made substantial purchases of materials, tools, arms and ammunition, seeds and plants. His transports travelled thousands and thousands of miles overland or came by sea after rounding Cape Horn. (Twenty-five years later, in the ranches in the hinterland, they still talked about a wagon pulled by sixty pairs of white oxen which, under heavy escort, crossed the entire American continent at its widest point; after crossing the prairies, the savannahs, the rivers, the fords, the mountain passes of the Rockies and the desert with its giant cactus-candelabra, it finally arrived safe and sound with its cargo, which consisted of the boiler and plant for the first steam-mill to be constructed in the United States. As will be seen later, it would have been better for John Augustus Sutter, then at the pinnacle of his success, wealth and prestige, if this wagon had never arrived, if it had foundered at the bottom of some river, if it had bogged down forever in some quagmire, if it had tumbled over some precipice or if its numerous teams of oxen had succumbed to an epidemic.)

· · · · ·

However, political events were hastening forward.

And although Sutter was now a man to be reckoned with, to be listened to with respect, he was by no means sheltered from contingencies. Quite the contrary. Revolutions occurred one after the other. The struggle between opposing factions was fiercer than ever. Everyone wanted Sutter on their side, as much for his moral ascendancy as for his social position. Ultimately, each camp was counting on the contribution of the little army of New Helvetia. But Sutter never allowed himself to be drawn into these civil wars, and although, more than once, he saw his estates on the point of being invaded, his crops burned, his flocks scattered, his stores and granaries looted by yelling hordes who had just laid waste everything for hundreds of miles around, and who were excited by the sight of so much well-ordered wealth, he also knew how to extricate himself from these predicaments thanks to his profound knowledge of the human heart, acquired during his years of poverty in New York, and it was this which, in moments of crisis, sharpened his wits, his insight and his powers of argument. At such times, he was of a rare perspicacity, never put a foot wrong, schemed and manoeuvred, promised everything that was asked of him, audaciously bribed the leaders at precisely the right moment, sweetened men with brilliant arguments and with alcohol. As a last resort, he was prepared to have recourse to arms, but it was not so much a military victory that he desired (although force was on his side), as the safeguarding of his work, his labours, for he had no wish to see everything that he had just built up destroyed. And, in spite of everything, he was often on the brink of losing it all in a single day.

He kept in constant touch with the United States, and it was precisely from that direction, from the government in Washington, that he had most to fear.

As early as 1841, Captain Graham, at the head of forty-six English and American adventurers, had hoped, by a bold stroke, to seize power and proclaim the independence of California. But Alvarado had got wind of the affair; he surprised the conspirators, massacred more than half of them and threw the rest into prison. Immediately, London and Washington seized on the incident to claim compensation for the murder of their subjects. London demanded 20,000 dollars and the United States 129,200 dollars for fifteen riflemen. A British corvette lay in wait off Vera Cruz. The Mexicans were forced to submit.

In the spring of 1842, the revolt led by the Dominican monk, Gabriel, was put down in a blood-bath.

In October 1843, a band of more than a hundred Americans arrived from Santa Fe and Governor Alvarado, unpopular because of his despotic rule and in fear of new disturbances, asked Mexico for aid. Santa Anna, the President and dictator, sent three hundred galley-slaves by sea. He had promised them land, tools, cattle and the restoration of their civil rights if they could succeed in kicking out the Americans. At the same time, he appointed a new Governor of California, General Manuel Micheltorena. This general was an honest man, full of good intentions, but he could do nothing to uphold the Mexican domination, which was rapidly disintegrating. He chose to set up his quarters in the old Mission buildings of Santa Clara, Los Angeles. He frequently visited New Helvetia to take counsel, but Sutter, for his part, was preoccupied with the unyielding attacks of the savages, which were causing terrible slaughter.

Five more years pass, years of struggles, uprisings, riots and revolutions fomented primarily by the Cabinet in Washington, then comes the war with Mexico and the cession of Texas and California to the United States.

Sutter has obtained a further grant of twenty-two square leagues of land from the last Mexican Governor.

He owns the largest domain in the States.

• • • • •

Peace at last.

A new era commences.

John Augustus Sutter will at last be able to enjoy, and rejoice in, his wealth and good fortune.

New seeds arrive from Europe and saplings of every kind of fruit-tree. He acclimatizes olive and fig-trees on the lower, more sheltered ground; apple and pear-trees on the hills. He starts the first cotton plantations and, on the banks of the Sacramento, experiments with rice and indigo.

And finally he realizes a desire that has long lain close to his heart: he plants vines. At great expense, he has vine-stock brought over from the Rhine and from Burgundy. In the northern part of his estates, on the banks of the Feather River, he has had built a sort of country seat or manor house. It is his retreat. The Hermitage. Clumps of tall trees shade the house. All around, there are gardens with huge beds of carnation and heliotrope. There his finest fruits grow, cherries, apricots, peaches and quinces. His choicest pedigree cattle graze in the meadows.

Now, every step leads him towards his vineyards. When he goes for a walk, it is to see his vines, his Hochheimer, his Chambertin, his Château-Chinon.

As he caresses his favourite dog in the shade of a pergola, he dreams of bringing his family over from Europe, of lavishly repaying his creditors, of regaining his civic rights and redeeming the honour of his name; also, of endowing his little birthplace, so far away...Sweet dreams.

My three sons will come, they will have work, they must be men by now. And my daughter, how is she? I know! I'll order a grand piano for her, from Pleyel in Paris. It will be brought along the route I travelled long ago, on the backs of bearers if need be...Maria...All my old friends...

Reverie.

His pipe has gone out. He gazes into the far distance. The first stars are coming out. His dog lies motionless.

Reverie. Calm. Repose.

It is Peace.

FORT ROSS STATE HISTORIC PARK

Perched on the fog-thick bluffs of the Sonoma Coast with the ocean foaming below, Fort Ross seems the perfect location for a ghost story. At its peak occupation, from 1812 to 1841, Fort Ross was the southernmost extension of Russian colonial efforts in North America. The fort was built as an agricultural outpost to provide food for starving colonies in Alaska, but it also served as a center for fur hunting and trading. Separate settlements of Coast Miwoks, Kashaya Pomos, Russians, and Native Alaskans were established near the fort, one of the few examples in early California of relatively successful multicultural cohabitation. Today, the Rotchev House—so named for the last manager of Fort Ross, Alexander Rotchev—has been restored to its late-1830s appearance, and several other buildings have been reconstructed on the 3,393 acres of parkland.

Gertrude Atherton moved in the literary circles of the likes of Oscar Wilde and Edith Wharton, but she was a California writer through and through, proud of her heritage and devoted to the exploration of its histories and personalities. The following story was inspired by a Kashaya Pomo tale reportedly based on a true incident. In Atherton's hands, Fort Ross is a haunted space, a dark Russian ghost story, mournfully weathering the wind and fog and echoing still with the memories of its occupants.

GERTRUDE ATHERTON
"NATALIE IVANHOFF: A MEMORY OF FORT ROSS"

At Fort Ross, on the northern coast of California, it is told that an astonishing sight may be witnessed in the midnight of the twenty-third of August. The present settlement vanishes. In its place the Fort appears as it was when the Russians abandoned it in 1841. The quadrilateral stockade of redwood beams, pierced with embrasures for carronades, is compact and formidable once more. The ramparts are paced by watchful sentries; mounted cannon are behind the iron-barred gates and in the graceful bastions. Within the enclosure are the low log buildings occupied by the Governor and his officers, the barracks of the soldiers, the arsenal, and storehouses. In one corner stands the Greek chapel, with its cupola and cross-surmounted belfry. The silver chimes have rung this night. The Governor, his beautiful wife, and their guest, Natalie Ivanhoff, have knelt at the jewelled altar.

At the right of the Fort is a small "town" of rude huts which accommodates some eight hundred Indians and Siberian convicts, the working-men of the company. Above the "town," on a high knoll, is a large grist-mill. Describing an arc of perfect proportions, its midmost depression a mile behind the Fort, a great mountain forms a natural rampart. At either extreme it tapers to the jagged cliffs. On its three lower tables the mountain is green and bare; then abruptly rises a forest of redwoods, tall, rigid, tenebrious.

The mountain is visible but a moment. An immense white fog-bank which has been crouching on the horizon rears suddenly and rushes across the ocean, whose low mutter rises to a roar. It sweeps like a tidal wave across cliffs and Fort. It halts abruptly against the face of the mountain. In the same moment the ocean stills. It would almost seem that Nature held her breath, awaiting some awful event.

Suddenly, in the very middle of the fog-bank, appears the shadowy figure of a woman. She is gliding—to the right—rapidly and stealthily. Youth is in her slender grace, her delicate profile, dimly outlined. Her long silver-blond hair is unbound and luminously distinct from the white fog. She walks swiftly across the lower table of the mountain, then disappears. One sees, vaguely, a dark figure crouching along the lower fringe of the fog. That, too, disappears.

For a moment the silence seems intensified. Then, suddenly, it is crossed by a low whir—a strange sound in the midnight. Then a shriek whose like is never heard save when a soul is wrenched without warning in frightfullest torture from its body. Then another and another and another in rapid succession, each fainter and more horrible in suggestion than the last. With them has mingled the single frenzied cry of a man. A moment later a confused hubbub arises from the Fort and town, followed by the flashes of many lights and the report of musketry. Then the fog presses downward on the scene. All sound but that of the ocean, which seems to have drawn into its loud dull voice all the angers of all the dead, ceases as though muffled. The fog lingers a moment, then drifts back as it came, and Fort Ross is the Fort Ross of to-day.

• • • • •

And this is the story:—

When the Princess Hélène de Gagarin married Alexander Rotscheff, she little anticipated that she would spend her honeymoon in the northern wilds of the Californias. Nevertheless, when her husband was appointed Governor of the Fort Ross and Bodega branch of the great Alaskan Fur Company, she volunteered at once to go with him—being in that stage of devotion which may be termed the emotionally heroic as distinguished from the later of non-resistance. As the exile would last but a few years, and as she was a lady of a somewhat adventurous spirit, to say nothing of the fact that she was deeply in love, her interpretation of wifely duty hardly wore the hue of martyrdom even to herself.

Notwithstanding, and although she had caused to be prepared a large case of books and eight trunks of ravishing raiment, she decided that life in a fort hidden between the mountains and the sea, miles away from even the primitive Spanish civilization, might hang burdensomely at such whiles as her husband's duties claimed him and books ceased to amuse. So she determined to ask the friend of her twenty-three years, the Countess Natalie Ivanhoff, to accompany her. She had, also, an unselfish motive in so doing. Not only did she cherish for the Countess Natalie a real affection, but her friend was as deeply wretched as she was happy.

Two years before, the Prince Alexis Mikhaïlof, betrothed of Natalie Ivanhoff, had been, without explanation or chance of parting word, banished to Siberia under sentence of perpetual exile. Later had come rumour of his escape, then of death, then of recapture. Nothing definite could be learned. When the Princess Hélène made her invitation, it was accepted gratefully, hope suggesting that in the New World might be found relief from the torture that was relived in every vibration of the invisible wires that held memory fast to the surroundings in which the terrible impressions, etchers of memory, had their genesis.

They arrived in summer, and found the long log house, with its low ceilings and rude finish, admirably comfortable within. By aid of the great case of things Rotscheff had brought, it quickly became an abode of luxury. Thick carpets covered every floor; arras hid the rough walls; books and pictures and handsome ornaments crowded each other; every chair had been designed for comfort as well as elegance; the dining table was hidden beneath finest damask, and glittered with silver and crystal. It was an unwritten law that every one should dress for dinner; and with the rich curtains hiding the gloomy mountain and the long sweep of cliffs intersected by gorge and gulch, it was easy for the gay congenial band of exiles to forget that they were not eating the delicacies of their French cook and drinking their costly wines in the Old World.

In the daytime the women—several of the officers' wives had braved the wilderness—found much diversion in riding through the dark forests or along the barren cliffs, attended always by an armed guard. Diego Estenega, the Spanish magnate of the North, whose ranchos adjoined Fort Ross, and who was financially interested in the Russian fur trade, soon became an intimate of the Rotscheff household. A Californian by birth, he was, nevertheless, a man of modern civilization, travelled, a student, and a keen lover of masculine sports. Although the most powerful man in the politics of his conservative country, he was an American in appearance and dress. His cloth or tweed suggested the colorous magnificence of the caballeros as little as did his thin nervous figure and grim pallid intellectual face. Rotscheff liked him better than any man he had ever met; with the Princess he usually waged war, that lady being clever, quick, and wedded to her own opinions. For Natalie he felt a sincere friendship at once. Being a man of keen sympathies and strong impulses, he divined her trouble before he heard her story, and desired to help her.

The Countess Natalie, despite the Governor's prohibition, was addicted to roving over the cliffs by herself, finding kinship in the sterile crags and futile restlessness of the ocean. She had learned that although change of scene lightened the burden, only death would release her from herself.

"She will get over it," said the Princess Hélène to Estenega. "I was in love twice before I met Alex, so I know. Natalie is so beautiful that some day some man, who will not look in the least like poor Alexis, will make her forget."

Estenega, being a man of the world and having consequently outgrown the cynicism of youth, also knowing women better than this fair Minerva would know them in twenty lifetimes, thought differently, and a battle ensued.

Natalie, meanwhile, wandered along the cliffs. She passed the town hurriedly. Several times when in its vicinity before, the magnetism of an intense gaze had given her a thrill of alarm, and once or twice she had met face to face the miller's son—a forbidding youth with the skull of the Tartar and the coarse black hair and furtive eyes of the Indian—whose admiration of her beauty had been annoyingly apparent. She was not conscious of observation to-day, however, and skirted the cliffs rapidly, drawing her gray mantle about her as the wind howled by, but did not lift the hood; the massive coils of silver-blond hair kept her head warm.

As the Princess Hélène, despite her own faultless blondinity, had pronounced, Natalie Ivanhoff was a beautiful woman. Her profile had the delicate effect produced by the chisel. Her white skin was transparent and untinted, but the mouth was scarlet. The large long eyes of a changeful blue-gray, although limpid of surface, were heavy with the sadness of a sad spirit. Their natural fire was quenched just as the slight compression of her lips had lessened the sensuous fulness of their curves.

But she had suffered so bitterly and so variously that the points had been broken off her nerves, she told herself, and, excepting when her trouble mounted suddenly like a wave within her, her mind was tranquil. Grief with her had expressed itself in all its forms. She had known what it was to be crushed into semi-insensibility; she had thrilled as the tears rushed and the sobs shook her until every nerve ached and her very fingers cramped; and she had gone wild at other times, burying her head, that her screams might not be heard: the last, as imagination pictured her lover's certain physical suffering. But of all agonies, none could approximate to that induced by Death. When that rumour reached her, she realized that hope had given her some measure of support, and how insignificant all other trouble is beside that awful blank, that mystery, whose single revelation is the houseless soul's unreturning flight from the only world we are sure of. When the contradicting rumour came, she clutched at hope and clung to it.

"It is the only reason I do not kill myself," she thought, as she stood on the jutting brow of the cliff and looked down on the masses of huge stones which, with the gaunt outlying rocks, had once hung on the face of the crags. The great breakers boiled over them with the ponderosity peculiar to the waters of the Pacific. The least of those breakers would carry her far into the hospitable ocean.

"It is so easy to die and be at peace; the only thing which makes life supportable is the knowledge of Death's quick obedience. And the tragedy of life is not that we cannot forget, but that we can. Think of being an old woman with not so much as a connecting current between the memory and the heart, the long interval blocked with ten thousand petty events and trials! It must be worse than this. I shall have gone over the cliff long before that time comes. I would go to-day, but I cannot leave the world while he is in it."

She drew a case from her pocket, and opened it. It showed the portrait of a young man with the sombre eyes and cynical mouth of the northern European, a face revealing intellect, will, passion, and much recklessness. Eyes and hair were dark, the face smooth but for a slight mustache.

Natalie burst into wild tears, revelling in the solitude that gave her freedom. She pressed the picture against her face, and cried her agony aloud to the ocean. Thrilling memories rushed through her, and she lived again the first ecstasy of grief. She did not fling herself upon the ground, or otherwise indulge in the acrobatics of woe, but she shook from head to foot. Between the heavy sobs her breath came in hard gasps, and tears poured, hiding the gray desolation of the scene.

Suddenly, through it all, she became conscious that some one was watching her. Instinctively she knew that it was the same gaze which so often had alarmed her. Fear routed every other passion. She realized that she was unprotected, a mile from the Fort, out of the line of its vision. The brutal head of the miller's son seemed to thrust itself before her face. Overwhelmed with terror, she turned swiftly and ran, striking blindly among the low bushes, her glance darting from right to left. No one was to be seen for a moment; then she turned the corner of a boulder and came upon a man. She shrieked and covered her face with her hands, now too frightened to move. The man neither stirred nor spoke; and, despite this alarming circumstance, her disordered brain, in the course of a moment, conceived the thought that no subject of Rotscheff would dare to harm her.

Moreover, her brief glance had informed her that this was not the miller's son; which fact, illogically, somewhat tempered her fear. She removed her hands and compelled herself to look sternly at the creature who had dared to raise his eyes to the Countess Natalie Ivanhoff. She was puzzled to find something familiar about him. His grizzled hair was long, but not unkempt. The lower part of his face was covered by a beard. He was almost fleshless; but in his sunken eyes burned unquenchable fire, and there was a determined vigour in his gaunt figure. He might have been any age. Assuredly, the outward seeming of youth was not there, but its suggestion still lingered tenaciously in the spirit which glowed through the worn husk. And about him, in spite of the rough garb and blackened skin, was an unmistakable air of breeding.

Natalie, as she looked, grew rigid. Then she uttered a cry of rapturous horror, staggered, and was caught in a fierce embrace. Her stunned senses awoke in a moment, and she clung to him, crying wildly, holding him with straining arms, filled with bitter happiness.

In a few moments he pushed her from him and regarded her sadly.

"You are as beautiful as ever," he said; "but I—look at me! Old, hideous, ragged! I am not fit to touch you; I never meant to. Go! I shall never blame you."

For answer she sprang to him again.

"What difference is it how you look?" she cried, still sobbing. "Is it not *you*? Are not you in here just the same? What matter? What matter? No matter what you looked through, you would be the same. Listen," she continued rapidly, after a moment. "We are in a new country; there is hope for us. If we can reach the Spanish towns of the South, we are safe. I will ask Don Diego Estenega to help us, and he is not the man to refuse. He stays with us to-night, and I will speak alone with him. Meet me to-morrow night—where? At the grist-mill at midnight. We had better not meet by day again. Perhaps we can go then. You will be there?"

"Will I be there? God! Of course I will be there."

And, the brief details of their flight concluded, they forgot it and all else for the hour.

• • • • •

II

Natalie could not obtain speech alone with Estenega that evening; but the next morning the Princess Hélène commanded her household and guest to accompany her up the hill to the orchard at the foot of the forest; and there, while the others wandered over the knolls of the shadowy enclosure, Natalie managed to tell her story. Estenega offered his help spontaneously.

"At twelve to-night," he said, "I will wait for you in the forest with horses, and will guide you myself to Monterey. I have a house there, and you can leave on the first barque for Boston."

As soon as the party returned to the Fort, Estenega excused himself and left for his home. The day passed with maddening slowness to Natalie. She spent the greater part of it walking up and down the immediate cliffs, idly watching the men capturing the seals and otters, the ship-builders across the gulch. As she returned at sunset to the enclosure, she saw the miller's son standing by the gates, gazing at her with hungry admiration. He inspired her with sudden fury.

"Never presume to look at me again," she said harshly. "If you do, I shall report you to the Governor."

And without waiting to note how he accepted the mandate, she swept by him and entered the Fort, the gates clashing behind her.

The inmates of Fort Ross were always in bed by eleven o'clock. At that hour not a sound was to be heard but the roar of the ocean, the soft pacing of the sentry on the ramparts, the cry of the panther in the forest. On the evening in question, after the others had retired, Natalie, trembling with excitement, made a hasty toilet, changing her evening gown for a gray travelling frock. Her heavy hair came unbound, and her shaking hands refused to adjust the close coils. As it fell over her gray mantle it looked so lovely, enveloping her with the silver sheen of mist, that she smiled in sad vanity, remembering happier days, and decided to let her lover see her so. She could braid her hair at the mill.

A moment or two before twelve she raised the window and swung herself to the ground. The sentry was on the rampart opposite: she could not make her exit by that gate. She walked softly around the buildings, keeping in their shadow, and reached the gates facing the forest. They were not difficult to unbar, and in a moment she stood without, free. She could not see the mountain; a heavy bank of white fog lay against it, resting, after its long flight over the ocean, before it returned, or swept onward to ingulf the redwoods.

She went with noiseless step up the path, then turned and walked swiftly toward the mill. She was very nervous; mingling with the low voice of the ocean she imagined she heard the moans with which beheaded convicts were said to haunt the night. Once she thought she heard a footstep behind her, and paused, her heart beating audibly. But the sound ceased with her own soft footfalls, and the fog was so dense that she could see nothing. The ground was soft, and she was beyond the sentry's earshot; she ran at full speed across the field, down the gorge, and up the steep knoll. As she reached the top, she was taken in Mikhaïlof's arms. For a few moments she was too breathless to speak; then she told him her plans.

"Let me braid my hair," she said finally, "and we will go."

He drew her within the mill, then lit a lantern and held it above her head, his eyes dwelling passionately on her beauty, enhanced by the colour of excitement and rapid exercise.

"You look like the moon queen," he said. "I missed your hair, apart from yourself."

She lifted her chin with a movement of coquetry most graceful in spite of long disuse, and the answering fire sprang into her eyes. She looked very piquant and a trifle diabolical. He pressed his lips suddenly on hers. A moment later something tugged at the long locks his hand caressed, and at the same time he became conscious that the silence which had fallen between them was shaken by a loud whir. He glanced upward. Natalie was standing with her back to one of the band-wheels. It had begun to revolve; in the moment it increased its speed; and he saw a glittering web on its surface. With an exclamation of horror, he pulled her toward him; but he was too late. The wheel, spinning now with the velocity of midday, caught the whole silver cloud in its spokes, and Natalie was swept suddenly upward. Her feet hit the low rafters, and she was whirled round and round, screams of torture torn from her rather than uttered, her body describing a circular right angle to the shaft, the bones breaking as they struck the opposite one; then, in swift finality, she was sucked between belt and wheel. Mikhaïlof managed to get into the next room and reverse the lever. The machinery stopped as abruptly as it had started; but Natalie was out of her agony.

Her lover flung himself over the cliffs, shattering bones and skull on the stones at their base. They made her a coffin out of the copper plates used for their ships, and laid her in the straggling unpopulous cemetery on the knoll across the gulch beyond the chapel.

"When we go, we will take her," said Rotscheff to his distracted wife.

But when they went, a year or two after, in the hurry of departure they forgot her until too late. They promised to return. But they never came, and she sleeps there still, on the lonely knoll between the sunless forest and the desolate ocean.

INDIAN GRINDING ROCK
STATE HISTORIC PARK

At Indian Grinding Rock State Historic Park in Amador County, a smooth expanse of limestone bedrock is pocked with over one thousand bowl-like indentations where for generations Miwok people cracked and pounded acorns into flour. Some of the holes are estimated to be three thousand years old, and many may be older still. Nearby is a reconstructed village of cedar-wood shelters.

While the location is rich in historical value, this 135-acre state park is not just a relic of the past. Near the village, modern Sierra Miwok people have built and rebuilt a ceremonial roundhouse where the Big Time festival is celebrated every September, at the traditional time of the acorn harvest. The roundhouse is made in the traditional style, with wild grapevines as rope, poles and shingles made of cedar, and a packed clay floor. Both the reconstructed village and the roundhouse are part of the attached Chaw'se Regional Indian Museum. The park also offers hiking, camping, and bird and wildlife viewing.

Malcolm Margolin is the publisher of Heyday and founder of *News from Native California*, a quarterly magazine dedicated to California Indian culture. He has been going to the annual Big Time at Chaw'se for nearly forty years.

MALCOLM MARGOLIN
from "BUILDING A ROUNDHOUSE"

Throughout much of north-central California—from Mendocino and Sonoma Counties east to the Sierra foothills—the roundhouse was (and in places still is) a major cultural and architectural attainment. In traditional times, this large communal building was mostly underground and served variously as a place of worship, a community center, and a university.

A few years ago I was at Chaw'se State Park, where the Sierra Mewuk community erected an especially graceful roundhouse in about 1970, then rebuilt it in the early 1990s. It is well used, especially at an annual September event called Big Time, when people come from all over California to celebrate the fall harvest, using the roundhouse for dancing, singing, praying, and otherwise honoring their culture. Here, especially at dawn when dancers enter the roundhouse to greet the rising sun, one can feel the mystery, beauty, ongoing vitality, and truthfulness of California's oldest cultures.

One day I was talking with my friend Dwight Dutschke, whose family had taken part in the original construction and who himself has been actively engaged in the annual Big Time. Our conversation turned to how the roundhouse had been constructed, and I was questioning him about certain details: how the entranceway had been oriented, how the posts had been put in, how the rafters had been secured, and so on. Finally he said, I know what you are getting at. You're getting at the fact that we could have constructed it better. No, no, I protested, that's not at all what I was getting at. Well, he went on, we could indeed have constructed it better. A lot of the people who worked on it were into construction and we know how to build. We could have put creosote on the posts when they went into the ground. There's nothing in the old laws that says you can't do that. There's nothing in the old laws that says you have to tie the rafters with grape vine; we could have used wire and nails. We could have built it so that it would last a hundred years. But we didn't. We didn't because there was another law we had to follow. When you build a roundhouse you construct it so that it falls apart every twenty years. That way every generation has the chance to rebuild it. Every generation has to learn the songs,' the ceremonies, the techniques. If you want to make a building last you do it one way. But if you want to make the knowledge last, you do it another way.

JACK LONDON
STATE HISTORIC PARK

Known for his rugged tales set in the wilderness of the West—
from *White Fang* to *The Call of the Wild*—as well as for his gritty
critiques of the Industrial Age *(The Iron Heel, The People of the
Abyss)*, Jack London is not often associated with bucolic set-
tings. Yet his home of more than fifteen years, and the seat of
much of his creative work, was the idyllic landscape near Glen
Ellen, in Sonoma County. Jack London and his wife Charmian
began purchasing land in Sonoma Valley in 1905, adding to it
over time until it eventually encompassed the redwood groves,
madrone forest, meadows, and creek that now make up Jack
London State Historic Park. In the selection that follows, London's fictionalized descriptions of the arrival of Billy and Saxon
at the site of their long-sought "place" in the country, shaded by
the purple sunset of Sonoma Mountain, closely mirror his own
journey to the land he and his wife would work and love for the
rest of their lives.

The 1,611 acres of Jack London State Historic Park feature
London's gravesite, the House of Happy Walls Museum, a memorial built by Charmian London to commemorate her husband's
life, the cottage where London wrote, and trails leading up the
ridges of Sonoma Mountain, where views of the Valley of the
Moon abound. Along the way visitors can enjoy madrone groves,
forests of bay and fir, vineyards, abandoned barns, and the lake
where Jack and Charmain often swam come summertime.

JACK LONDON
from *THE VALLEY OF THE MOON*

South they held along the coast, hunting, fishing, swimming, and horse buying. Billy shipped his purchases on the coasting steamers. Through Del Norte and Humboldt counties they went, and through Mendocino into Sonoma—counties larger than Eastern states—threading the giant woods, whipping innumerable trout-streams, and crossing countless rich valleys. Ever Saxon sought the valley of the moon. Sometimes, when all seemed fair, the lack was a railroad, sometimes madroño and manzanita trees, and, usually, there was too much fog.

"We do want a sun cocktail once in a while," she told Billy.

"Yep," was his answer. "Too much fog might make us soggy. What we're after is betwixt an' between, an' we'll have to get back from the coast a ways to find it."

This was in the fall of the year, and they turned their backs on the Pacific at old Fort Ross and entered the Russian River Valley, far below Ukiah, by way of Cazadero and Guerneville. At Santa Rosa, Billy was delayed with the shipping of several horses, so that it was not until afternoon that he drove south and east for Sonoma Valley.

"I guess we'll no more than make Sonoma Valley when it'll be time to camp," he said, measuring the sun with his eye. "This is called Bennett Valley. You cross a divide from it and come out at Glen Ellen. Now this is a mighty pretty valley if anybody should ask you. An' that's some nifty mountain over there."

Rising from rolling stubble fields, Bennett Peak towered hot in the sun, a row of bastion hills leaning against its base. But hills and mountain on that side showed bare and heated, though beautiful with the sunburnt tawniness of California.

They took a turn to the right and began crossing a series of steep foothills. As they approached the mountain there were signs of a greater abundance of water. They drove beside a running stream, and though the vineyards on the hills were summer-dry, the farmhouses in the hollows and on the levels were grouped about with splendid trees.

"Maybe it sounds funny," Saxon observed, "but I'm beginning to love that mountain already. It almost seems as if I'd seen it before, somehow; it's so all-around satisfying—oh!"

Crossing a bridge and rounding a sharp turn, they were suddenly enveloped in a mysterious coolness and gloom. All about them arose stately trunks of redwood. The forest floor was a rosy carpet of autumn fronds. Occasional shafts of sunlight, penetrating the deep shade, warmed the somberness of the grove. Alluring paths led off among the trees and into cozy nooks made by circles of red columns growing around the dust of vanished ancestors—witnessing the titanic proportions of those ancestors by the girth of the circles in which they stood.

Out of the grove they pulled to the steep divide, which was no more than a buttress of Sonoma Mountain. The way led on through rolling uplands and across small dips and canyons, all well wooded and adrip with water. In places the road was muddy from wayside springs.

"The mountain's a sponge," said Billy. "Here it is, the tail end of a dry summer, an' the ground's just leakin' everywhere."

"I know I've never been here before," Saxon communed aloud. "But it's all so familiar! So I must have dreamed it. And there's madroños—a whole grove! And manzanita! Why, I feel just as if I was coming home. Oh, Billy, if it should turn out to be our valley!"

"Plastered against the side of a mountain?" he queried, with a skeptical laugh.

"No; I don't mean that. I mean on the way to our valley. Because the way—all ways—to our valley must be beautiful. And this—I've seen it all before, dreamed it."

They passed a large and comfortable farmhouse surrounded by wandering barns and cow-sheds, went on under forest arches, and emerged beside a field with which Saxon was instantly enchanted. It flowed in a gentle concave from the road up the mountain, its farther boundary an unbroken line of timber. The field glowed like rough gold in the approaching sunset, and near the middle of it stood a solitary great redwood, with blasted top suggesting a nesting eyrie for eagles. The timber beyond clothed the mountain in solid green to what they took to be the top. But as they drove on, Saxon, looking back upon what she called *her* field, saw the real summit of Sonoma towering beyond, the mountain behind her field a mere spur upon the side of the larger mass.

Ahead and toward the right across sheer ridges of the mountains, separated by deep green canyons and broadening lower down into rolling orchards and vineyards, they caught their first sight of Sonoma Valley and the wild mountains that rimmed its eastern side. To the left they gazed across a golden land of small hills and valleys. Beyond, to the north, they glimpsed another portion of the valley, and, still beyond, the opposing wall of the valley—a range of mountains, the highest of which reared its red and battered ancient crater against a rosy and mellowing sky. From north to southeast, the mountain rim curved in the brightness of the sun, while Saxon and Billy were already in the shadow of evening. He looked at Saxon, noted the ravished ecstasy of her face, and stopped the horses. All the eastern sky was blushing to rose, which descended upon the mountains, touching them with wine and ruby. Sonoma Valley began to fill with a purple flood, laving the mountain bases, rising, inundating, drowning them in its purple. Saxon pointed in silence, indicating that the purple flood was the sunset shadow of Sonoma Mountain. Billy nodded, then chirruped to the mares, and the descent began through a warm and colorful twilight.

On the elevated sections of the road they felt the cool, delicious breeze from the Pacific, forty miles away; while from each little dip and hollow came warm breaths of autumn earth, spicy with sunburnt grass and fallen leaves and passing flowers.

They came to the rim of a deep canyon that seemed to penetrate to the heart of Sonoma Mountain. Again, with no word spoken, merely from watching Saxon, Billy stopped the wagon. The canyon was wildly beautiful. Tall redwoods lined its entire length. On its farther rim stood three rugged knolls, covered with dense woods of spruce and oak. From between the knolls, a feeder to the main canyon and likewise fringed with redwoods, emerged a smaller canyon. Billy pointed to a stubble-field that lay at the feet of the knolls.

"It's in fields like that I've seen my mares a-pasturing," he said.

They dropped down into the canyon, the road following a stream that sang under maples and alders. The sunset fires, refracted from the cloud-driftage of the autumn sky, bathed the canyon with crimson, in which ruddy-limbed madroños and wine-wooded manzanitas burned and smoldered. The air was aromatic with laurel. Wild grapevines bridged the stream from tree to tree. Oaks of many sorts were veiled in lacy Spanish moss. Ferns and brakes grew lush beside the stream.

"I've got a hunch," said Billy.

"Let me say it first," Saxon begged.

He waited, his eyes on her face as she gazed about her in rapture.

"We've found our valley," she whispered. "Was that it?"

He nodded, but checked speech at sight of a small boy driving a cow up the road, a preposterously big shotgun in one hand, in the other as preposterously big a jackrabbit.

"How far to Glen Ellen?" Billy asked.

"Mile an' a half," was the answer.

"What creek is this?" inquired Saxon.

"Wild Water. It empties into Sonoma Creek, half a mile down."

"Trout?"—this from Billy.

"If you know how to ketch 'em," grinned the boy.

"Deer up the mountain?"

"It ain't open season," the boy evaded.

"I guess you never shot a deer," Billy slyly baited, and was rewarded with, "I got the horns to show."

"Deer sheds their horns," Billy teased on. "Anybody can find 'em."

"I got the meat on mine. It ain't dry yet—"

The boy broke off, gazing with shocked eyes into the pit Billy had dug for him.

"It's all right, sonny," Billy laughed, as he drove on. "I ain't the game-warden. I'm buyin' horses."

More ruddy madroños, more fairy circles of redwoods, and, still beside the singing stream, they passed a gate by the roadside. Before it stood a rural mailbox, on which was lettered "Edmund Hale." Standing under the rustic arch, leaning upon the gate, a man and woman composed a picture so arresting and beautiful that Saxon caught her breath. They were side by side, the delicate hand of the woman curled in the hand of the man, which looked as if made to confer benedictions. His face bore out this impression—a beautiful-browed countenance, with large, benevolent gray eyes under a wealth of white hair that shone like spun glass. He was fair and large; the little woman beside him was daintily wrought. She was saffron brown, as a woman of the white race can well be, with smiling eyes of bluest blue. In quaint sage-green draperies, she seemed a flower, with her small, vivid face irresistibly reminding Saxon of a springtime wake-robin.

Perhaps the picture made by Saxon and Billy was equally arresting and beautiful, as they drove down through the golden end of day. The two couples had eyes only for each other. The little woman beamed joyously. The man's face glowed into the benediction that had trembled there. To Saxon, like the field up the mountain, like the mountain itself, it seemed that she had always known this adorable pair. She knew that she loved them.

"How d'ye do," said Billy.

"You blessed children," said the man. "I wonder if you know how dear you look sitting there."

That was all. The wagon had passed by, rustling down the road which was carpeted with fallen leaves of maple, oak, and alder. Then they came to the meeting of the two creeks.

"Oh, what a place for a home," Saxon cried, pointing across Wild Water. "See, Billy, on that bench there, above the meadow."

"It's a rich bottom, Saxon, and so is the bench rich. Look at the big trees on it. An' they's sure to be springs."

"Drive over," she said.

Forsaking the main road, they crossed Wild Water on a narrow bridge and continued along an ancient, rutted road that ran beside an equally ancient worm fence of split redwood rails. They came to a gate, open and off its hinges, through which the road led out on the bench.

"This is it—I know it," Saxon said with conviction. "Drive in, Billy."

A small, whitewashed farmhouse with broken windows showed through the trees.

"Talk about your madroños—"

Billy pointed to the father of all madroños, six feet in diameter at its base, sturdy and sound, which stood before the house.

They spoke in low tones as they passed around the house under great oak trees and came to a stop before a small barn. They did not wait to unharness. Tying the horses, they started to explore. The pitch from the bench to the meadow was steep yet thickly wooded with oaks and manzanita. As they crashed through the underbrush they startled a score of quail into flight.

"How about game?" Saxon queried.

Billy grinned, and fell to examining a spring which bubbled a clear stream into the meadow. Here the ground was sunbaked and wide open in a multitude of cracks.

Disappointment leaped into Saxon's face, but Billy, crumbling a clod between his fingers, had not made up his mind.

"It's rich," he pronounced. "But—"

He broke off, stared all about, studying the configuration of the meadow, crossed it to the redwood trees beyond, then came back.

"It's no good as it is," he said. "But it's the best ever if it's handled right. All it needs is a little common sense an' a lot of drainage. This meadow's a natural basin not yet filled level. Come on; I'll show you."

They went through the redwoods and came out on Sonoma Creek. At this spot was no singing. The stream poured into a quiet pool. The willows on their side brushed the water. The opposite side was a steep bank. Billy measured the height of the bank with his eye, the depth of the water with a driftwood pole.

"Fifteen feet," he announced. "That allows all kinds of high divin' from the bank."

They followed down the pool. It emptied into a riffle, across exposed bedrock, into another pool. As they looked, a trout flashed into the air and back, leaving a widening ripple on the quiet surface.

"This place was specially manufactured for us," Billy said. "In the morning I'll find out who owns it."

Half an hour later, feeding the horses, he called Saxon's attention to a locomotive whistle.

"You've got your railroad," he said. "That's a train pulling into Glen Ellen, an' it's only a mile from here."

Saxon was dozing off to sleep under the blankets when Billy aroused her.

"Suppose the guy that owns it won't sell?"

"There isn't the slightest doubt," Saxon answered with unruffled certainty. "This is our place. I know it."

SONOMA STATE
HISTORIC PARK

Sonoma State Historic Park, a grouping of six sites situated within the town of Sonoma, provides a rich cross-section of California history. Among the historical structures visitors can explore are a mission, soldiers' barracks, a gold rush saloon, and two homes that belonged to General Mariano Vallejo, founder of the town in 1833. Adobe and stone buildings dating back almost two centuries are lovingly preserved, and nearby, vineyards swathe the Sonoma Valley with their green ribbons of vine against a background of hills thick with coast live oak and native grassland.

The California Republic began at this very location: the original Bear Flag was raised in the heart of what is now Sonoma State Historic Park on June 14, 1846, and many of the Bear Flag followers—Americans opposing Mexican rule of California—stayed in the Sonoma Barracks during the following month. Rosalía Vallejo Leese, General Vallejo's sister, witnessed the takeover. In this interview from June 27, 1874, conducted by Henry Cerruti, an agent of historian Hubert Howe Bancroft, she recollects the moments before and after a new, handpainted flag was raised in the plaza near the old mission. Her account stands in sharp contrast to those who in later years would depict the creation of the Bear Flag Republic as a noble act of political liberation.

ROSALÍA VALLEJO LEESE
(Translated by Rose Marie Beebe and Robert M. Senkewicz)
REMINISCENCES

Q. Please madam Lease, tell me what you know with reference to the hoisting of the Bear Flag in Sonoma.

A. About half past five in the morning of June 14th 1846, an old gentleman called Don Pepe de la Rosa came to my house and notified me that a band of seventy two rough looking desperadoes, many of them runaway sailors from whale ships, had surrounded the house of General Vallejo and had arrested him, Captain Salvador Vallejo and Victor Prudón. On hearing this alarming piece of intelligence, I dressed in a hurry and hastened to the streets for the purpose of ascertaining the truth of such report—the first thing which met my eyes was Colonel Prudón hastening to the rescue of Captain Salvador Vallejo, whom a ruffian called Benjamin Kelsey was trying to murder in cold blood. I don't believe that you can give a different name to the killing of an unarmed prisoner by a stalwart bully who had seventy men of his own ilk at his back. The timely arrival of Prudón saved the life of the defenseless Captain whom the companions of Kelsey hurried off towards the party under Doctor Semple, to all appearance the least inhuman of that godforsaken crowd. I also perceived ex-Commander General Vallejo dressed in the uniform of a general of the Mexican army, a prisoner of a large group of rough looking men, some wearing on their heads caps made with the skins of coyotes or wolfs, some wearing slouched hats full of holes, some wearing straw hats as black as charcoal. The majority of this marauding band wore buck-skin pants, some blue pants that reached only to the knees, several had no shirts, shoes were only to be seen on the feet of fifteen or twenty among the whole lot.

After some parleying among themselves, a great many of them mounted their horses and escorted General Vallejo, Captain Salvador Vallejo, Colonel Victor Prudón and my husband

Jacob Leese to Sacramento where they were delivered to the tender mercy of the arch fiend John A. Sutter, a man who though married in Europe where he had left a wife and several children, was living in open concubinage with two black women whom he had brought in his vessel from the Sandwich Islands.

After General Vallejo had been hurried away, the remaining robbers hoisted in the square of Sonoma, on the flag staff that was standing in the corner of the plaza near the old mission church, a piece of linen about the size of a large towel; in it was painted a red bear and a lone star. It is fair to presume that John C. Frémont, the man who had planned the wholesale robbery of California, though an officer of the United States army, was afraid to compromise the honor of his government if his party pursued their thieving operations under the flag, that lovers of liberty throughout the world hold dear, hence his reason for resorting to the adoption of a flag unknown to civilized nations. As soon as the flag of the Bear had been hoisted, the robbers interpreter, Solís (formerly a servant of my husband) notified me that I was a prisoner, and he pointed towards four ill-looking desperadoes who stood near me with drawn pistols. Resistance being useless, I yielded and at their request gave them the key of the storehouse of my husband. No sooner I gave them the key, they called their friends and began ransacking the storehouse where were deposited provisions and liquor sufficient to feed two hundred men during two years. Few days after the departure of my husband, arrived in Sonoma John C. Frémont, who as he then said, came for the sole and only purpose of arranging matters so as to give general satisfaction, and protect every one against extortion or oppression. That man, whom many paid writers have dubbed with many an endearing epitet, was a great coward. I say so with good reason—hear me—on the 20th of June, news reached Sonoma that Captain Padilla at the head of one hundred men was coming to the rescue of Sonoma; no sooner Frémont heard this than he sent for me and ordered me to address Padilla a letter requesting him to return to San José, and not to approach Sonoma. I flatly refused, but Frémont, who was bent on having his way, told me that he would burn our houses with us inside of them if I refused to address Padilla in the manner he wished me to do so ("mandaré quemar las casas con ustedes adentro si Padilla se acerca a Sonoma"). I consented, not for the purpose of saving my life, but being then in the family way, I had no right to endanger the life of my unborn baby; moreover I judged that a man who had already gone so far would not stop at anything which may be a barrier to his ends, and being desirous of saving trouble to my countrywomen, I wrote the fatal letter which induced Captain Padilla to retrace his steps—while on the alert for Padilla, Frémont changed his shining uniform for a blue blouse, put away his hat and wrapped his head with a common handkerchief—he adopted this fantastic style of dress for the purpose of avoiding recognition. Is this the conduct becoming a brave man?

During the whole time Frémont and his gang were in Sonoma, robberies were very common. Ladies dared not go out for a walk unless escorted by their husband and brothers. Among my maid servants I had a young Indian girl about seventeen years of age; and I assure you that many a time John C. Frémont sent me orders to deliver her to the officers of the barracks, but by resorting to artifices I managed to save the unhappy girl from the fate decreed to her by the lawless band who had imprisoned my husband. During the whole time of my husband's imprisonment I forwarded him delicacies and gold, but the recreant Sutter, who on more than one occasion had been compelled to acknowledge the superiority of Mr. Leese, arranged matters so that during the two months of his imprisonment he never received a single dollar. He kept him during one whole week sleeping on the bare floor, and appointed as jailer of this room in which he was confined an uncouth Missourian who whenever he opened the door insulted the prisoners, whom a band of ungrateful horse thieves, trappers and runaway sailors had deprived of their liberty. I could relate many a misdeed of the Bear Flag crowd, but not wishing to detain you any longer I will close with the remark that those hated men inspired me with such a large dosis of hate against their race, that though twenty eight years have elapsed since that time, I have not yet forgotten the insults they heaped upon me, and not being desirous of coming in contact with them I have abstained from learning their language.

BENICIA CAPITOL STATE HISTORIC PARK

This dignified brick edifice standing just off Benicia's main street was California's third capital building and is the state's oldest to survive to the present day. It was used as the center of government from 1853 to 1854, when the state legislature left Benicia for Sacramento.

In the autumn of 1850, the infamous California humorist George Horatio Derby (alias John P. Squibob) paid a visit to Benicia. Tongue in cheek, he dubs the place "the world-renowned sea-port of Benicia" and proceeds to regale the reader with the magnificence of the modest town of forty-two houses, three billiard tables, and very nearly twelve hundred residents.

Today, the Benicia Capitol has been restored to match the time period in which it was used, complete with ponderosa pine flooring and period desks, topped each with candlestick, quill pen, newspaper, and top hat.

GEORGE HORATIO DERBY

from *PHOENIXIANA*

Benicia, October 1st, 1850

Leaving the metropolis last evening by the gradually-increasing-in-popularity steamer, *West Point*, I "skeeted" up Pablo Bay with the intention of spending a few days at the world-renowned sea-port of Benicia. Our Captain (a very pleasant and gentlemanly little fellow by the way) was named Swift, our passengers were emphatically a fast set, the wind blew like well-watered rosebushes, and the tide was strong in our favor. All these circumstances tended to impress me with the idea that we were to make a wonderfully quick passage, but alas, "the race is not always to the Swift," the *Senator* passed us ten miles from the wharf, and it was nine o'clock, and very dark at that, when we were roped in by the side of the "ancient and fishlike" smelling hulk that forms the broad wharf of Benicia.

As I shouldered my carpet-bag, and stepped upon the wharf among the dense crowd of four individuals that were there assembled, and gazing upon the mighty city whose glimmering lights, feebly discernible through the Benician darkness, extended over an area of five acres, an overpowering sense of the grandeur and majesty of the great rival of San Francisco affected me.—I felt my own extreme insignificance, and was fain to lean upon a pile of watermelons for support. "Boy!" said I, addressing an intelligent specimen of humanity who formed an integral portion of the above-mentioned crowd, "Boy! can you direct me to the best hotel in this city?"—"Ain't but one," responded the youth, "Winn keeps it; right up the hill thar." Decidedly, thought I, I will go in to Winn, and reshouldering my carpet-bag, I blundered down the ladder, upon a plank foot-path leading over an extensive morass in the direction indicated, not noticing, in my abstraction, that I had inadvertently retained within my grasp the melon upon which my hand had rested. *"Saw yer!"* resounded from the wharf as

I retired—"*Saw yer!*" repeated several individuals upon the foot-path. For an instant my heart beat with violence at the idea of being seen accidentally appropriating so contemptible an affair as a watermelon; but hearing a man with a small white hat and large white mustache shout "Hello!" and immediately rush with frantic violence up the ladder, I comprehended that Sawyer was his proper name, and by no means alluded to me or my proceedings; so slipping the melon in my carpet-bag, I tranquilly resumed my journey.

A short walk brought me to the portal of the best and only hotel in the city, a large two-story building dignified by the title of the "Solano Hotel," where I was graciously received by mine host, who welcomed me to Benicia in the most *winning* manner. After slightly refreshing my inner man with a feeble stimulant, and undergoing an introduction to the oldest inhabitant, I calmly seated myself in the bar-room, and contemplated with intense interest the progress of a game of billiards between two enterprising citizens; but finding, after a lapse of two hours, that there was no earthly probability of its ever being concluded, I seized a candle-stick and retired to my room. Here I discussed my melon with intense relish, and then seeking my couch, essayed to sleep. But, oh! the fleas! skipping, hopping, crawling, biting! "Won't someone establish an agency for the sale of D. L. Charles & Co.'s Fleabane, in Benicia?" I agonizingly shouted, and echo answered through the reverberating halls of the "Solano Hotel," "Yes, they won't!" What a night!

But everything must have an end (circles and California gold excepted), and day at last broke over Benicia. Magnificent place! I gazed upon it from the attic window of the "Solano Hotel," with feelings too deep for utterance. The sun was rising in its majesty, gilding the red wood shingles of the U.S. Store-houses in the distance; seven deserted hulks were riding majestically at anchor in the bay; clothes-lines, with their burdens, were flapping in the morning breeze; a man with a wheelbarrow was coming down the street!—Everything, in short, spoke of the life, activity, business, and bustle of a great city. But in the midst of the excitement of this scene, an odoriferous smell of beefsteak came, like a holy calm, across my olfactories, and hastily drawing in my *cabeza*, I descended to breakfast. This operation concluded, I took a stroll in company with the oldest inhabitant, from whom I obtained much valuable information (which I hasten to present), and who cheerfully volunteered to accompany me as a guide to the lions of the city.

There are no less than forty-two wooden houses, many of them two stories in height, in this great place—and nearly 1200 inhabitants, men, women and children! There are six grocery, provision, drygoods, auction, commission, and where-you-can-get-almost-any-little-thing-you-want stores, one hotel, one school-house—which is also a *brevet* church—three billiard-tables, a post-office—from which I actually saw a man get a letter—and a tenpin-alley, where I am told a man once rolled a whole game, paid $1.50 for it, and walked off chuckling. Then there is a "monte bank"—a Common Council, and a Mayor, who, my guide informed me, was called *"Carne,"* from a singular habit he has of eating roast beef for dinner.—But there isn't a tree in all Benicia. "There was one," said the guide, "last year—only four miles from here, but they chopped it down for firewood for the 'post.' Alas! why didn't the woodman spare that tree?" The dwelling of one individual pleased me indescribably—he had painted it a vivid green! Imaginative being. He had evidently tried to fancy it a tree, and in the enjoyment of this sweet illusion, had reclined beneath its grateful shade, secured from the rays of the burning sun, and in the full enjoyment of rural felicity even among the crowded streets of this great metropolis.

· · · · ·

As I sit here looking from my airy chamber upon the crowds of two or three persons thronging the streets of the great city; as I gaze upon that man carrying home a pound and a half of fresh beef for his dinner; as I listen to the bell of the *Mary* (a Napa steam packet of four cat power) ringing for departure, while her captain in a hoarse voice of authority requests the passengers to "step over the other side, as the larboard paddle-box is under water"; as I view all these unmistakable signs of the growth and prosperity of Benicia, I cannot but wonder at the infatuation of the people of your village, who will persist in their absurd belief that San Francisco will become a *place,* and do not hesitate to advance the imbecile idea that it may become a successful rival of this city. Nonsense! Oh Lord! at this instant there passed by my window the—prettiest—little—I can't write any more this week; if this takes, I'll try it again.

Yours for ever, Squibob

MONO LAKE TUFA
STATE NATURAL RESERVE

Despite the fact that the dramatic views of ghostly tufa towers rising from pale Mono Lake are considered among the wonders of the American West, Mark Twain wasn't much taken with this mountaintop inland sea. Nevertheless, in *Roughing It*, Twain's lively and at times outrageous descriptions of the lake's salty water, the bubbling hot springs, and the unique limestone formations still capture something of the area's bizarre and otherworldly beauty.

Located near the eastern Sierra town of Lee Vining, Mono Lake has been called California's Dead Sea. While it is very salty, it is in fact teeming with life, mainly brine shrimp, which provide food for the numerous birds—including gulls, grebes, and red-necked phalaropes—that use the lake as nesting and feeding grounds. The California gull flies all the way from the coast to Mono Lake to breed on its sharp-cut islands; it is estimated that 90 percent of California gulls are hatched there.

The 55,300-acre state natural reserve offers many trails from which to appreciate the famed tufa towers—calcite deposits formed into spires over millennia—as well as longer walks along the lakeshore that boast stunning views of the surrounding snowy Sierra. The reserve also hosts boating, bird watching, swimming, and crosscountry skiing.

MARK TWAIN
from *ROUGHING IT*

We held a council and decided to make the best of our misfortune and enjoy a week's holiday on the borders of the curious Lake. Mono, it is sometimes called, and sometimes the "Dead Sea of California." It is one of the strangest freaks of Nature to be found in any land, but it is hardly ever mentioned in print and very seldom visited, because it lies away off the usual routes of travel and besides is so difficult to get at that only men content to endure the roughest life will consent to take upon themselves the discomforts of such a trip. On the morning of our second day, we traveled around to a remote and particularly wild spot on the borders of the Lake, where a stream of fresh, ice-cold water entered it from the mountain side, and then we went regularly into camp. We hired a large boat and two shotguns from a lonely ranchman who lived some ten miles further on, and made ready for comfort and recreation. We soon got thoroughly acquainted with the Lake and all its peculiarities.

· · · · ·

Mono Lake lies in a lifeless, treeless, hideous desert, eight thousand feet above the level of the sea, and is guarded by mountains two thousand feet higher, whose summits are always clothed in clouds. This solemn, silent, sailless sea—this lonely tenant of the loneliest spot on earth—is little graced with the picturesque. It is an unpretending expanse of grayish water, about a hundred miles in circumference, with two islands in its centre, mere upheavals of rent and scorched and blistered lava, snowed over with gray banks and drifts of pumice stone and ashes, the winding sheet of the dead volcano, whose vast crater the lake has seized upon and occupied.

The lake is two hundred feet deep, and its sluggish waters are so strong with alkali that if you only dip the most hopelessly soiled garment into them once or twice, and wring it out, it will be found as clean as if it had been through the ablest of washerwomen's hands. While we camped there our laundry work was easy. We tied the week's washing astern of our boat, and sailed a quarter of a mile, and the job was complete, all to the wringing out. If we threw the water on our heads and gave them a rub or so, the white lather would pile up three inches high. This water is not good for bruised places and abrasions of the skin. We had a valuable dog. He had raw places on him. He had more raw places on him than sound ones. He was the rawest dog I almost ever saw. He jumped overboard one day to get away from the flies. But it was bad judgment. In his condition, it would have been just as comfortable to jump into the fire. The alkali water nipped him in all the raw places simultaneously, and he struck out for the shore with considerable interest. He yelped and barked and howled as he went—and by the time he got to the shore there was no bark to him—for he had barked the bark all out of his inside, and the alkali water had cleaned the bark all off his outside, and he probably wished he had never embarked in any such enterprise. He ran round and round in a circle, and pawed the earth and clawed the air, and threw double summersets, sometimes backwards and sometimes forwards, in the most extraordinary manner. He was not a demonstrative dog, as a general thing, but rather of a grave and serious turn of mind, and I never saw him take so much interest in anything before. He finally struck out over the mountains, at a gait which we estimated at about two hundred and fifty miles an hour, and he is going yet. This was about nine years ago. We look for what is left of him along here every day.

A white man cannot drink the water of Mono Lake, for it is nearly pure lye. It is said that the Indians in the vicinity drink it sometimes, though. It is not improbable, for they are among the purest liars I ever saw. [There will be no additional charge for this joke, except to parties requiring an explanation of it. This joke has received high commendation from some of the ablest minds of the age.]

There are no fish in Mono Lake—no frogs, no snakes, no polliwogs—nothing, in fact, that goes to make life desirable. Millions of wild ducks and sea-gulls swim about the surface, but no living thing exists *under* the surface, except a white feathery sort of worm, one half an inch long, which looks like a bit of white thread frayed out at the sides. If you dip up a gallon of water, you will get about fifteen thousand of these. They give to the water a sort of grayish-white appearance. Then there is a fly, which looks something like our house fly. These settle on the beach to eat the worms that wash ashore—and any time, you can see there a belt of flies an inch deep and six feet wide, and this belt extends clear around the lake—a belt of flies one hundred miles long. If you throw a stone among them, they swarm up so thick that they look dense, like a cloud. You can hold them under water as long as you please—they do not mind it—they are only proud of it. When you let them go, they pop up to the surface as dry as a patent office report, and walk off as unconcernedly as if they had been educated especially with a view to affording instructive entertainment to man in that particular way. Providence leaves nothing to go by chance. All things have their uses and their part and proper place in Nature's economy: the ducks eat the flies—the flies eat the worms—the Indians eat all three—the wild cats eat the Indians—the white folks eat the wild cats—and thus all things are lovely.

Mono Lake is a hundred miles in a straight line from the ocean—and between it and the ocean are one or two ranges of mountains—yet thousands of sea-gulls go there every season to lay their eggs and rear their young. One would as soon expect to find sea-gulls in Kansas. And in this connection let us observe another instance of Nature's wisdom. The islands in the lake being merely huge masses of lava, coated over with ashes and pumice stone, and utterly innocent of vegetation or anything that would burn; and sea-gulls' eggs being entirely useless to anybody unless they be cooked, Nature has provided an unfailing spring of boiling water on the largest island, and you can put your eggs in there, and in four minutes you can boil them as hard as any statement I have made during the past fifteen years. Within ten feet of the boiling spring is a spring of pure cold water, sweet and wholesome. So, in that island you get your board and washing free of charge—and if nature had gone further and furnished a nice American hotel clerk who was crusty and disobliging, and didn't know anything about the time tables, or the railroad routes—or—

anything—and was proud of it—I would not wish for a more desirable boarding house.

Half a dozen little mountain brooks flow into Mono Lake, but *not a stream of any kind flows out of it.* It neither rises nor falls, apparently, and what it does with its surplus water is a dark and bloody mystery.

There are only two seasons in the region round about Mono Lake—and these are, the breaking up of one winter and the beginning of the next. More than once (in Esmeralda) I have seen a perfectly blistering morning open up with the thermometer at ninety degrees at eight o'clock, and seen the snow fall fourteen inches deep and that same identical thermometer go down to forty-four degrees under shelter, before nine o'clock at night. Under favorable circumstances it snows at least once in every single month in the year, in the little town of Mono. So uncertain is the climate in summer that a lady who goes out visiting cannot hope to be prepared for all emergencies unless she takes her fan under one arm and her snow shoes under the other. When they have a Fourth of July procession it generally snows on them, and they do say that as a general thing when a man calls for a brandy toddy there, the bar-keeper chops it off with a hatchet and wraps it up in a paper, like maple sugar. And it is further reported that the old soakers haven't any teeth—wore them out eating gin cocktails and brandy punches. I do not endorse that statement—I simply give it for what it is worth—and it is worth—well, I should say, millions, to any man who can believe it without straining himself. But I do endorse the snow on the Fourth of July—because I know that to be true.

• • • • •

About seven o'clock one blistering hot morning—for it was now dead summer time—Higbie and I took the boat and started on a voyage of discovery to the two islands. We had often longed to do this, but had been deterred by the fear of storms; for they were frequent, and severe enough to capsize an ordinary row-boat like ours without great difficulty—and once capsized, death would ensue in spite of the bravest swimming, for that venomous water would eat a man's eyes out like fire, and burn him out inside, too, if he shipped a sea. It was called twelve miles, straight out to the islands—a long pull and a warm one—but the morning was so quiet and sunny, and the lake so smooth and glassy and dead, that we could not resist the temptation. So we filled two large tin canteens with water (since we were not acquainted with the locality of the spring said to exist on the large island), and started. Higbie's brawny muscles gave the boat good speed, but by the time we reached our destination we judged that we had pulled nearer fifteen miles than twelve.

We landed on the big island and went ashore. We tried the water in the canteens, now, and found that the sun had spoiled it; it was so brackish that we could not drink it; so we poured it out and began a search for the spring—for thirst augments fast as soon as it is apparent that one has no means at hand of quenching it. The island was a long, moderately high hill of ashes—nothing but gray ashes and pumice stone, in which we sunk to our knees at every step—and all around the top was a forbidding wall of scorched and blasted rocks. When we reached the top and got within the wall, we found simply a shallow, far-reaching basin, carpeted with ashes, and here and there a patch of fine sand. In places, picturesque jets of steam shot up out of crevices, giving evidence that although this ancient crater had gone out of active business, there was still some fire left in its furnaces. Close to one of these jets of steam stood the only tree on the island—a small pine of most graceful shape and most faultless symmetry; its color was a brilliant green, for the steam drifted unceasingly through its branches and kept them always moist. It contrasted strangely enough, did this vigorous and beautiful outcast, with its dead and dismal surroundings. It was like a cheerful spirit in a mourning household.

We hunted for the spring everywhere, traversing the full length of the island (two or three miles), and crossing it twice—climbing ash-hills patiently, and then sliding down the other side in a sitting posture, plowing up smothering volumes of gray dust. But we found nothing but solitude, ashes and a heart-breaking silence. Finally we noticed that the wind had risen, and we forgot our thirst in a solicitude of greater importance; for, the lake being quiet, we had not taken pains about securing the boat. We hurried back to a point overlooking our landing place, and then—but mere words cannot describe our dismay—the boat was gone! The chances were that there was not another boat on the entire lake. The situation was not comfortable—in truth, to speak plainly, it was frightful. We were prisoners on a desolate island, in aggravating proximity to friends who were for the present helpless to aid us; and what was still more uncomfortable was the reflection that we had neither food nor water. But presently we sighted the boat. It was drifting along, leisurely, about fifty yards from shore, tossing in a foamy sea. It drifted, and continued to drift, but at the same safe distance from land, and we walked along abreast it and waited for fortune to favor us. At the end of an hour it approached a jutting cape, and Higbie ran ahead and posted himself on the utmost verge and prepared for the assault. If we failed there, there was no hope for us. It was driving gradually shoreward all the time, now; but whether it was driving fast enough to make the connection or not was the momentous question. When it got within thirty steps of Higbie I was so excited that I fancied I could hear my own heart beat. When, a little later, it dragged slowly along and seemed about to go by, only one little yard out of reach, it seemed as if my heart stood still; and when it was exactly abreast him and began to widen away, and he still standing like a watching statue, I knew my heart did stop. But when he gave a great spring, the next instant, and lit fairly in the stern, I discharged a war-whoop that woke the solitudes!

But it dulled my enthusiasm, presently, when he told me he had not been caring whether the boat came within jumping distance or not, so that it passed within eight or ten yards of him, for he had made up his mind to shut his eyes and mouth and swim that trifling distance. Imbecile that I was, I had not thought of that. It was only a long swim that could be fatal.

The sea was running high and the storm increasing. It was growing late, too—three or four in the afternoon. Whether to venture toward the mainland or not, was a question of some moment. But we were so distressed by thirst that we decided to try it, and so Higbie fell to work and I took the steering-oar. When we had pulled a mile, laboriously, we were evidently in serious peril, for the storm had greatly augmented; the billows ran very high and were capped with foaming crests, the heavens were hung with black, and the wind blew with great fury. We would have gone back, now, but we did not dare to turn the boat around, because as soon as she got in the trough of the sea she would upset, of course. Our only hope lay in keeping her head-on to the seas. It was hard work to do this, she plunged so, and so beat and belabored the billows with her rising and falling bows. Now and then one of Higbie's oars would trip on the top of a wave, and the other one would snatch the boat half around in spite of my cumbersome steering apparatus. We were drenched by the sprays constantly, and the boat occasionally shipped water. By and by, powerful as my comrade was, his great exertions began to tell on him, and he was anxious that I should change places with him till he could rest a little. But I told him this was impossible; for if the steering-oar were dropped a moment while we changed, the boat would slue around into the trough of the sea, capsize, and in less than five minutes we would have a hundred gallons of soap-suds in us and be eaten up so quickly that we could not even be present at our own inquest.

But things cannot last always. Just as the darkness shut down we came booming into port, head-on. Higbie dropped his oars to hurrah—I dropped mine to help—the sea gave the boat a twist, and over she went!

The agony that alkali water inflicts on bruises, chafes and blistered hands, is unspeakable, and nothing but greasing all over will modify it—but we ate, drank and slept well, that night, notwithstanding.

MOUNT TAMALPAIS
STATE PARK

The silhouette of 2,574-foot Mount Tamalpais, likened by more than one person to the profile of a sleeping maiden, dominates the skyline of Marin County, just north of San Francisco. In a single afternoon walking on the mountain, one can pass through redwood forest thick with fog, dry chaparral of tangled manzanita, coastal sage and sticky monkeyflower, and windy coast live oak savannah overlooking a cloud-blanketed Pacific. The great variety of microclimates contained within the 6,243 acres of this state park—created by Mount Tam's location between ocean and bay, and its numerous canyons, valleys, and faces—make the area rich and diverse in plant and animal life. Tamalpais is one of many peaks in the Northern California Coast Ranges, but its proximity to the urban centers of the Bay Area, as well as its bay laurel–spiced hillsides and rushing redwood streams, have made it wildly popular with hikers since the first summer houses were built in its canyons by San Francisco residents as early as the 1860s.

Among its more famous hikers is poet Gary Snyder, who in the spring of 1956 invited his buddy Jack Kerouac to stay for a few months with him in his hillside shack, Marin-an. Together they wandered the trails, meadows, and groves of the great mountain. This trip, Mount Tamalpais, and Snyder himself (in the form of Japhy Ryder), became immortalized in Kerouac's Beat classic *The Dharma Bums*.

JACK KEROUAC

from *THE DHARMA BUMS*

The party went on for days; the morning of the third day people were still sprawled about the grounds when Japhy and I sneaked our rucksacks out, with a few choice groceries, and started down the road in the orange early-morning sun of California golden days. It was going to be a great day, we were back in our element: trails.

Japhy was in high spirits. "Goddammit it feels good to get away from dissipation and go in the woods. When I get back from Japan, Ray, when the weather gets really cold we'll put on our long underwear and hitchhike through the land. Think if you can of ocean to mountain Alaska to Klamath a solid forest of fir to bhikku in, a lake of a million wild geese. Woo! You know what woo means in Chinese?"

"What?"

"Fog. These woods are great here in Marin. I'll show you Muir Woods today, but up north is all the real old Pacific Coast mountain and ocean land, the future home of the Dharma-body. Know what I'm gonna do? I'll do a new long poem called 'Rivers and Mountains Without End' and just write it on and on on a scroll and unfold on and on with new surprises and always what went before forgotten, see, like a river, or like one of them real long Chinese silk paintings that show two little men hiking in an endless landscape of gnarled old trees and mountains so high they merge with the fog in the upper silk void. I'll spend three thousand years writing it, it'll be packed full of information on soil conservation, the Tennessee Valley Authority, astronomy, geology, Hsuan Tsung's travels, Chinese painting theory, reforestation, Oceanic ecology and food chains."

"Go to it, boy." As ever I strode on behind him and when we began to climb, with our packs feeling good on our backs as though we were pack animals and didn't feel right without a burden, it was the same old lonesome old good old thwap thwap up the trail, slowly, a mile an hour. We came to the end of the steep road where we had to go through a few houses built near steep bushy cliffs with waterfalls trickling down, then up to a high steep meadow, full of butterflies and hay and a little seven a.m. dew, and down to a dirt road, then to the ends of the dirt road, which rose higher and higher till we could see vistas of Corte Madera and Mill Valley far away and even the red top of the Golden Gate Bridge.[...]

"What are you thinking about?" [I asked Japhy.]

"Just makin up poems in my head as I climb toward Mount Tamalpais. See up there ahead, as beautiful a mountain as you'll see anywhere in the world, a beautiful shape to it, I really love Tamalpais. We'll sleep tonight way around the back of it. Take us till late afternoon to get there."

The Marin country was much more rustic and kindly than the rough Sierra country we'd climbed last fall: it was all flowers, flowers, trees, bushes, but also a great deal of poison oak by the side of the trail. When we got to the end of the high dirt road we suddenly plunged into the dense redwood forest and went along following a pipeline through glades that were so deep the fresh morning sun barely penetrated and it was cold and damp. But the odor was pure deep rich pine and wet logs. Japhy was all talk this morning. He was like a little kid again now that he was out on the trail.[...]

We came up out of the gladey redwood forest onto a road, where there was a mountain lodge, then crossed the road and dipped down again through bushes to a trail that probably nobody even knew was there except a few hikers, and we were in Muir Woods. It extended, a vast valley, for miles before us. An old logger road led us for two miles, then Japhy got off and scrambled up the slope and got onto another trail nobody dreamed was there. We hiked on this one, up and down along a tumbling creek, with fallen logs again where you crossed the creek, and sometimes bridges that had been built Japhy said by the Boy Scouts, trees sawed in half the flat surface for walking. Then we climbed up a steep pine slope and came out to the highway and went up the side of a hill of grass and came out in some outdoor theater, done up Greek style with stone seats all around a bare stone arrangement for four-dimensional presentations of Aeschylus and Sophocles. We drank water and sat down and took our shoes off and watched the silent play from the upper stone seats. Far away you could see the Golden Gate Bridge and the whiteness of San Francisco.

Japhy began to shriek and hoot and whistle and sing, full of pure gladness. Nobody around to hear him.[...]

He picked up his pack and started off. In a half-hour we were in a beautiful meadow following a dusty little trail over shallow creeks and finally we were at Potrero Meadows camp. It was a National Forest camp with a stone fireplace and picnic tables and everything but no one would be there till the weekend. A few miles away, the lookout shack on top of Tamalpais looked right down on us. We undid our packs and spent a quiet late afternoon dozing in the sun or Japhy ran around looking at butterflies and birds and making notes in his notebook and I hiked alone down the other side, north, where a desolate rocky country much like the Sierras stretched out toward the sea.

At dusk Japhy lit a good big fire and started supper. We were very tired and happy. He made a soup that night that I shall never forget and was really the best soup I'd eaten since I was a lionized young author in New York eating lunch at the Chambord or in Henri Cru's kitchen. This was nothing but a couple of envelopes of dried pea soup thrown into a pot of water with fried bacon, fat and all, and stirred till boiling. It was rich, real pea taste, with that smoky bacon and bacon fat, just the thing to drink in the cold gathering darkness by a sparkling fire. Also, while poking about he'd found puffballs, natural mushrooms, not the umbrella type, just round grapefruit-size puffs of white firm meat, and these he sliced and fried in bacon fat and we had them on the side with fried rice. It was a great supper. We washed the dishes in the gurgling creek. The roaring bonfire kept the mosquitoes away. A new moon peeked down through the pine boughs. We rolled out our sleeping bags in the meadow grass and went to bed early, bone weary.

"Well Ray," said Japhy, "pretty soon I'll be far out to sea and you'll be hitchhiking up the coast to Seattle and on through the Skagit country. I wonder what'll happen to all of us."

We went to sleep on this dreamy theme. During the night I had a vivid dream, one of the most distinct dreams I ever had, I clearly saw a crowded dirty smoky Chinese market with beggars and vendors and pack horses and mud and smokepots and piles of rubbish and vegetables for sale in dirty clay pans on the ground and suddenly from the mountains a ragged hobo, a little seamed brown unimaginable Chinese hobo, had come down and was just standing at the end of the market, surveying it with an expressionless humor. He was short, wiry, his face leathered hard and dark red by the sun of the desert and mountains; his clothes were nothing but gathered rags; he had a pack of leather on his back; he was bare-footed. I had seen guys like that only seldom, and only in Mexico, maybe coming into Monterrey out of those stark rock mountains, beggars who probably live in caves. But this one was a Chinese twice-as-poor, twice-as-tough and infinitely mysterious tramp and it was Japhy for sure. It was the same broad mouth, merry twinkling eyes, bony face (a face like Dostoevsky's death mask, with prominent eyebrow bones and square head); and he was short and compact like Japhy. I woke up at dawn, thinking, "Wow, is *that* what'll happen to Japhy? Maybe he'll leave that monastery and just disappear and we'll never see him again, and he'll be the Han Shan ghost of the Orient mountains and even the Chinese'll be afraid of him he'll be so raggedy and beat."

I told Japhy about it. He was already up stoking the fire and whistling. "Well don't just lay there in your sleeping bag pullin your pudding, get up and fetch some water. Yodelayhee hoo! Ray, I will bring you incense sticks from the coldwater temple of Kiyomizu and set them one by one in a big brass incense bowl and do the proper bows, how's about that. That was some dream you had. If that's me, then it's me. Ever weeping, ever youthful, hoo!" He got out the hand-ax from the rucksack and hammered at boughs and got a crackling fire going. There was still mist in the trees and fog on the ground. "Let's pack up and take off and dig Laurel Dell camp. Then we'll hike over the trails down to the sea and swim."

"Great." On this trip Japhy had brought along a delicious combination for hiking energy: Ry-Krisp crackers, good sharp Cheddar cheese a wedge of that, and a roll of salami. We had this for breakfast with hot fresh tea and felt great. Two grown men could live two days on that concentrated bread and that salami (concentrated meat) and cheese and the whole thing only weighed about a pound and a half. Japhy was full of great ideas like that. What hope, what human energy, what truly American optimism was packed in that neat little frame of his! There he was clomping along in front of me on the trail and shouting back "Try the meditation of the trail, just walk along looking at the trail at your feet and don't look about and just fall into a trance as the ground zips by."

We arrived at Laurel Dell camp at about ten, it was also supplied with stone fireplaces with grates, and picnic tables, but the surroundings were infinitely more beautiful than Potrero Meadows. Here were the real meadows: dreamy beauties with soft grass sloping all around, fringed by heavy deep green timber, the whole scene of waving grass and brooks and nothing in sight.

"By God, I'm gonna come back here and bring nothing but food and gasoline and a primus and cook my suppers smokeless and the Forest Service won't even know the difference."

"Yeah, but if they ever catch you cooking away from these stone places they put you out, Smith."

"But what would I do on weekends, join the merry picknickers? I'd just hide up there beyond that beautiful meadow. I'd stay there forever."

"And you'd only have two miles of trail down to Stinson Beach and your grocery store down there." At noon we started for the beach. It was a tremendously grinding trip. We climbed way up high on meadows, where again we could see San Francisco far away, then dipped down into a steep trail that seemed to fall directly down to sea level; you had sometimes to run down the trail or slide on your back, one. A torrent of water fell down at the side of the trail. I went ahead of Japhy and began swinging down the trail so fast, singing happily. I left him behind about a mile and had to wait for him at the bottom. He was taking his time enjoying the ferns and flowers. We stashed our rucksacks in the fallen leaves under bushes and hiked freely down the sea meadows and past seaside farmhouses with cows browsing, to the beach community, where we bought wine in a grocery store and stomped on out into the sand and waves. It was a chill day with only occasional flashes of sun. But we were making it. We jumped into the ocean in our shorts and swam swiftly around then came out and spread out some of our salami and Ry-Krisp and cheese on a piece of paper in the sand and drank wine and talked. At one point I even took a nap. Japhy was feeling very good. "Goddammit, Ray, you'll never know how happy I am we decided to have these last two days hiking. I feel good all over again. I *know* something good's gonna come out of all this!"

"All what?"

"I dunno—out of the way we feel about life. You and I ain't out to bust anybody's skull, or cut someone's throat in an economic way, we've dedicated ourselves to prayer for all sentient beings and when we're strong enough we'll really be able to do it, too, like the old saints. Who knows, the world might wake up and burst out into a beautiful flower of Dharma everywhere."

After dozing awhile he woke up and looked and said, "Look at all that water out there stretching all the way to Japan." He was getting sadder and sadder about leaving.

ANGEL ISLAND STATE PARK

From 1910 until 1940, the mile-square Angel Island, situated in the middle of the San Francisco Bay, served as the main immigration station for the entire West Coast. More than one million people, the vast majority of whom were from China, passed through Angel Island. Often wreathed in thick ocean fog, the island today is a beautiful place to camp, hike, cycle, picnic, and enjoy views of the city, the bay, and the Golden Gate Bridge through banners of mist. But back when it was a necessary stopover for California-bound immigrants, the station was often seen as a prison little better than its neighbor, Alcatraz Island. Exclusionary laws placed severe restrictions on entry into the United States, especially for those coming from Asia, and immigrants were frequently detained and interrogated at Angel Island while officials determined whether they had the right to enter the country. Although the median length of detention was about four days, the length of individual stays varied wildly—especially for Chinese immigrants, many of whom were held for weeks, months, or even years.

Still visible today on the preserved immigration station are more than 135 poems etched into the wooden barracks walls by men waiting for appeal hearings, for deportation, or for reunions with family and loved ones just on the other side of the bay. (The administrative building that was used to hold female immigrants burned down in 1940, but one woman recalled seeing "plenty of poems on the wall" of the women's building as well.) The overwhelming majority of the poems are written in Chinese and, in the style of classical poetry from the Tang Dynasty period, their voices describe wind and fog and loneliness in tones at once despairing and beautiful. Composed in states of limbo and anxiety, these lines of poetry reach into the present with enduring lyricism and strength.

VARIOUS AUTHORS
(Edited by Him Mark Lai, Genny Lim, and Judy Yung)
Poems from *ISLAND: POETRY AND HISTORY OF CHINESE IMMIGRANTS ON ANGEL ISLAND, 1910–1940*

The sea-scape resembles lichen twisting
    and turning for a thousand *li*.
There is no shore to land and it is difficult to
    walk.
With a gentle breeze I arrived at the city
    thinking all would be so.
At ease, how was one to know he was to live in a
    wooden building?

· · · · ·

RANDOM THOUGHTS DEEP AT NIGHT

In the quiet of night, I heard, faintly,
    the whistling of wind.
The forms and shadows saddened me; upon
    seeing the landscape, I composed a poem.
The floating clouds, the fog, darken the sky.
The moon shines faintly as the insects chirp.
Grief and bitterness entwined are heaven sent.
The sad person sits alone, leaning by a window.

Written by Yu of Taishan

· · · · ·

The west wind ruffles my thin gauze clothing.
On the hill sits a tall building with a room of
wooden planks.
I wish I could travel on a cloud far away,
reunite with my wife and son.
When the moonlight shines on me alone, the
nights seem even longer.
At the head of the bed there is wine and my
heart is constantly drunk.
There is no flower beneath my pillow and
my dreams are not sweet.
To whom can I confide my innermost
feelings?
I rely solely on close friends to relieve my
loneliness.

• • • • •

This place is called an island of immortals,
When, in fact, this mountain wilderness is a
prison.
Once you see the open net, why throw
yourself in?
It is only because of empty pockets I can do
nothing else.

• • • • •

I have infinite feelings that the ocean
has changed into a mulberry grove.
My body is detained in this building.
I cannot fly from this grassy hill,
And green waters block the hero.

Impetuously, I threw away my writing brush.
My efforts have all been in vain.
It is up to me to answer carefully.
I have no words to murmur against the east
  wind.

By Ruan

• • • • •

POEM BY ONE NAMED XU,

FROM XIANGSHAN, CONSOLING HIMSELF

Over a hundred poems are on the walls.
Looking at them, they are all pining at the
  delayed progress.
What can one sad person say to another?
Unfortunate travellers everywhere wish to
  commiserate.
Gain or lose, how is one to know what is
  predestined?
Rich or poor, who is to say it is not the will
  of heaven?
Why should one complain if he is detained
  and imprisoned here?
From ancient times, heroes often were the
  first ones to face adversity.

MOUNT DIABLO STATE PARK

Rising suddenly from the relatively flat Central Valley to the east and the San Francisco Bay region to the west, Mount Diablo's 3,864-foot summit affords views that have inspired generations of adventurers to wax poetic. Indeed, legend once had it that the panorama from the top of Mount Diablo encompassed more area than the view from any other mountain peak except Mount Kilimanjaro, a good 16,000 feet taller, and although contemporary geographers have denied the claim, the view is no less impressive.

Botanist and explorer William H. Brewer trekked up and down California in the 1860s, a time when hiking the steep, dry slopes of Mount Diablo was already a weekend treat for San Franciscans. The following excerpt from Brewer's expedition notes is a delicious foray back to a time when the Bay Area was still connected by dusty horse tracks and when ladies in gowns adventured atop mules through the rocky and wildflower-thick canyons of Mount Diablo to gape at the views of the snowcapped Sierra, the bay and delta, the green expanse of the Central Valley, and the blue Pacific on the horizon.

Located in Contra Costa County, Mount Diablo State Park includes more than 19,000 acres of rocky slopes, oak woodlands, grasslands, and chaparral, and adjacent open space preserves and regional parks extend Mount Diablo's wild-space to some 90,000 acres, home to numerous coyotes, bobcats, mountain lions, rattlesnakes, and San Joaquin kit foxes, as well as migrating bald and golden eagles in wintertime. At the summit, a visitors' center provides an overview of the mountain's natural and cultural history, and an observation deck offers magnificent views of the Bay Area and beyond.

WILLIAM H. BREWER

from *UP AND DOWN CALIFORNIA IN 1860–1864*

Tuesday last, April 22, I sent on the party to go into camp here, near Martinez, and I followed the next day.[…]

Professor Whitney [Josiah Whitney, chief of the California Geological Survey from 1860 to 1874] joined us, and on Wednesday, April 30, we moved about nine miles up the valley, south. The next day [topographer Charles] Hoffmann and I visited a ridge about two thousand feet high, about six miles from camp, quite a hard day's tramp. Heavy clouds wreathed the whole summit of Mount Diablo, but we had a fine view of the green hills near and around us. A shower caught us on our return and wet us, but how unlike the rains of the city. The smell of the rain on the fresh soil and green grass was decidedly refreshing.

That night the wind was high, and for three days we had intermittent but heavy rains. We stuck to our tents, but on Friday, May 2, Professor Whitney left for San Francisco. It rained too hard to cook outdoors, so that day and Saturday we got our meals at a tavern near. On Sunday, May 4, we got a fire lit and dinner half cooked when a heavy shower put it out. We went to the tavern again. In the afternoon there was less rain and I sent [assistant Chester] Averill to Pacheco, seven miles, for letters.

The rain was a godsend to the farmers. The soil had begun to bake and crack so that the growing grain could not get on farther. Everything has "greened up" marvelously, and this region, so brown, dry, dusty, and parched when we visited it last fall, is now green and lovely, as only California can be in the spring. Flowers in the greatest profusion and richest colors adorn hills and valleys and the scattered trees are of the liveliest and richest green.

Tuesday, May 6, the camp came on here, about ten or twelve miles. I waited to observe barometer to get the height of the camp above the sea, then footed it across here, a part of the way across hills, the rest across the Pacheco Valley, a plain of many thousand acres, several miles wide, sloping gently from Mount Diablo northwest to the Straits of Carquinez.

The plain is covered for miles with intervals of scattered oaks; not a forest, but scattered trees of the California white oak (*Quercus hindsii*) [now *Quercus lobata*], the most magnificent of trees, often four to five feet in diameter, branching low. They are worthless for timber, but grand, yes magnificent, as ornamental trees, their great spreading branches often forming a head a hundred feet in diameter. Across this great park the trail ran.

On arriving I found the camp pitched in one of the loveliest localities, a pure rippling stream for water, plenty of wood, fine oak trees around, in a sheltered valley, but with the grand old mountain rising just behind us.

Professor Whitney had met us, and a party was here from San Francisco to visit us and climb the mountain. A little town, consisting of a tavern, store, etc., is rapidly growing up scarce twenty rods from camp, where a "hotel" accommodated them. The party consisted of Rev. T. Starr King, the most eloquent divine and, at the same time, one of the best fellows in the state, Mrs. Whitney, Mr. and Mrs. Tompkins (a lawyer whose wedding I had attended last winter), Mr. Blake (a relative of Mrs. Whitney and an intimate friend), and a Mr. Cleaveland (one of the officers in the United States Mint)—a better party could not have been selected.

That evening, a lovely moonlight May evening, we lighted a great camp fire, and our visitors enjoyed it, so new to them, ever so charming to us. The moon lit up the dim outline of the mountain behind, while our fire lit up the group around it. We "talked of the morrow," spun yarns, told stories, and the old oaks echoed with laughter.

Wednesday, May 7, dawned and all bid fair. We were off in due season. I doubt if there are half a dozen days in the year so favorable—everything was *just right,* neither too hot nor too cold, a gentle breeze, the atmosphere of matchless purity and transparency.

Five of our party, Professor Whitney, Averill, Gabb, Rémond, and I, accompanied our visitors. They rode mules or horses; we (save Averill, who was to see to the ladies) went on foot. First, up a wild rocky canyon, the air sweet with the perfume of the abundant flowers, the sides rocky and picturesque, the sky above of the intensest blue; then, up a steep slope to the height of 2,200 feet, where we halted by a spring, rested, filled our canteens, and then went onward.

The summit was reached, and we spent two and a half hours there. The view was one never to be forgotten. It had nothing of grandeur in it, save the almost unlimited extent of the field of view. The air was clear to the horizon on every side, and although the mountain is only 3,890 feet high, from the peculiar figure of the country probably but few views in North America are more extensive—certainly nothing in Europe.

To the west, thirty miles, lies San Francisco; we see out the Golden Gate, and a great expanse of the blue Pacific stretches beyond. The bay, with its fantastic outline, is all in sight, and the ridges beyond to the west and northwest. Mount St. Helena, fifty or sixty miles, is almost lost in the mountains that surround it, but the snows of Mount Ripley (northeast of Clear Lake), near a hundred miles, seem but a few miles off. South and southwest the view is less extensive, extending only fifty or sixty miles south, and to Mount Bache, seventy or eighty miles southwest.

The great features of the view lie to the east of the meridian passing through the peak. First, the great central valley of California, as level as the sea, stretches to the horizon both on the north and to the southeast. It lies beneath us in all its great expanse for near or quite *three hundred miles of its length!* But there is nothing cheering in it—all things seem blended soon in the great, vast expanse. Multitudes of streams and bayous wind and ramify through the hundreds of square miles—yes, I should say *thousands* of square miles—about the mouths of the San Joaquin and Sacramento rivers, and then away up both of these rivers in opposite directions, until nothing can be seen but the straight line on the horizon. On the north are the Marysville Buttes, rising like black masses from the plain, over a hundred miles distant; while still beyond, rising in sharp clear outline against the sky, stand the snow-covered Lassen's Buttes, over *two hundred miles in air line distant from us*—the longest distance I have ever seen.

Rising from this great plain, and forming the horizon for three hundred miles in extent, possibly more, were the snowy crests of the Sierra Nevada. What a grand sight! The peaks of that mighty chain glittering in the purest white under the bright sun, their icy crests seeming a fitting helmet for their black and furrowed sides! There stood in the northeast Pyramid Peak (near Lake Bigler), 125 miles distant, and Castle Peak (near Lake Mono), 160 miles distant, and hundreds of other peaks without names but vieing with the Alps themselves in height and sublimity—all marshaled before us in that grand panorama! I had carried up a barometer, but I could scarcely observe it, so enchanting and enrapturing was the scene.

Figures are dull, I admit, yet in no other way can we convey accurate ideas. I made an estimate from the map, based on the distances to known peaks, and found that the extent of land and sea embraced between the extreme limits of vision amounted to eighty thousand square miles, and that forty thousand square miles, or more, were spread out in tolerably plain view—over 300 miles from north to south, and 260 to 280 miles from east to west, between the extreme points.

We got our observations, ate our lunch, and lounged on the rocks for two and a half hours, and then were loath to leave. We made the descent easily and without mishap or accident—a horse falling once, a girth becoming loose and a lady tumbling off at another time, were the only incidents. The shadows were deep in the canyon as we passed down it, but we were back at sunset.

GREAT VALLEY GRASSLANDS STATE PARK

It might be hard to believe now, passing through the Great Central Valley of California on Interstate 5, that this agricultural heartland was once a vast and rich alluvial plain so covered in wildflowers, so thick with brambles and wild roses along its riparian corridors, that John Muir himself called it "the bee-pastures." But there's a reason the Central Valley is now essentially one huge patchwork of corporate agribusiness: this is the old flood-grounds of the Sacramento and San Joaquin Rivers, and the earth is rich with silt. Even at the time of its writing in 1882, Muir's essay "The Bee-Pastures" predicted the transformation of the "noble valley" into one huge, heavily tilled "garden" because of its incredible fertility.

Pieces of the valley's wild abundance still remain, including the 2,826-acre Great Valley Grasslands State Park, extended on either side by wildlife refuges. Just twenty-eight miles west of Merced, swathes of native bunchgrass prairie flourish intact, spotted with vernal pools that host migrating waterfowl in spring and then turn to colorful rings of wildflowers come the dry heat of summer. A portion of the San Joaquin River flows through the park, its bank lined with cottonwoods and the thickets of blackberry so deliciously described by Muir in the excerpt that follows. A six-mile roundtrip meander through the high grass and gentle riparian woods of the park will transport any visitor, at least momentarily, to an older Central Valley, where time falls away into one endless prairie of nectar, grass, and soft wind. [Note: Some of the scientific names Muir uses have since been changed or updated.]

JOHN MUIR

from "THE BEE-PASTURES"

The Great Central Plain of California, during the months of March, April, and May, was one smooth, continuous bed of honey-bloom, so marvelously rich that, in walking from one end of it to the other, a distance of more than 400 miles, your foot would press about a hundred flowers at every step. Mints, gilias, nemophilas, castilleias, and innumerable compositae were so crowded together that, had ninety-nine per cent of them been taken away, the plain would still have seemed to any but Californians extravagantly flowery. The radiant, honeyful corollas, touching and overlapping, and rising above one another, glowed in the living light like a sunset sky—one sheet of purple and gold, with the bright Sacramento pouring through the midst of it from the north, the San Joaquin from the south, and their many tributaries sweeping in at right angles from the mountains, dividing the plain into sections fringed with trees.

Along the rivers there is a strip of bottom-land, counter-sunk beneath the general level, and wider toward the foot-hills, where magnificent oaks, from three to eight feet in diameter, cast grateful masses of shade over the open, prairie-like levels. And close along the water's edge there was a fine jungle of tropical luxuriance, composed of wild-rose and bramble bushes and a great variety of climbing vines, wreathing and interlacing the branches and trunks of willows and alders, and swinging across from summit to summit in heavy festoons. Here the wild bees reveled in fresh bloom long after the flowers of the drier plain had withered and gone to seed. And in midsummer, when the "blackberries" were ripe, the Indians came from the mountains to feast—men, women, and babies in long, noisy trains, often joined by the farmers of the neighborhood, who gathered this wild fruit with commendable appreciation of its superior flavor, while their home orchards were full of ripe peaches, apricots, nectarines, and figs, and their vineyards were laden with grapes. But, though these luxuriant, shaggy river-beds were thus distinct from the smooth, treeless plain, they made no heavy dividing lines in general views. The whole appeared as one continuous sheet of bloom bounded only by the mountains.

When I first saw this central garden, the most extensive and regular of all the bee-pastures of the State, it seemed all one sheet of plant gold, hazy and vanishing in the distance, distinct as a new map along the foot-hills at my feet.

Descending the eastern slopes of the Coast Range through beds of gilias and lupines, and around many a breezy hillock and bush-crowned headland, I at length waded out into the midst of it. All the ground was covered, not with grass and green leaves, but with radiant corollas, about ankle-deep next the foot-hills, knee-deep or more five or six miles out. Here were bahia, madia, madaria, burrielia, chrysopsis, corethrogyne, grindelia, etc., growing in close social congregations of various shades of yellow blending finely with the purples of clarkia, orthocarpus, and oenothera, whose delicate petals were drinking the vital sunbeams without giving back any sparkling glow.

Because so long a period of extreme drought succeeds the rainy season, most of the vegetation is composed of annuals, which spring up simultaneously, and bloom together at about the same height above the ground, the general surface being but slightly ruffled by the taller phacelias, pentstemons, and groups of *Salvia carduacea,* the king of the mints.

Sauntering in any direction, hundreds of these happy sun-plants brushed against my feet at every step, and closed over them as if I were wading in liquid gold. The air was sweet with fragrance, the larks sang their blessed songs, rising on the wing as I advanced, then sinking out of sight in the polleny sod, while myriads of wild bees stirred the lower air with their monotonous hum—monotonous, yet forever fresh and sweet as every-day sunshine. Hares and spermophiles showed themselves in considerable numbers in shallow places, and small bands of antelopes were almost constantly in sight, gazing curiously from some slight elevation, and then bounding swiftly away with unrivaled grace of motion. Yet I could discover no crushed flowers to mark their track, nor, indeed, any destructive action of any wild foot or tooth whatever.

The great yellow days circled by uncounted, while I drifted toward the north, observing the countless forms of life thronging about me, lying down almost anywhere on the approach of night. And what glorious botanical beds I had! Oftentimes on awaking I would find several new species leaning over me and looking me full in the face, so that my studies would begin before rising.

All the seasons of the great plain are warm or temperate, and bee-flowers are never wholly wanting; but the grand spring-time—the annual resurrection—is governed by the rains, which usually set in about the middle of November or the beginning of December. Then the seeds, that for six months have lain on the ground dry and fresh as if they had been gathered into barns, at once unfold their treasured life. The general brown and purple of the ground, and the dead vegetation of the preceding year, give place to the green of mosses and liverworts and myriads of young leaves. Then one species after another comes into flower, gradually overspreading the green with yellow and purple, which lasts until May.

The "rainy season" is by no means a gloomy, soggy period of constant cloudiness and rain. Perhaps nowhere else in North America, perhaps in the world, are the months of December, January, February, and March so full of bland, plant-building sunshine. Referring to my notes of the winter and spring of 1868–69, every day of which I spent out of doors, on that section of the plain lying between the Tuolumne and Merced rivers, I find that the first rain of the season fell on December 18th. January had only six rainy days—that is, days on which rain fell; February three, March five, April three, and May three, completing the so-called rainy season, which was about an average one. The ordinary rain-storm of this region is seldom very cold or violent. The winds, which in settled weather come from the northwest, veer round into the opposite direction, the sky fills gradually and evenly with one general cloud, from which the rain falls steadily, often for days in succession, at a temperature of about 45° or 50°.

• • • • •

In 1855, two years after the time of the first arrivals from New York, a single swarm was brought over from San Jose, and let fly in the Great Central Plain. Bee-culture, however, has never gained much attention here, notwithstanding the extraordinary abundance of honey-bloom, and the high price of honey during the early years. A few hives are found here and there among settlers who chanced to have learned something about the business before coming to the State. But sheep, cattle, grain, and fruit raising are the chief industries, as they require less skill and care, while the profits thus far have been greater. In 1856 honey sold here at from one and a half to two dollars per pound. Twelve years later the price had fallen to twelve and a half cents. In 1868 I sat down to dinner with a band of ravenous sheep-shearers at a ranch on the San Joaquin, where fifteen or twenty hives were kept, and our host advised us not to spare the large pan of honey he had placed on the table, as it was the cheapest article he had to offer. In all my walks, however, I have never come upon a regular bee-ranch in the Central Valley like those so common and so skilfully managed in the southern counties of the State. The few pounds of honey and wax produced are consumed at home, and are scarcely taken into account among the coarser products of the farm. The swarms that escape from their careless owners have a weary, perplexing time of it in seeking suitable homes. Most of them make their way to the foot-hills of the mountains, or to the trees that line the banks of the rivers, where some hollow log or trunk may be found. A friend of mine, while out hunting on the San Joaquin, came upon an old coon trap, hidden among some tall grass, near the edge of the river, upon which he sat down to rest. Shortly afterward his attention was attracted to a crowd of angry bees that were flying excitedly about his head when he discovered that he was sitting upon their hive, which was found to contain more than 200 pounds of honey. Out in the broad, swampy delta of the Sacramento and San Joaquin rivers, the little wanderers have been known to build their combs in a bunch of rushes, or stiff, wiry grass, only slightly protected from the weather, and in danger every spring of being carried away by floods. They have the advantage, however, of a vast extent of fresh pasture, accessible only to themselves.

The present condition of the Grand Central Garden is very different from that we have sketched. About twenty years ago, when the gold placers had been pretty thoroughly exhausted, the attention of fortune-seekers—not home-seekers—was, in great part, turned away from the mines to the fertile plains, and many began experiments in a kind of restless, wild agriculture. A load of lumber would be hauled to some spot on the free wilderness, where water could be easily found, and a rude box-cabin built. Then a gang-plow was procured, and a dozen mustang ponies, worth ten or fifteen dollars apiece, and with these hundreds of acres were stirred as easily as if the land had been under cultivation for years, tough, perennial roots being almost wholly absent. Thus a ranch was established, and from these bare wooden huts, as centers of desolation, the wild flora vanished in ever-widening circles. But the arch destroyers are the shepherds, with their flocks of hoofed locusts, sweeping over the ground like a fire, and trampling down every rod that escapes the plow as completely as if the whole plain were a cottage garden-plot without a fence. But notwithstanding these destroyers, a thousand swarms of bees may be pastured here for every one now gathering honey. The greater portion is still covered every season with a repressed growth of bee-flowers, for most of the species are annuals, and many of them are not relished by sheep or cattle, while the rapidity of their growth enables them to develop and mature their seeds before any foot has time to crush them. The ground is, therefore, kept sweet, and the race is perpetuated, though only as a suggestive shadow of the magnificence of its wildness.

The time will undoubtedly come when the entire area of this noble valley will be tilled like a garden, when the fertilizing waters of the mountains, now flowing to the sea, will be distributed to every acre, giving rise to prosperous towns, wealth, arts, etc. Then, I suppose, there will be few left, even among botanists, to deplore the vanished primeval flora. In the mean time, the pure waste going on—the wanton destruction of the innocents—is a sad sight to see, and the sun may well be pitied in being compelled to look on.

PESCADERO STATE BEACH

William Everson, better known as Brother Antoninus, the "Beat Friar" poet and hand-press printer of the San Francisco Renaissance, was initially inspired to study poetry—and eventually to write it himself—after he read the work of Robinson Jeffers, bard of the Monterey coast. Everson registered as a conscientious objector during World War II, and it was at a work camp for objectors that he learned the printing trade and wrote his first volume of poetry. Everson was a member of the Catholic Church's Dominican Order during the 1950s and '60s, until he left it to marry. He spent many years teaching at UC Santa Cruz, running a small press, and enjoying life in a cabin by Big Creek that he named Kingfisher Flat. His poetry is a heady mix of ecstatic spirituality and the wild, earthly world of salmon, gooseberry, rain, dry coastal grass, and environmental revolution.

Pescadero State Beach is one of several preserves along the Monterey County coastline that protects the mouths of the creeks that drain from the Santa Cruz Mountains. The park is made up of 699 acres of both wild sandy beach and rich marsh preserve on the side of Highway 1. There, the Pescadero and Butano Creeks pool together, making a lagoon and estuary where birdlife abounds. Such creek- and river-mouths draw in coho salmon, steelhead trout, and other anadromous fish. The steelhead, unlike salmon, spawn and then return to the ocean instead of expiring—all of them, that is, except the mysterious fish described in tones at once holy and profane by the masterful Brother Antoninus.

WILLIAM EVERSON

"STEELHEAD"

Incipient summer, scorch of the sun,
And the great steelhead shows up in our creek.
He lies in a pool, the shallow basin of a thin rock weir,
Impassively waiting. Ten days go by
And still he lingers. His presence
Is inscrutable. No one around here
Recalls such a thing: steelhead
Landlocked in summer.

                For the tag-end of April
Sees the last of them. Unlike all salmon,
Rising in winter to die at the spawn,
Steelhead commonly wrig back to sea,
Reclimbing the river-path year after year:
Continuous the trek, the journey joined;
Indomitable the will, the life-thrust.

But this? This aberration?
What is its meaning, and why here?
Deeper hideouts, below and above,
Where salmon and steelhead alike at the spawn
Await their time—those same deep holes
Are perfect places to bide out the drought
Were such his purpose. But no. Dangerously exposed,
In window-pane water he lies alone,
And waits. Inexplicably waits.

Dreaming last night I stiffly arose,
Groped my way down through scarred slopes
To a shallow pool. I knew it for his.
The moon, gibbous, lacked light to see by,
But sensing him there I made vaguely out,
Alone on the bottom like a sunken stick—
No, like a God-stoned monk prostrate in his cell—
That enigmatic shape, sleeplessly intent.
Daunted, I left him alone in that hapless place
And crept back to bed.

              To go down in the dawn,
Seeking him out as in my dream,
Holding him there in my mind's eye,
Still pointed upstream, smelling the high
Headwaters, while all about him
The dance of life sweeps rapturously on—

Giddy with delight the moths fly double.
In a spasm of joy the mayflies breed.
Above on the bank our Labrador bitch,
Massively in heat, hears her elkhound lover
Yelp on the hill and will not heel;
While under the weir the phlegmatic crayfish,
Gnome of these waters, ponderously grapples his viscid consort,
All fever aslake....

Only myself,
Stooping to fathom his meaning here,
Know the tightening nerves....

What his time portends
I dare not guess. But much or little,
Brief or prolonged, in this recondite presence
I am favored in my life—honored in my being,
Illuminated in my fate. As hieratic gesture
He sounds the death-pang of abnegation,
Witness to the world.

Segregate,
Wrenched out of context, bearing the suppressed
Restlessness of all disjunction, subsumed
In the abstract dimension this bloodlife abhors—
Out of time, out of season,
Out of place and out of purpose—
Ineluctable pariah, he burns in my dream
And calls me from sleep.

Who am hardly surprised
To find by the water his scattered remains
Where the raccoons flung him: tore gill from fin,
Devoured the life-sustaining flesh, and left in clay
The faint skeletal imprint—as fossil
Etched in stone spans time like myth—
The glyph of God.

PACHECO STATE PARK

In the Diablo Range just south of Highway 152, Pacheco State Park straddles Merced and Santa Clara Counties. The highway cuts through the range via a mountain pass that connects the Central Valley to the coast. It is called Pacheco Pass for Francisco Perez Pacheco, a carriage maker turned soldier who went on to become one of the major landowners in California. In 1850, pioneer and military man William Mayfield led his family over Pacheco Pass on his way to the goldfields, and one of his sons, Thomas Jefferson Mayfield, then six years old, later published his memories of the trip, excerpted below.

Pacheco State Park was once part of a 48,821-acre Mexican land grant deeded in 1843 to José María Ramos Mejía and Francisco's son Juan Perez Pacheco. The land remained in the family until 1992, when the last descendant of Francisco Pacheco, Paula Fatjo, bequeathed the land to the state. This 6,868-acre expanse of windy ridges and long rolling hills is known for its displays of spring wildflowers and is home to a surprising variety of wildlife, from feral pigs to bald eagles. The western 2,600 acres of the park are open to the public for hiking, mountain biking, and horseback riding.

THOMAS JEFFERSON MAYFIELD

from *INDIAN SUMMER*

Of our whole trip from Texas to Kings River I remember the Pacheco Pass portion the best. In fact, my first real clear recollection begins as we were ascending the western slope leading toward the pass. We were all so anxious for our first glimpse of the Valle de San Joaquin, as our Californian acquaintances had called it, that I am sure we all remembered the Pacheco Pass and the first view it gave us at the summit.

After we had almost reached the summit, I begged to be allowed to ride on one of the pack animals. I had been riding on the folded blanket behind my mother's saddle, and from there could not see ahead. She did not like to have me ride the pack animals, as they were loose and might brush me off when they passed under low branches. But as the country grew more level and we came to a large, flat meadow, she had my oldest brother place me on top of one of the packs.

I remember that there were five or six deer feeding in the meadow, and that they did not run away, but watched us closely as we passed at a distance of about two hundred yards.

As we left the meadow and again entered the timber to the east, I remember the scene so well. My daddy and brother, Ben, were riding ahead. Then came the three pack animals, mine being the third. Brother John came behind me driving the loose animals. Then came my mother, the last of the procession, interested in the new valley we were about to enter, but watching me most of the time. I remember that I proudly smiled back at her from my perch on the pack ahead, and that she returned my smile. I can see her yet. This is the last real picture I have of my mother, as she died within a year.

Within a few minutes after we entered the timber, we came to the eastern slope, and through an opening in the trees we could see a large canyon through which my daddy concluded ran El Arroyo de San Luis Gonzaga.

We followed down a long ridge to our right on the south side of the canyon. Here, for the first time, we noticed that a passage had been made with wagons just a short time previous to our coming. Brush had been cleared away, and a few trees had been felled and dragged to one side. The leaves on the felled trees were still partly green. We followed the wagon trail down the ridge.

So far we were all disappointed because we could not see the valley, and we were growing more restless and anxious all the time. There were always trees and brush in the way and there seemed to be a high range of bare hills fifteen or twenty miles further on. In addition, the view ahead was obscured by a purplish haze. Finally we rode out on a bare point, and halted in order to rest the animals and talk. We could see that there was a fairly extensive, bowl-shaped valley between us and the bare hills to the east. There was a strong west wind blowing, and it was waving the tall grasses in the valley and changing its floor into shifting splotches of a green and yellowish green.

Suddenly my daddy pointed over the tops of the bare hills ahead of us and exclaimed, "Look there!" And there in the distance, until then lost to us in the haze, was our valley. A shining thread of light marked El Rio de San Joaquin flowing, as my mother said, "through a crazy quilt of color."

How excited we all were. Everyone wanted to talk at once. Then someone noticed, still farther to the east, that what we had first taken for clouds was a high range of snow-covered peaks, their bases lost in the purple haze.

Finally we started on and passed down the long ridge, which my daddy called a "hog's back," to the small valley below. There we found the grass we had seen from above to be wild oats. They stood as high as our stirrups and were as thick as they could grow. My daddy said that was the finest country he had ever seen.

We followed along El Arroyo de San Luis to where it passed through a narrow opening in the bare hills to the San Joaquin plains below. There, under a grove of large cottonwoods and sycamores, we found the buildings of El Rancho de San Luis. Of the ranch buildings I remember only a long, low adobe with loopholed walls. Here we were made welcome by a pretty native Californian, who talked Spanish to us and took my mother and me inside with her.

The inside of the building was of interest to me as I had not been in one just like it before. There was an earthen floor which had been smoothed and beaten hard. In one corner was a raised adobe platform about the size of a modern blacksmith's forge. There the cooking was done. In the opposite corner was a crude bed made of a cowhide stretched over a rough wooden frame. There were two chairs in the room, and a few garments hanging on the wall.

After a short visit we made camp under a large cottonwood tree on the bank of the creek a few yards northeast of the building. Here there was a large deep pool of water. I have always remembered that place as one of the most ideal I have ever seen. The tall, green grass, the cool, clear water, and the trees with their fresh leaves made as pretty a spot as one could wish.

We left Rancho de San Luis early the next morning before anyone was stirring at the adobe house, and passed down the creek about three miles. By this time we were out on the level plains, and the creek was a wide shallow bed of gravel with a small stream of water wandering about it.

Leaving the stream, we started across the plains in an easterly direction. We had been told at El Rancho de San Luis that we would in this way arrive at El Rio de San Joaquin where there was a ford. By this time we could see what had caused the mass of color so noticeable from the mountain the day before. The entire plain, as far as we could see, was covered with wild flowers. Almost all of the flowers were new to us.

Along the creek were many blue lupines, some of them growing on bushes six and eight feet high. The low foothills were covered with two pretty, lily-like flowers, one tall and straight-stemmed with a cluster of lavender, bell-shaped flowers at the top and the other a purple, ball-shaped blossom on a similar stem.

As we passed below the hills the whole plain was covered with great patches of rose, yellow, scarlet, orange and blue. The colors did not seem to mix to any great extent. Each kind of flower liked a certain kind of soil best and some of the patches of one color were a mile or more across.

I believe that we were more excited out there on the plains among the wild flowers than we had been when we saw the valley for the first time from the mountains the day before. Several times we stopped to pick the different kinds of flowers and soon we had our horses and packs decorated with masses .of all colors.

My daddy had traveled a great deal and it was not easy to get him excited about wild flowers, or pretty scenery. But he said that he would not have believed that such a place existed if he had not seen it himself. And my mother cried with joy, and wanted to make a home right here in the midst of it all.

For my own part, I have never seen anything equal to the virgin San Joaquin Valley before there was a plow or fence within it. I have always loved nature and have liked to live close to her. Many times when traveling alone and night has overtaken me, I have tied my horse and rolled up in my saddle blanket and slept under a bank, or among the wild flowers, or in the desert under a bush. I remember those experiences as the greatest in my life. The two most beautiful remembrances I have are the virgin San Joaquin and my mother.

MILLERTON LAKE STATE RECREATION AREA

When the Friant Dam was constructed across the San Joaquin River in 1944, Millerton Lake was born. Lewis Barnes, several-time tribal chair of the Table Mountain Rancheria in Fresno County, witnessed the building of the dam as a boy, and with it the transformation of his home. He knew the land around present-day Millerton Lake—about thirty-five miles northeast of Fresno—like the back of his hand. From the fruit groves to the old school-house, from the railroad ties to the San Joaquin River crowded with salmon, Barnes brings to life the stories of that landscape and river, both far older than the dammed lake.

Today, three quarters of a million people visit Millerton Lake every year, drawn to the ample boating, fishing, waterskiing, camping, and hiking opportunities in the area. During the winter, bald and golden eagles can be seen winging overhead as they reach the final destination on their southern migration tour.

LEWIS BARNES
REMINISCENCES

I was born in 1933. I grew up on tribal land at Table Mountain. We kids liked it because we had the free run of the whole mountain. It was good then. It's good now. I've lived there all my life.

I never learned the old language. My mom didn't either. Well, I guess she spoke it for a while but then they sent her to the Sherman Institute in Los Angeles; it was an Indian school in Riverside. Every time the kids would start to speak their own language they'd tape their mouths or slap their hands or send them into the corner. Quite a few of my friends went there but I didn't have to go. My mother was just a little girl when they sent her down there and the students weren't treated very well, not at all. It was bad. My mother didn't want me to have that same experience, so I got to stay here.

My dad was from the Tollhouse area. He never told me many stories. I really don't remember my mother or father telling any stories at all; I think they were busy doing other things. But I do remember many things about them. My dad and uncles would fish in the riffles where the dam is now. They used to mine for gold there, too, and my father had a mining tunnel where the fish hatchery is now. They'd take whatever gold they could find—not much—but enough to help support the family. That was in the late 1930s during the Depression, so any little thing helped.

We were fruit pickers. I remember that we worked for Mr. Joe Moore in Clovis; he had about eighty acres out there on Fowler. We took care of it for him through the harvest season. It wasn't so bad; what I hated most was picking up the raisins and stacking the wooden trays when it started raining. Lizards would run up your pant legs. I remember that.

I went to the Millerton School, right there at Table Mountain. The school was on Sky Harbor Road. There was probably room for about twenty children—one room for all eight classes. But around 1945, I helped tear my own school down. They said there weren't enough kids to keep it going, so they got the older boys to take it all apart, and they had me rip the nails out to keep anybody from stepping on them. They paid us to do that, to pull our own school down. Come the fall season, they had to send us to school in Auberry on buses. It was a long ride up there and back every day.

The San Joaquin River was very important to us. Every year, in the fall, we'd set up our salmon camp on the banks of the river. Mr. Rank owned all that property along there. He had a road that went all the way back to the river, and we had permission to use it. There must have been eight or ten families that would go there every year. We camped together, everybody we knew. The Walker family, the Smith family, and I think the Tex family from North Fork. I think the Pomonas and the Samples from Auberry were there too. We fished with spears at night with a big basket made out of chicken wire that we used for light. We'd put the basket at the end of a pole and light it; then somebody would have to go out into the water and hold the lantern up. The salmon would come into that light and then the guys would spear them. I was holding the pole one night and a big salmon came by and hit my legs and knocked me down. I fell down and the fire went out. I remember that like it was yesterday.

While the men went to work during the day, picking fruit or whatever, the ladies set up lines to dry the salmon on. They would clean up the salmon heads and boil them and that's what we would eat for lunch sometimes, the meat from the heads. We had a lot of salmon; every day there'd be fish to eat. Everybody would get all the salmon they needed.

As kids we'd try to go see what was happening while the dam was going up. They wouldn't let anybody all the way down in there, but of course we kids would sneak on to the high points on the hills and look down and watch. I remember playing around the buildings that were left from the town of Millerton, but it didn't seem like a town then because they were in the process of cleaning everything away and getting ready to make the lake. As the dam was built and the lake started coming up, I remember we went out in the winter and picked from the orange trees that were left in the old town. There were lemons and oranges. We picked those while we still could. Then the dam was built and the lake started coming up. Another stage.

I didn't graduate from high school. In 1950 the Korean War had just started, so I joined the service. I'd just turned seventeen and I went home and told my mom I was leaving town. She said, "Where you going?" I said, "I'm going to Korea." She didn't like that, but she had to go down and sign the papers for me. She signed them but she didn't want to.

I came back home to Table Mountain after the war and I got into the logging industry. I started working first around Shaver Lake and Blue Canyon. It was pretty hard work. I was a logger until 1983, when I went to work for State Parks and Recreation. First I went to Lake Tahoe; I worked there for about three years. Then a job opened up at Millerton so I transferred back home. I was a maintenance worker in charge of the Madera side of the lake—all the maintenance work over there. I liked it; it was a nice job for me. I saw a lot of river life during that time: coyotes, eagles, mountain lions, bobcats, and rattlesnakes. There were river otters too. People would sometimes go and shoot around the lake. They'd even shoot the otters. People will shoot at whatever moves.

I did all the railroad tie work that's down around the lake. I remember one night I dreamt about what I was going to do the next day. You know how sometimes you dream about your work? Well, I saw myself falling and I had railroad ties in my arms. I fell on the banks and broke both my legs—all this happened in my dream. The next day I was doing the work I had dreamed about, and I was pulling this railroad tie backwards. I remembered my dream and thought, "That might happen. I better not be doing this." So I did the job in another way, to make sure I wouldn't have to live that dream. I've always thought about that, how that dream came to me, warning me of something that was going to happen.

I think that messages like that do come to us. My sister lived out by the river where the road goes back to where we used to fish. When they had that big earthquake in Tehachapi, her old dog and her horse went just about crazy before it hit. The horse was running around and the dog was jumping and barking; then all of a sudden it got real quiet and that's when my sister felt it rumbling, heard the noise. Those animals knew what was coming.

SANTA CRUZ MISSION
STATE HISTORIC PARK

Only one building from the original Misión de la Exaltación de la Santa Cruz remains standing: the dormitory that housed native California Indian neophytes for some thirty years. It has been carefully restored and today accommodates the museum for the Santa Cruz Mission State Historic Park, in downtown Santa Cruz. Two hundred years ago, in those very adobe chambers, began Mission Santa Cruz's very own murder mystery: the plot to assassinate Father Andrés Quintana. It was an act of vengeance in response to the father's having whipped a neophyte with an iron-tipped bullwhip. On October 12, 1812, led by the mission gardener, cook, and their wives, a group of Indians murdered Father Quintana in the dark of night and secreted him back to his own bed, where his death, for many years, was assumed to have been from natural causes.

In 1877, Lorenzo Asisara, a local Indian who was born at the mission, gave his account of the murder to Thomas Savage, who was conducting interviews for Hubert Howe Bancroft's massive history of the Pacific West.

LORENZO ASISARA
REMINISCENCES

The following story which I shall convey was told to me by my
dear father in 1818. He was a neophyte of the Mission of Santa
Cruz. He was one of the original founders of that mission. He
was an Indian from the *ranchería* of Asar on the Jarro coast,
up beyond Santa Cruz. He was one of the first neophytes baptized at the founding, being about twenty years of age. He was
called Venancio Asar and was the gardener of the Mission of
Santa Cruz.

My father was a witness to the happenings that follow.
He was one of the conspirators who planned to kill Father
Quintana. When the conspirators were planning to kill Father
Quintana, they gathered in the house of Julián the gardener
(the one who made the pretense of being ill). The man who
worked inside the plaza of the mission, named Donato, was
punished by Father Quintana with a whip with wire. With
each blow it cut his buttocks. Then the same man, Donato,
wanted vengeance. He was the one who organized a gathering
of fourteen men, among them the cook and the pages serving
the Father. The cook was named Antonio, the eldest page was
named Lino, the others were named Vicente and Miguel Antonio. All of them gathered in the house of Julián to plan how
they could avoid the cruel punishments of Father Quintana.
One man present, Lino, who was more capable and wiser than
the others, said, "The first thing we should do today is to see
that the Father no longer punishes the people in that manner.
We aren't animals. He [Quintana] says in his sermons that God
does not command these [punishments], but only examples
and doctrine. Tell me now, what shall we do with the Father?
We cannot chase him away, nor accuse him before the Judge,
because we do not know who commands him to do with us as
he does." To this, Andrés, father of Lino the page, answered,
"Let's kill the Father without anyone being aware—not the
servants, or anyone, except us that are here present." (This Lino
was a pure-blooded Indian, but as white as a Spaniard and a
man of natural abilities.) And then Julián the gardener said,

"What shall we do in order to kill him?" His wife responded, "You, who are always getting sick—only this way can it be possible—think if it is good this way." Lino approved the plan and asked that all present also approve it. "In that case, we shall do it tomorrow night." That was Saturday. It should be noted that the Father wished all the people gather in the plaza on the following Sunday in order to test the whip that he had made with pieces of wire, to see if it was to his liking.

All of the conspirators present at the meeting concurred that it should be done as Lino had recommended. On the evening of Saturday at about six o'clock [October 12] of 1812, they went to tell the Father that the gardener was dying. The Indians were already posted between two trees on both sides so that they could grab the Father when he passed. The Father arrived at the house of Julián, who pretended to be in agony. The Father helped him, thinking that he was really sick and about to die. When the Father was returning to his house, he passed close to where the Indians were posted. They didn't have the courage to grab him, and they allowed him to pass. The moribund gardener was behind him, but the Father arrived at his house. Within an hour, the wife of Julián arrived [again] to tell the Father that her husband was dying. With this news the Father returned to the orchard, the woman following behind, crying and lamenting. He saw that the sick man was dying. The Father took the man's hand in order to take his pulse. He felt the pulse and could find nothing amiss. The pulse showed there was nothing wrong with Julián. Not knowing what it could be, the Father returned to pray for him. It was night when the Father left. Julián arose and washed away the sacraments (oil) that the Father had administered, and he followed behind to join the others and see what his companions had done. Upon arriving at the place where they were stationed, Lino lifted his head and looked in all directions to see if they were coming out to grab the Father. The Father passed and they didn't take him. The Father arrived at his house.

Later, when the Father was at his table, dining, the conspirators had already gathered at the house of the allegedly sick man to ascertain why they hadn't seized Father Quintana. Julián complained that the Father had placed herbs on his ears, and because of them, now he was really going to die. Then the wife of Julián said, "Yes, you all did not carry through with your promised plans; I am going to accuse you all, and I will not go back to the house." They all answered her, "All right, now, go and speak to the Father." The woman again left to fetch Father Quintana, who was at supper. He got up immediately and went, where he found the supposedly sick man. This time he took with him three pages, two who walked ahead lighting his way with lanterns, and behind him followed his majordomo Lino. The other two were Vicente and Miguel Antonio. The Father arrived at the gardener's house and found him unconscious. He couldn't speak. The Father prayed the last orations without administering the oils and said to the wife, "Now your husband is prepared to live or die. Don't come to look for me again." Then the Father left with his pages, to return to his house. Julián followed him. Arriving at the place where the two trees were (since the Father was not paying attention to his surroundings, but only the path in front of him), Lino grabbed him from behind, saying these words: "Stop here, Father, you must speak for a moment." When the other two pages who carried the lanterns turned around and saw the other men come out to attack the Father, they fled with their lanterns. The Father said to Lino, "Oh, my son, what are you going to do to me?" Lino answered, "Your assassins will tell you."

"What have I done to you children for which you would kill me?"

"Because you have made a horsewhip tipped with iron," Andrés answered him. Then the Father replied, "Oh, children, leave me, so that I can go from here now, at this moment." Andrés asked him why he had made this horsewhip. Quintana said that it was only for transgressors. Then someone shouted, "Well, you are in the hands of those evil ones, make your peace with God." Many of those present (seeing the Father in his affliction) cried and pitied his fate, but could do nothing to help him, because they were themselves compromised. He pleaded much, promising to leave the mission immediately if they would only let him.

"Now you won't be going to any part of the earth from here, Father, you are going to heaven." This was the last plea of the

Father. Some of them, not having been able to lay hands on the Father, reprimanded the others because they talked too much, demanding that they kill him immediately. They then covered the Father's mouth with his own cape to strangle him. They had his arms tightly secured. After the Father had been strangled, [they did not beat him but] took a testicle so that it would not be obvious that he had been attacked, and in a moment Father expired. Then Lino and the others took him to his house and put him in his bed.

When the two little pages, Vicente and Miguel Antonio, arrived at the house, the former wanted to tell the guard, but the others dissuaded him by saying, "No, the soldiers will also kill your mother, father, all of the others, and you, yourself, and me. Let them, the conspirators, do what they want." The two hid themselves. After the Indians had put the Father in his bed, Lino looked for the two pages, and he found them hidden. They undressed the body of Father Quintana and placed him in the bed as if he were going to sleep. All of the conspirators, including Julián's wife, were present. Andrés asked Lino for the keys to the storeroom. He handed them over, saying, "What do you want?" And they said silver and beads. Among the group there were three Indians from the Santa Clara Mission. These proposed that they investigate to see how much money there was. Lino opened the box and showed them the accumulated gold and silver. The three Indians from Santa Clara took as much as they could carry to their mission. (I don't know what they have done with that money.) The others took their portions as they saw fit.

Then they asked for the keys to the convent, or nunnery [women's dormitory]. Lino gave the keys to the *jayunte,* or barracks of the single men, to one of them in order to free the men and gather them together, below in the orchard, with the unmarried women. They gathered in the orchard so that neither the people in the plaza, nor in the *ranchería,* nor in the guardhouse would hear them. The single men left and without a sound gathered in the orchard at the same place where the Father was assassinated. There was a man there cautioning them not to make any noise, that they were going to have a good time. After a short time the young unmarried women arrived in order to spend the night there. The young people of both sexes got together and had their pleasure. At midnight Lino, being in the Father's living room with one of the girls from the single women's dormitory, entered the Father's room in order to see if he was really dead. He found him reviving. He was already on the point of arising. Lino went to look for his accomplices to tell them that the Father was coming to. The Indians returned, and they crushed the Father's other testicle. This last act put an end to the life of Father Quintana. Donato, the one who had been whipped, walked around the room with the plural results of his operation in hand, saying, "I shall bury these in the outdoor privy."

Donato told Lino that they should close the treasure chest: "Close the trunk with the colored silver (that is the name that the Indians gave to gold), and let's see where we shall bury it." The eight men carried it down to the orchard and buried it secretly, without the others knowing.

At about two o'clock in the morning, the young girls returned to their convent and the single men to their *jayunte,* without making any noise. The assassins gathered once more after everything had occurred, in order to hear the plans of Lino and Donato. Some wanted to flee, and others asked, "What for? No one except us knows." Lino asked them what they wanted to take to their houses—sugar, *panocha,* honey, or any other things—and suggested that they lie down to sleep for a while. Finally everything was ready. Donato proposed to return to where the Father was, to check on him. They found him not only lifeless, but completely cold and stiff. Lino then showed them the new whip that the Father was planning to use for the first time the next day, assuring them that he (Father Quintana) would not use it now. He sent them to their houses to rest, remaining in the house with the keys. He asked them to be very careful. He arranged the room and the Bible in the manner in which the Father was accustomed to doing before retiring, telling them that he was not going to toll the bells in the morning until the majordomo and corporal of the guard came and he had talked to them. All went through the orchard very silently.

This same morning (Sunday), the bells should have been rung at about eight o'clock. At that hour the people from the *Villa de* Branciforte began to arrive in order to attend the Mass. The majordomo, Carlos Castro, saw that the bells were not being rung and went to Lino, who was the first assistant of the Father, to ask why the Father had not ordered him (to toll the bells). Lino was in the outer room feigning innocence and answered the majordomo that he couldn't tell him anything about the Father because he was still inside, sleeping or praying, and that the majordomo should wait until he should speak to him first. The majordomo returned home. Soon the corporal of the guard arrived, and Lino told him the same thing he had told the majordomo. The majordomo returned to join in the conversation. They decided to wait a little while longer. Finally, Lino told them that in their presence he would knock on the door of the room, observing, "If he is angry with me, you will stand up for me." And so he did, calling to the Father. As he didn't hear noise inside, the majordomo and corporal asked Lino to knock again, but he refused. They then left, charging him with calling the Father again, because the hour was growing late. All of the servants were busy at their jobs, as always, in order not to cause any suspicion. The majordomo returned after ten o'clock and asked Lino to call the Father to see what was wrong. Lino, with the keys in his pocket, knocked at the door. Finally the majordomo insisted that Lino enter the room, but Lino refused. At this moment, the corporal, old Nazario Galindo, arrived. Lino (although he had the key to the door in his pocket) said, "Well, I am going to see if I can get the door open," and he pretended to look for a key to open the door. He returned with a ring of keys, but he didn't find one that opened the lock. The majordomo and the corporal left to talk to some men who were there. Later, Lino took the key that opened the door, saying that it was for the kitchen. He opened another door that opened into the plaza (the key opened three doors), and through there he entered. Then he opened the main door from inside, in front of which the others waited. Lino came out screaming and crying and carrying on in an uncontrolled manner, saying that the Father was dead. They asked him if he was certain, and he responded, "As this light that illuminates us. By God, I'm going to toll the bells." The three entered, the corporal, the majordomo, and Lino. He didn't allow anyone else to enter. The corporal and the majordomo and the other people wrote to the other missions and to Monterey to Father Marcelino Marquínez. (This Marquínez was an expert horseman and a good friend.) The poor elderly neophytes, and many other Indians who never suspected that the Father was killed, thought he had died suddenly. They cried bitterly. Lino was roaring inside the Father's house like a bear.

The Fathers from Santa Clara and from other missions came, and they held the Father's funeral, all believing that he had died a natural death, but not before examining the corpse in the entrance room and opening the stomach in order to be certain that the Father had not been poisoned. Officials, sergeants, and many others participated in these acts, but nothing was discovered. Finally, by chance, one of those present noted that the testicles were missing, and they were convinced that this had been the cause of death. Through modesty they did not reveal the fact, and buried the body with everyone convinced that the death had been a natural one.

A number of years after the death, Emiliana, the wife of Lino, and María Tata, the wife of the cook Antonio, became mutually jealous. They were both seamstresses and they were at work. This was around August, at the time of the lentil harvest. Carlos Castro was with his men, working in the cornfields. Shortly before eleven o'clock he returned to his house for the meal. He understood the language of the Indians. Returning from the cornfields, he passed behind one of the plaza walls near where these women were sewing and heard one tell the other that she was secretly eating *panocha*. Castro stopped and heard the second woman reply to the first, "How is it that you have so much money?" The first replied, "You also have it, because your husband killed the Father." Then the second accused the husband of the first woman of the same crime. The war of words continued, and Castro was convinced that Father

Quintana had been assassinated, and he went to tell Father Ramón Olbes, who was the missionary at Santa Cruz, what he had heard. Father Ramón went to tell Father Marquínez. The latter sent one of his pages to the orchard to warn Julián and his accomplices that they were going to be caught. At noon, at about the time of the midday meal, Father Olbes spoke to Lino and asked him to send for his wife to come there to cut some pieces of cloth. Emiliana arrived, and Father Olbes placed her in a room where there was clothing and gave her some scissors with which to cut some pieces, telling her, "You will eat here." Then he sent a page to bring María Tata to take some dirty clothing out of the church to wash. The majordomo was observing the maneuverings of the Father. He made María Tata stay to eat there. He placed her in another room to cut some suits for the pages. The majordomo and the two Fathers went to eat. After the meal, and when the two women had also eaten, Father Olbes said to Emiliana, "Do you know who eats a lot of white sugar?" She answered that it was María Tata, "because her husband had killed Father Quintana." The Father made her return to the room and called for María Tata. The Father asked her, "Tell me if you know who it was that killed Father Quintana, tell me the truth so that nothing will happen to you." Lino and Antonio often took their meal in the kitchen. María Tata replied, "Lino, Father." Father Olbes then sent the women to their houses to rest, offering them a present. Then the Father sent for the corporal, Nazario Galindo, to arrest the assassins. They began with the orchard workers and the cook, without telling them why they were under arrest. Antonio was the first prisoner. They put him in jail and asked him who his accomplice was. He said who his accomplice was, and the man was arrested, and they asked each one the name of their respective accomplices. In this way they were all arrested, except Lino, who was looked upon as a valiant man of great strength. He was taken through the deceit of his own *compadre* Carlos Castro, who handed him a knife to trim some black and white mares, in order to make a hackamore for the animal of the Father. Suspiciously, Lino said to Castro, "*Compadre,* why are you deceiving me? I know that you are going to arrest me." There were already two soldiers hidden behind the corral. "Here, take your knife, *compadre*, that which I thought is already done. I am going to pay for it—and if I had wanted to, I could have finished off the soldiers, the majordomos, and any others that might have been around on the same night that I killed the Father."

The result of all this was that the accused were sent to San Francisco, and among them was my father. There they were judged, and those who killed the Father were sentenced to receive a *novenano* (nine days in succession) of fifty lashes for each one, and to serve in public works at San Diego. The rest, including my father, were freed because they had served as witnesses, and it was not proven that they had taken part in the assassination.

All returned, after many years, to their mission.

The Spanish Fathers were very cruel toward the Indians. They abused them very much. They had bad food, bad clothing, and they made them work like slaves. I also was subject to that cruel life. The Fathers did not practice what they preached in the pulpit. The same Father Olbes was once stoned by the Indians for all his cruelties.

FREMONT PEAK
STATE PARK

Sometimes looking back into the past is like climbing a peak covered with manzanita and toyon, thick with lupine, to look down upon a bay, a mountain range, a valley. From that distance, the landscape becomes smaller, something one could almost hold. It is simpler, more beautiful, and it also inspires inexplicable longing because, of course, it can never truly be held. John Steinbeck's relationship with Fremont Peak, as described in his *Travels with Charley* (Charley being his poodle), is as much about his own childhood as it is about the hawk-passed hilltop swaying with knee-high grasses and the orange arms of madrone trees. Each landmark he looks out upon is marked with the stories of his own life, and the passing of time. Beyond what we have from Steinbeck, Fremont Peak has given us many stories, including, of course, that of the man who gave the peak its name: Captain John Charles Frémont, who in 1846 resisted the demands of Mexican military leaders ordering him to leave Alta California and instead defiantly planted an American flag on the tallest nearby peak.

The 162-acre state park is located about thirty-two miles northeast of Salinas. Camping and picnicking is available, and at night, straight up, the panorama of stars is magnificent, especially aided by the lens of a thirty-inch Challenger telescope housed at the Fremont Peak Observatory.

JOHN STEINBECK
from *TRAVELS WITH CHARLEY*

In my flurry of nostalgic spite, I have done the Monterey Peninsula a disservice. It is a beautiful place, clean, well run, and progressive. The beaches are clean where once they festered with fish guts and flies. The canneries which once put up a sickening stench are gone, their places filled with restaurants, antique shops, and the like. They fish for tourists now, not pilchards, and that species they are not likely to wipe out. And Carmel, begun by starveling writers and unwanted painters, is now a community of the well-to-do and the retired. If Carmel's founders should return, they could not afford to live there, but it wouldn't go that far. They would be instantly picked up as suspicious characters and deported over the city line.

The place of my origin had changed, and having gone away I had not changed with it. In my memory it stood as it once did and its outward appearance confused and angered me.

What I am about to tell must be the experience of many in this nation where so many wander and come back. I called on old and valued friends. I thought their hair had receded a little more than mine. The greetings were enthusiastic. The memories flooded up. Old crimes and old triumphs were brought out and dusted. And suddenly my attention wandered, and looking at my ancient friend, I saw that his wandered also. And it was true what I had said to Johnny Garcia—I was the ghost. My town had grown and changed and my friend along with it. Now returning, as changed to my friend as my town was to me, I distorted his picture, muddied his memory. When I went away I had died, and so became fixed and unchangeable. My return caused only confusion and uneasiness. Although they could not say it, my old friends wanted me gone so that I could take my proper place in the pattern of remembrance—and I wanted to go for the same reason. Tom Wolfe was right. You can't go home again because home has ceased to exist except in the mothballs of memory.

My departure was flight. But I did do one formal and sentimental thing before I turned my back. I drove up to Fremont's

Peak, the highest point for many miles around. I climbed the last spiky rocks to the top. Here among these blackened granite outcrops General Fremont made his stand against a Mexican army, and defeated it. When I was a boy we occasionally found cannon balls and rusted bayonets in the area. This solitary stone peak overlooks the whole of my childhood and youth, the great Salinas Valley stretching south for nearly a hundred miles, the town of Salinas where I was born now spreading like crab grass toward the foothills. Mount Toro, on the brother range to the west, was a rounded benign mountain, and to the north Monterey Bay shone like a blue platter. I felt and smelled and heard the wind blow up from the long valley. It smelled of the brown hills of wild oats.

I remembered how once, in that part of youth that is deeply concerned with death, I wanted to be buried on this peak where without eyes I could see everything I knew and loved, for in those days there was no world beyond the mountains. And I remembered how intensely I felt about my interment. It is strange and perhaps fortunate that when one's time grows nearer one's interest in it flags as death becomes a fact rather than a pageantry. Here on these high rocks my memory myth repaired itself. Charley, having explored the area, sat at my feet, his fringed ears blowing like laundry on a line. His nose, moist with curiosity, sniffed the windborne pattern of a hundred miles.

"You wouldn't know, my Charley, that right down there, in that little valley, I fished for trout with your namesake, my Uncle Charley. And over there—see where I'm pointing—my mother shot a wildcat. Straight down there, forty miles away, our family ranch was—old starvation ranch. Can you see that darker place there? Well, that's a tiny canyon with a clear and lovely stream bordered with wild azaleas and fringed with big oaks. And on one of those oaks my father burned his name with a hot iron together with the name of the girl he loved. In the long years the bark grew over the burn and covered it. And just a little while ago, a man cut that oak for firewood and his splitting wedge uncovered my father's name and the man sent it to me. In the spring, Charley, when the valley is carpeted with blue lupines like a flowery sea, there's the smell of heaven up here, the smell of heaven."

I printed it once more on my eyes, south, west, and north, and then we hurried away from the permanent and changeless past where my mother is always shooting a wildcat and my father is always burning his name with his love.

MONTEREY STATE
HISTORIC PARK

With all the intrigue and romance of any good historical adventure, Chilean author Isabel Allende's *Zorro* brings to life a rough-and-tumble backstory for the infamous fictional outlaw of Alta California. During Zorro's time, the capital of Spanish California was then situated in Monterey at the hewn-stone presidio, described here as cold, lonely, and wreathed in fog, with only the seagull cries and the sound of waves for company. In Allende's rapid scenes of interpersonal conflict we see Pedro Fages, the first military commander of Spanish California, spring into action at a dark dining table while outside an icy wind howls and the Pacific Ocean stretches more vast and lonesome than we can now fathom.

Today, Monterey State Historic Park preserves buildings spanning the time between the early mission era and the gold rush. Visitors can take guided tours inside the oldest adobes, and the Monterey Path of History winds through the park area, from the landing site of Spanish explorers in 1602 to the whalebone sidewalks of the coastal whaling era to the numerous gold rush–period houses, passing a total of fifty-five historical sites.

ISABEL ALLENDE
from *ZORRO*

Alejandro de la Vega reached Monterey in less time than was normally required for a rider to cover that distance; he was in a hurry to carry out his project, and he wanted to avoid the raiding Indians. He traveled alone, and at a gallop, stopping at missions along the road to change his horse and sleep a few hours. He had followed that trail before, and he knew it well, but he was always awed by the magnificence of nature: endless forests, a thousand varieties of animals and birds, streams and gentle slopes, the white sands of the beaches of the Pacific. He had no unpleasant encounters with Indians: they were wandering around in the hills without a chief and without a purpose, demoralized. If Padre Mendoza's predictions were correct, their enthusiasm had been punctured completely, and it would take years for them to reorganize. The Presidio, built on an isolated promontory seven hundred leagues from Mexico City and half the world away from Madrid, was as gloomy as a dungeon, a monstrosity of stone and mortar that served as headquarters for a small contingent of soldiers, the only company of the governor and his family. That day a thick fog amplified the cries of the seagulls and the crashing of waves upon the rocks.

Pedro Fages received the captain in a nearly bare room in which small windows admitted very little light but failed, on the other hand, to keep out the icy wind off the sea. The walls were covered with mounted bear heads, swords, pistols, and Doña Eulalia de Callís's coat of arms, embroidered in gold but worn now, and almost humble. In the way of furniture, there were a dozen bare wood chairs, an enormous armoire, and a military table. The ceiling was black with soot and the floor was tamped-down earth, the same as in the rudest barracks. The governor was a corpulent man with a colossal voice and the rare virtue of being immune to flattery and corruption. He wielded power with a quiet conviction that it was his accursed fate to lead Alta California out of barbarism, whatever the price. He compared himself to the first Spanish conquistadors, who had added a great part of the world to the empire, and he carried out his obligation with a sense of history, although if truth be known, he would have preferred to enjoy his wife's fortune in Barcelona, as she asked him daily to do. An orderly served them red wine in crystal goblets from Bohemia carried thousands of miles in the trunks of Eulalia de Callís, a refinement in strong contrast to the rude furnishings of the fort. The two men toasted the far-off homeland and their friendship, commenting on the revolution in France, in which the people had taken up arms against the king. That had happened more than a year before, but the news had just reached Monterey. They agreed that there was no reason to be alarmed; surely by this time order would have been restored, and King Louis XVI would be back on the throne, though they thought he was a poor specimen of a man and not worthy of their sympathy. Deep down, they were happy that the French were killing each other, but good manners prevented them from expressing that aloud. Somewhere in the distance they could hear the muted sound of voices and yelling, which gradually grew so loud that it was impossible to ignore.

"Forgive me, Captain. These women…," said Pedro Fages, with a gesture of impatience.

"And is Her Excellency, Doña Eulalia, well?" inquired Alejandro de la Vega, blushing to his ear tips.

Pedro Fages pierced him with a steely glance, trying to make out his intentions. He was up to date on what people were saying about this handsome captain and his wife; he wasn't deaf. No one could understand, he least of all, why it should take Doña Eulalia six months to reach Monterey when the trip could be made in much less time. It was said that the journey was drawn out on purpose because the two wanted to be together. Added to that was the exaggerated version of an assault by bandits in which supposedly de la Vega had risked his life to save hers. That was not the real story, but Pedro Fages never learned that. The attackers were a half dozen Indians, fired up by alcohol, who went tearing off the moment they heard the first shots; nothing more. And as far as the injury to de la Vega's leg went, that had not come about in defending Doña

Eulalia de Callís, as rumor had it, but from a minor goring from a wild cow. Pedro Fages prided himself on being a good judge of human nature—he had not been exercising power for many years for nothing—and after studying Alejandro de la Vega, he decided that it was pointless to waste suspicions on this man; he was sure that the captain had delivered his wife to him with her virtue intact. He knew his wife very well. If those two had really fallen in love, no human or divine power would have persuaded Eulalia to leave her lover and go back to her husband. Perhaps there had been a kind of platonic affinity between them, but nothing that would cause him to lose sleep, the governor concluded.

In the meantime, the uproar of servants running through the corridors, doors slamming, and shouting continued. Alejandro de la Vega, like the whole world, knew of the couple's fights, as epic as their reconciliations. He had heard that in their fits the Fages threw crockery at each other's heads, and that on more than one occasion Don Pedro had drawn his sword against her, but also that afterward they locked themselves in their room for several days to make love. The robust governor thumped the table, making the cups dance, and confessed to his guest that Eulalia had been in her room for five days in a white-hot rage.

"She misses the refinement she is used to," he said, just as a maniacal howl shook the walls.

"Perhaps she feels a little lonely, Excellency," muttered de la Vega, just to fill the awkward silence.

"I have promised her that in three years we will return to either Mexico City or Spain, but she doesn't want to hear that. My patience has run out, Captain de la Vega. I am going to send her to the nearest mission so the friars can put her to work with the Indians. We'll see then whether she learns to respect me!" Fages roared.

"Will you allow me to have a few words with your lady, Excellency?" the captain inquired.

During those five stormy days the governor's wife had refused to see anyone, including her three-year-old son. The teary-eyed child was sniveling, curled up on the floor outside her door, so frightened that he wet himself every time his father beat on the door with his cane. The only person allowed to cross the threshold was the Indian girl who carried in food and carried out the chamber pot. However, when Eulalia learned that Alejandro de la Vega had come to visit and wanted to see her, her hysteria disappeared in a minute. She washed her face, put up her long braid, and dressed in a mauve-colored gown, with all her pearls. Pedro Fages watched her enter, as splendid and smiling as on her best days, and he entertained hope for a steamy reconciliation, even though he was not ready to forgive her too quickly; the woman deserved some punishment. That night during the austere dinner, in a dining room as gloomy as the hall of weapons, Eulalia de Callís and Pedro Fages, casting their guest in the role of witness, threw recriminations in each other's faces that would curdle the soul. Alejandro de la Vega took refuge in an uncomfortable silence until the moment dessert was served. By then the wine had taken effect, and the wrath of husband and wife was beginning to cool, so the captain set forth the reason for his visit. He explained that Toypurnia had Spanish blood. He described her bravery and intelligence, although he avoided mention of her beauty, and he begged the governor to be indulgent, praising his reputation for being compassionate and asking for clemency in the name of their mutual friendship. Pedro Fages did not need further pleading; the rosy glow of Eulalia's décolletage had begun to distract him, and he consented to change the death penalty to a sentence of twenty years in prison.

"In prison that woman will become a martyr for the Indians," Eulalia interrupted. "Simply saying her name will be enough to cause them to rebel again. I have a better solution. First of all, she must be baptized, as God wills. Then you bring her to me and I will take charge of the problem. I wager that in a year's time I will have converted this Toypurnia, Daughter-of-Wolf, wild Indian, into a Christian Spanish lady. In that way we will destroy her influence over the Indians once and for all."

"And in doing so, you will have something to do, and someone to keep you company," her husband added good-naturedly.

And so it was done. It was left to Alejandro de la Vega himself to go to San Gabriel to collect the prisoner and bring her back to Monterey—to the relief of Padre Mendoza, who could not be rid of her too quickly. She was a volcano waiting to explode in the mission, where the neophytes still had not recovered from the tumult of war. Toypurnia was baptized under the name of Regina María de la Inmaculada Concepción, but she immediately forgot most of it and went only by Regina. Padre Mendoza dressed her in the rough cloth robe the neophytes wore, strung a medal of the Virgin around her neck, helped her onto her horse, since her hands were tied, and gave her his blessing. As soon as they had left the low buildings of the mission behind, Captain de la Vega untied the captive's hands and, with a sweeping gesture indicating the immensity of the horizon, invited her to escape. Regina thought it over for a few minutes, and must have calculated that if she were captured a second time there would be no mercy, for she shook her head no. Or perhaps it was not merely fear but the same burning emotion that clouded the mind of the Spaniard. In any case, without a trace of rebellion, she followed him throughout the trip, which he strung out as long as possible because he imagined he would never see her again. Alejandro de la Vega savored every step they took along the Camino Real, every night they slept under the stars without touching, every time that they waded together in the ocean, all the while waging stubborn combat against desire and imagination. He knew that a de la Vega, an hidalgo, a man of honor and lineage, could never dream of living his life with a mestiza woman. If he had hoped that those days on horseback with Regina, traveling through the solitudes of California, would cool his ardor, he was in for a disappointment; when, inevitably, they reached the Presidio at Monterey, he was as wildly in love as a teenager. He had to call upon his long discipline as a soldier to be able to say good-bye to the woman, and silently swear by all that was holy that he would never try to communicate with her again.

POINT LOBOS STATE NATURAL RESERVE

The poetry of Robinson Jeffers is drenched in Pacific fogs, great granite bluffs, the mournful winging of gulls and cormorants, and the ancient silhouettes of Monterey cypress trees. It is hard to read this early-twentieth-century master's verse without tasting salt on your lips. Jeffers lived near Carmel with his wife in a house built from hand-cut granite stones, called Tor House, for most of his life. His short verse as well as his epic and narrative poetry are renowned for their reverence for the more-than-human world, for their tragic beauty, and for the way they capture the untamable and sometimes savage splendor of the central California coast.

At Point Lobos State Natural Reserve, which encompasses a marine reserve and conservation area as well as the cypress-wreathed headlands and meadow-covered coastal bluffs, a walk along the Cypress Grove Trail or the slightly longer North Shore Trail will feel like something right out of Jeffers's poetry. From the shore or underwater, you will find the coast teeming with life, including orcas, passing whales, sea otters, thriving kelp forests, and a multitude of sea lions. In fact, the park itself was named in Spanish "Punta de los Lobos Marinos" for the barking of the "sea wolves," or sea lions, that was so loud it could be heard for miles inland. Artists of many disciplines have been drawn since the late nineteenth century to the rocky, sea-spray grandeur of this landscape, and it's not hard to see why.

ROBINSON JEFFERS
POEMS

BIRDS

The fierce musical cries of a couple of sparrowhawks hunting
 on the headland,
Hovering and darting, their heads northwestward,
Prick like silver arrows shot through a curtain the noise of the
 ocean
Trampling its granite; their red backs gleam
Under my window around the stone corners; nothing gracefuller,
 nothing
Nimbler in the wind. Westward the wave-gleaners,
The old gray sea-going gulls are gathered together, the northwest
 wind wakening
Their wings to the wild spirals of the wind-dance.
Fresh as the air, salt as the foam, play birds in the bright wind,
 fly falcons
Forgetting the oak and the pinewood, come gulls
From the Carmel sands and the sands at the river-mouth, from
 Lobos and out of the limitless
Power of the mass of the sea, for a poem
Needs multitude, multitudes of thoughts, all fierce, all flesh-eaters,
 musically clamorous
Bright hawks that hover and dart headlong, and ungainly
Gray hungers fledged with desire of transgression, salt slimed
 beaks, from the sharp
Rock-shores of the world and the secret waters.

• • • • •

THE CYCLE

The clapping blackness of the wings of pointed cormorants,
    the great indolent planes
Of autumn pelicans nine or a dozen strung shorelong,
But chiefly the gulls, the cloud-caligraphers of windy spirals
    before a storm,
Cruise north and south over the sea-rocks and over
That bluish enormous opal; very lately these alone, these and the
    clouds
And westering lights of heaven, crossed it; but then
A hull with standing canvas crept about Point Lobos...now
    all day long the steamers
Smudge the opal's rim; often a seaplane troubles
The sea-wind with its throbbing heart. These will increase, the
    others diminish; and later
These will diminish; our Pacific has pastured
The Mediterranean torch and passed it west across the fountains
    of the morning;
And the following desolation that feeds on Crete
Feed here; the clapping blackness of the wings of pointed
    cormorants, the great sails
Of autumn pelicans, the gray sea-going gulls,
Alone will streak the enormous opal, the earth have peace like the
    broad water, our blood's
Unrest have doubled to Asia and be peopling
Europe again, or dropping colonies at the morning star: what
    moody traveler

Wanders back here, watches the sea-fowl circle
The old sea-granite and cemented granite with one regard, and
       greets my ghost,
One temper with the granite, bulking about here?

PFEIFFER BIG SUR
STATE PARK

With the Pacific Ocean spreading blue and far below, the coastal-scrub-covered mountains and bluffs of Big Sur are indeed "like a dreamland." Spanish novelist and linguist Jaime de Angulo, fantasizing about living somewhere steep and wild and far from human company, writes here about his first foray into the canyons and coastal forests of Big Sur. He evokes all the bliss of wheeling vultures, blue sky, magnificent redwoods, fruited madrones, and steep, dizzying views of the ocean, as well as the odd and hardy characters of his time—the early 1900s, before highways were paved through the area.

Pfeiffer Big Sur State Park is quintessential Big Sur, with the Big Sur River wending five miles through the redwood forest before it meets the wild breakers of the ocean. Located in southern Monterey County, this 1,391-acre state park features camping cabins and the Big Sur Lodge Hotel, as well as a lovely hike along the Pfeiffer Falls and Valley Views Trails past a sixty-foot waterfall and through oak woodland to the ocean.

In his later life, de Angulo moved to Berkeley, where he continued until his death in 1950 to research California Indian languages and write about his life "rolling in ditches with shamans." Ezra Pound called him "the American Ovid" and Berkeley poets Jack Spicer and Robert Duncan, along with other members of the beat movement, were powerfully influenced by de Angulo, perhaps even moreso by his life than his writing.

JAIME DE ANGULO

from "FIRST SEEING THE COAST"

It was Sam Seward who first told me about the Big Sur country.
Sam taught English and literature at Stanford. He had just
returned from a ten-day hike on foot from Monterey in the
north to San Luis Obispo in the south. "You never saw such a
landscape!" he had said, "I did not imagine it was possible...
like a dreamland, somewhere, not real...imagine: only a trail,
for a hundred miles, bordering the Ocean, but suspended above
it a thousand feet, clinging half-way up the side of the sea-wall,
and that wall at an incredible angle of forty-five degrees, a
green wall of grass (he had seen it in winter—throughout the
summer the green is brown-yellow) and canyons with oaks,
redwoods, pines, madronyos, bluejays, quail, deer, and to one
side the blue ocean stretching away to China, and over all that
an intense blue sky with eagles and vultures floating about...
and nobody, no humans there, solitude, solitude, for miles and
miles—why! in one place I walked thirty miles between one
ranch and the next!—what a wilderness, what beauty, it's a
dreamland, you must go there...."

I somewhat discounted the lyricism of a professional liter-
ateur (although I found it subsequently to be all of what Sam
had promised, and more!), still my curiosity was aroused, all
the moreso because I was looking for a place in the country
where to settle and raise cattle and horses.

I said to Sam: "Why should the country have remained so
wild?" "I think it is because when the first expedition was sent
out of Mexico with Portolá to rediscover Monterey, they traveled along the sea-shore all the way up to San Luis Obispo and
a little beyond; well, there were about a hundred Spaniards and
Indians and two or three hundred horses and pack-animals—
quite an expedition to tackle a totally unknown country without roads or even trails!...and I imagine when they got into
that tangle and labyrinth of mountains that fall plumb into
the ocean without even a beach, they just got discouraged, and
tried going around that clump of mountains; they turned east
away from the sea, and found the Salinas valley which led them

ultimately to Monterey. That first trip of Portolá established the route for the Camino Real and the Missions. Then Monterey became the capital of California Alta and the center of development—and as there was plenty of good flat land around it, north and west, nobody bothered with that rough land to the south."

Sam was right. That is why that country was always known to the paisanos of Monterey as "la costa del Sur," the coast to the south; a wild, little known land, with two rivers; and these two rivers, naturally, were known as "los ríos al sur," the rivers to the south—and to distinguish them: sur grande and sur chico, the little river to the south and the big river to the south. Then came the Gringos, and that not very felicitous combination of "Big Sur." We still receive an occasional letter addressed to "Big Sewer!"

But to go back to my story. It was around Christmas time of '15, and I was loafing in Carmel (which at that time was not much more than two score houses or so); and one day, as I was riding my horse along the road, I saw two vaqueros on horseback. But these two were real vaqueros, and dressed up for going to town—nothing funny or clownish, but the real old stuff: angora chaps, big rowel spurs that tinkled with the gait of the horse, wide sombreros (but not ridiculous); they were riding half-broken colts with jáquimas and fine horsehair mecates... and were they good-looking, the whole outfit of them, horses, men, and equipment!

Since they were paisanos I needed no introduction, and I stopped them: "Where do you come from?" "Allá, de la costa del Sur, allá lojos al Diablo...from the coast to the south, from down there to the devil...we are on our way to town to spend Christmas with our mother." "Is there free land down there?" "Plenty of it, hermano, but too wild, too steep, too far from everywhere...nothing but coyotes and deer...." "Fine!" I said, "that's just what I am looking for....Will you take me down there, when you go back?"

And that's how I made the acquaintance of El Mocho, as we used to call him (like so many vaqueros he had lost a thumb in the coils of the reata), the best horse-breaker I ever knew, and the most reckless, daredevil plenipotentiary whose laughter could be heard half-a-mile away.

He called for me, a week or so later, one morning, on horseback. And although we started early we did not reach his home, at the very end of the wagon-road, until nightfall. Nowadays, when you average sixty miles an hour on smooth highways, people do not realize what traveling horseback meant. A horse does not walk much faster than a man; I must have owned some hundred and fifty horses in my time—and I can only remember three who averaged a steady six-mile an hour walking gait under the saddle. Such a horse is a benediction on a long trip; you are carried along in bliss. But take a slow poke of a horse under you; you keep urging him, urging him, urging him—at the end of the day you are worn out! I should say that most horses average four miles an hour at a steady walk.

That was the end of the wagon-road. The next morning we started on the TRAIL! I shall never forget my first impression when I saw that Coast. I was aghast. I stood still. I looked and looked. What a panorama. The coast made a gentle curve so that I was able to see it for all of thirty miles or so—a wall of green rising abruptly out of the sea, not really perpendicular but half-way so. Headland succeeded headland, like the wings on a stage. And along that wall, a thousand feet above the ocean, the trail.

"Well, what are you waiting for? Are you bemused? encantado?"

"Yes…estoy emocionado…que hermosura!…yes, this is the country I was looking for."

"Wait, you haven't seen anything yet. Wait until I show you the place I have in mind for you."

● ● ● ● ●

So we started again on the trail. But I was not used to such height and I felt dizzy. I had to get off my horse and lead him. We came to a bad place: there had been a slide, there was practically no trail left. But the Mocho never got off his colt. Then the colt lost his footing, went off the trail, and started to plunge down that slide of loose rocks....My heart was in my mouth....In all the years I have spent around cowboy camps and horse-ranches, I have never seen a rider like this Mocho... he was off the saddle like lightning, the colt turned a somersault and started to roll down toward the ocean, and the Mocho leaping twenty feet at a time, after him...he managed somehow to get hold of the horse's head by the jáquima and keep him from turning over again. Then they scrambled back to the trail, and we went on.

After some riding we arrived at a cabin and dismounted. That's where I first met Clarence, ex-Mormon, not much over 5-foot but strong as an ox, with the flat voice of the nearly deaf, a little wizened face and a heart of gold—but alas, a rather inconsequential type of mind. He wasn't really a moron; it was rather that his mind did not follow the usual grooves and patterns. He came to live with me later on, and I got to know him quite well and appreciate his intimate knowledge of wild nature. He could make a lot of trouble, though, due to a complete ignorance of the cussedness of human nature—with charming naivete and the best intentions, coupled with a penchant for repeating tales, he finally succeeded in getting the whole Coast embroiled in a mix-up of feuds and counter-feuds that lasted twenty-five years—but that's another story, as the fellow said.

Clarence lived there all alone with a pet pig whom he had trained to sit on a chair at table. He also kept bees. He showed us a small churn he had just made out of a 3-lb can of lard and a few sticks whittled with a pocket-knife. His butter was excellent. We had a cup of coffee with him, and remounted our horses.

• • • • •

We followed the Country Trail again for two or three hours. Hanging on the mountainside, a thousand feet above the ocean, then dipping into a wooded canyon with giant redwoods, oaks, madronyos, maples (maples!); I was struck by the diversity of trees; then out again onto grasslands, the trail curving around

these "knees of the gods"; then in again into the next canyon...
in, out...in, out....

At last the Mocho said: "Here we go up to the place I have
in mind for you to homestead" (he said *esquatar*—a barbaric
neologism, from squatter, to squat!!). So we turned off the
County Trail and started straight up the mountainside...and I
must confess I got dizzy and had to get off my horse and lead
him, much to the Mocho's amusement. Another hour's climb,
and we were there, sixteen hundred feet above the ocean...but
I mean above the ocean—the ocean, the blue Pacific, was there,
practically under us (not more than a rifle-shot away), sixteen
hundred feet below...and gulls flying, and we looking down on
them so far down that they were the size of white pigeons.

What a scene! Yes, I lost my heart to it, right there and then.
This is the place for a freedom loving anarchist. There will
never be a road into this wilderness...it's impossible! Alas,
nothing is impossible to modern man and his infernal progress:
they came with bulldozers and tractors before very long, and
raped the virgin. Roads and automobiles, greasy lunch-papers
and beer-cans, and their masters. And the shy Masters of the
Wilderness receded to the depths of the canyadas, and back
over the Ridge, into the yet unraped country of the Forest
Reserve—but even there they are not safe; the well-meaning
Rangers (boy-scouts of the forest, one good deed a day) are
opening trails, and "restricted" camping grounds, and you must
not smoke or swear. A Guide Book to the Wilderness, complete
with figures and estimates! Lo, the untamed, adieu....

COLONEL ALLENSWORTH
STATE HISTORIC PARK

In 1908, Lieutenant Colonel Allen Allensworth, a former slave who became the army's highest-ranking black officer of his time, founded the only California town to be fully financed and governed by African Americans. Families from across the state gave up their previous homes for this dream of a life without discrimination in Tulare County. They grew grain and sugar beets, raised livestock, and were supplied with their own water from nearby wells. The town of three hundred settlers was indeed self-sufficient, boasting its own school, drugstore, post office, livery stable, church, and barbershop, as well as community organizations like a Debating Society, a Theater Club, and a group of Campfire Girls. The settlement was a social success, but by 1914 a combination of factors led to its decline: the shallow water tables could not support the town, the Santa Fe Railroad built a line that caused rail traffic to bypass Allensworth, and Colonel Allensworth himself was struck and killed by a motorcycle in Los Angeles. By World War II, the town was empty.

In the oral histories that follow, former residents remember Allentown, their narratives capturing both the strength and tireless dignity of the human spirit and the everyday reality of this brief but remarkable community.

HENRY SINGLETON AND JOSEPHINE HACKETT
REMINISCENCES

Henry Singleton (son of store owner and town leader Joshua Singleton):

In 1910, when we came to Allensworth, there was a great deal of prejudice against Negroes. When we came down to Allensworth there was a lot of fear in those days. This particular group of pioneers didn't know how the people in these little white towns were going to react toward them. Allensworth, being an Army man, was interested in having soldiers settle in Allensworth. There were eight or ten sergeants there. Sergeant Phillips lived behind the Colonel's house. Other sergeants were named Bird, May, Hickson, Carver. Sergeant Carver was first baseman on our baseball team.

Since so many ex-soldiers were here, they formed protective groups. They even went so far as to drill, and they had signals so if something happened in the town and we had to get together for protection, they had signals they'd give, and people a mile and a half away would get together. They trained and got real good, but they never once said anything about the little towns—but they were ready. But the most interesting thing that makes it lovely is that every one of these little towns became extraordinarily friendly to Allensworth. There was never one difficulty, racially.

· · · · ·

Josephine Hackett (youngest daughter in the Hackett Family):

As I recall, it was our soon-to-be-next-door neighbor, Mr. Stockett, who met us with his horse and buggy and drove us to our house.

We had a great deal to do that afternoon and evening to prepare ourselves to meet curious townsfolk the next day. Mama made a fire in the kitchen range and, before it got too hot, drew our ribbons back and forth across the stovepipe to iron out the wrinkles. It was unthinkable for a proper young girl to go out into polite society without a hair ribbon. Though her flatirons were not yet unpacked, Mama was not about to let that deter her from doing the correct thing.

At first we found much in the colony to engage our interest. There were eight public buildings to look into. Very close to our house was the Baptist church, a well-built structure in which we were later to visit the Baptist Young People's Union, which was the counterpart to the Varick Christian Endeavor of our own Methodist denomination.

The drugstore was operated jointly by Mr. William Scott and Mrs. Mary Gross, one of the town's practical nurses. Mr. Scott lived in the back room of the store and Mrs. Gross in the house next door. These buildings were also near our house, slightly to the northwest.

We soon wore a beaten path to the library, which was kept fairly current by the county. Residents could make requests for books not in the library. Whenever possible, these were delivered with the next consignment.

Allensworth had two grocery stores. Mr. Hindsman's was on a corner lot across the road from the Santa Fe Railroad. His house was next door, just to the west of the store.

The Singleton store was diagonally across the road from the hotel. Between it and the Hindsman house was the post office. When we first came to town the mail was handled by Mr. and Mrs. Oscar Wells. I have never known which was the official postmaster; one seemed as responsible as the other.

For a few weeks these places and persons were of absorbing interest to us, but we soon began to realize that we had learned just about as much as we were capable of learning about them. Inevitably, we began to develop an awareness of the flat landscape around us and to be a little uneasy about it.

One starlit night, Alice, Grace, and I were out in the yard when I suddenly felt unusually oppressed by the sense of confinement. I thought of the butter dish sitting on our dining table, with its flat plate and dome-shaped cover. It seemed to me that the land around us was that plate, the sky coming down all around it like a huge, transparent dome. I turned to the other girls and said, "We're in a butter dish!"

When we left Alameda, we children thought it was for a lark, a temporary change of atmosphere. After a few weeks in Allensworth we asked, "Mama, when are we going home?" Only then did we learn that we *were* home.

There was no merciful glimpse into the future, that we might see how greatly enlarged our borders would be one day; how circumstances would take us individually to many "faraway places with strange-sounding names." Now, Allensworth was the center and circumference, the be-all and end-all and, as far as we knew, the forever Omega of our lives.

HEARST SAN SIMEON STATE HISTORICAL MONUMENT

In the 1930s Hearst Castle was, it seemed, the choice rendezvous spot of every major movie star in Hollywood. Located overlooking the Pacific Ocean between Los Angeles and San Francisco, the "Golden People"—along with many notable political, social, and cultural figures of the day—were either flown in via private plane or loaded onto a private railcar headed toward a luxurious weekend on the lavish property, which included the Mediterranean-style castle known as Casa Grande, plus gardens, pavilions, a private zoo (which is today still full of zebras), and the guest villas, modestly called "cottages," the smallest of which had ten rooms. Visitors included Howard Hughes, Greta Garbo, P. G. Wodehouse, Winston Churchill, and the very first American movie columnist—dubbed "the Queen of Hollywood"—Louella Parsons.

Newspaper and publishing tycoon William Randolph Hearst called his estate La Cuesta Encantada—"The Enchanted Hill"—and the castle's 90,000 square feet and surrounding 208 acres remain in beautiful condition, their original extravagance and opulence preserved for their many visitors. Several different tours of the buildings are available, and the extensive gardens and grounds can be explored at one's leisure.

SAMANTHA BARBAS

from *THE FIRST LADY OF HOLLYWOOD*

Louella's most cherished weekends were spent away from Hollywood, with Hearst and [his mistress Marion] Davies on the California coast. Hearst called it "the ranch." A sprawling Spanish-style castle overlooking the Pacific and set on a vast plot of land the size of Rhode Island, Hearst's San Simeon, 250 miles north of Los Angeles, was the largest and most extravagant residence in the United States. It featured acres of gardens, panoramic views, and, in each of its 165 rooms, priceless European antiques from Hearst's twenty-five-million-dollar art collection. The grand assembly room in the estate's main building, Casa Grande, featured authentic wooden pews from Renaissance churches; the dining room was ornamented with Siennese battle flags, and throughout the living quarters hung sixteenth-century French tapestries, some worth tens of thousands of dollars.

"The facade looked like a combination of Rheims Cathedral and a gigantic Swiss chalet," recalled Charlie Chaplin. "Surrounding it like vanguards were five Italian villas, set in on the edge of the plateau, each housing six guests. They were furnished in Italian style with baroque ceilings from which carved seraphs and cherubs smiled down at you." Photographer Cecil Beaton, another regular guest, described it as something "right out of a fairy story. The sun poured down with theatrical brilliance on tons of white marble and white stone. There seemed to be a thousand marble statues, pedestals, urns. The flowers were unreal in their ordered profusion." It was Hearst's "little hideaway," his "little hilltop at San Simeon," and for over two decades, he and Davies called it home.

In public, Hearst may have been modest about his seaside residence, but it was one of the consuming passions of his life. Built on land originally purchased by his father, George, the castle was the result of a joint collaboration by Hearst and architect Julia Morgan. Though the majority of the construction was completed in the 1920s, in time for Hearst and Davies to move in in 1926, it remained a work in progress. Never quite satisfied with it, Hearst constantly added rooms and cottages, pools and gardens, more precious antiques and more elaborate facades. Hearst had an "edifice complex," pundits joked.

Each weekend during the late 1920s and 1930s, Hearst dispatched telegrams to the MGM studio ordering Louis B. Mayer to send up ten or twenty actors for a weekend at the ranch. Most stars were afraid to decline the offer, lest they offend Louella, Mayer, and Hearst, so the turnout was always healthy. Weekends at San Simeon became a regular feature of Hollywood celebrity life in the 1930s.

On Friday evenings at 6:30, guests assembled at the Southern Pacific station in Los Angeles. They took the train to San Luis Obispo, the town nearest San Simeon, and were taken up to the castle by a fleet of Hearst's private cars. The somber procession of automobiles climbing slowly up the foggy hill looked like a "funeral procession," recalled Hedda Hopper, who was one of Hearst's regular weekend guests. Along the road were areas for large grazing animals, including antelope, deer, bison, elk, mountain sheep, and zebras—Hearst had the world's largest private zoo and game preserve, which housed over 120 varieties of animals. In 1928 an inventory of his zoo reported twenty-seven antelope, five kinds of deer, forty-four bison, three cougars, five lions, two bobcats, a leopard, a cheetah, three kinds of bears, a chimpanzee, three Java monkeys, a tapir, sheep, goats, two llamas, two kangaroos, and a wallaby. Often the animals strayed onto the path, causing delays. Once when Louella was being driven up the hill, a moose who had settled on the road refused to budge. She and her driver waited almost an hour until it decided to leave.

On Saturdays, Hearst planned a full morning of tennis matches, hikes, and ocean swims, and the participants were expected to enjoy themselves—or at least give the appearance— lest they insult the host. According to Hearst reporter Adela Rogers St. Johns, Hearst loved to picnic, and he regularly had his weekend guests join him for pheasant and caviar beneath the shady oaks on the estate. "A picnic consisted of leaving . San Simeon after lunch and stopping in a pleasant valley by a running stream. Servants went ahead with chuck wagons filled to overflowing...with pate de fois gras, thick filet mignon, and sparkling burgundy. After sleeping on cots under army tents, guests rode all next day to one of Mr. Hearst's faraway ranches for a dinner of chicken with all the trimmings. Automobiles waited to whisk you home in the usual luxury," recalled Hopper. Hearst also led his guests on grueling daylong horseback rides, humiliating ordeals in which the vigorous septuagenarian outpaced sore, tired actors half his age. Director King Vidor described them as "sadistic." In the afternoons, guests swam in the pool, a sparkling grotto of white marble flanked by Roman columns, or read one of the nine thousand volumes in the castle's two libraries.

The focal point of a weekend at San Simeon was the Saturday evening dinner in the refectory, a dim, cavernous dining room that resembled the inside of a medieval cathedral. From the center of the long wooden table, which seated more than seventy guests, Hearst and Davies presided over the extravagant multicourse meal. Though the dinners were cooked in gourmet style and featured fine cheeses and meats—"pheasant, wild duck, partridge and venison," recalled Chaplin in his autobiography—guests received paper napkins and were offered ketchup and mustard, in their original bottles, as condiments. (A fanatic about germs, Hearst thought such arrangements more "sanitary" than more elegant serving options.) After dinner, guests were ushered to Hearst's private theater, where they watched Davies's old films.

Concerned by Davies's alcoholic tendencies, Hearst banned liquor from the castle, and guests who brought their own private bottles had them promptly confiscated by the servants. But Davies always had a stash of gin hidden in her bedroom, and when Hearst had gone to bed, the guests made merry. Davies "would get a bottle after dinner and snag two or three cronies and withdraw to the mirrored ladies' room for a pleasant aftermath," remembered actress Ilka Chase. One night Davies and a group of female guests were imbibing in the bathroom, and "Mr. Hearst came and threw [in] our robes and our toothbrushes," Adela St. Johns recalled. Furious, "he just opened the door and said, 'if you girls are going to stay in there all night, you'll need these!'"

Louella first went to San Simeon not long after her arrival in Hollywood, and by the late 1920s she was a regular weekend guest. According to the gardener, Louella "would come up here with her twenty-seven trunks even if she was going to stay three or four days. But she was up here a lot of the time." "She would like attention and sometimes she would call for me to come over, and it was only to decide which necklace she should wear, amethyst or some other necklace," recalled a housekeeper. Louella often used the San Simeon weekends to collect Hollywood news, and she spent much of her time working on her column, which she dispatched to the *Examiner* office by wire. "She was always there, and she was talking to Miss Davies about what gossip was going on in Hollywood; who was doing what, who was sleeping with whom and all that sort of stuff. That was always going on," remembered another member of the San Simeon staff. Hearst frequently held editorial meetings at San Simeon, and on any given weekend Hearst editors and executives Arthur Brisbane, George Young, Ray Van Ettisch, and James Richardson of the *Examiner;* Bill Curley, editor of the *New York Journal American;* and Walter Howey of the *Chicago Herald Examiner* could be found discussing finances, politics, and circulation in the refectory.

Hearst also conducted his Hollywood business at San Simeon. In the early 1930s, Hearst, Davies, and actress Constance Bennett, after watching several screen tests in Hearst's private theater, made the decision to star actor Joel McCrea in an upcoming Cosmopolitan-MGM film. McCrea was also staying at San Simeon that weekend, but he was unaware of the decision until Louella told him the following morning. "Well congratulations," she said. "I gave you the [headline] in the *Examiner* this morning." Louella had been there when the decision was made, and the news was in print before McCrea had even heard it. Actress Louise Brooks recalled that female visitors had to avoid being caught alone with Hearst. Though Hearst was never known to have seduced any of his guests, Davies was always suspicious. One weekend Hearst entered the library when Brooks was alone reading, and Brooks immediately shut the book and "fled from the room." "Had Marion come upon us," Brooks said, "she would not only have deported me from the lunch but have ordered Louella Parsons to exterminate me from the column."

Louella's regular attendance at San Simeon cemented her position among Hollywood's elite. Virtually every major film star of the 1920s and 1930s vacationed at San Simeon, as did major political, social, and literary figures, including Charles Lindbergh, Herbert Hoover, George Bernard Shaw, Winston Churchill, and Calvin Coolidge, among others. By the early 1930s, Louella had also become an important member of Hearst's "inner circle." According to Adela Rogers St. Johns, Louella was one of the few people whom Hearst felt he could really trust.

ARTHUR B. RIPLEY DESERT WOODLAND STATE PARK

The sight of a roadrunner dashing past, feet awhirl above the cracked earth beside a two-lane highway, is quintessential to the deserts of Southern California. Naturalist Edmund C. Jaeger, whose study of the desert flora and fauna of the American West spanned seven decades, writes with particular warmth and humor about the California roadrunner, whom he calls the "desert's bird wag," a fellow at once comical and wise.

Located in Los Angeles County against the backdrop of the Tehachapi Range, the oft-overlooked Arthur B. Ripley Desert Woodland State Park is rich in jackrabbits, rattlesnakes, kangaroo rats, quails, coyotes, ground squirrels, and of course the ubiquitous roadrunner. Additionally, the 566 acres of park land formerly belonging to farmer Arthur Ripley protects the woodland habitat of Joshua trees and junipers, which once covered the Antelope Valley. Because the sandy soil is low in nutrients, Joshua trees here tend to be small—rarely taller than fourteen feet—and their forms twist and bend, creating eerie silhouettes against the sky. The landscape is replete with sage, beavertail cactus, buckwheat, and springtime wildflowers, together creating a wooded desert haven for visitor and roadrunner alike.

EDMUND C. JAEGER

from "CALIFORNIA ROAD RUNNER"

Of all the feathered dwellers in the desert there is none that has such an amazing stock of peculiarities as the California road runner. He is the desert's bird wag, as full of comical manners and as mischievous as the jay or the nutcracker; yet, unlike these birds, he is never obtrusive in his familiarity. Every morning he goes down on the trail below my shanty and saunters along, waiting for me to come with my pail for water, well knowing that I will chase him and give him the fun of beating me to the corner. Just as I am almost upon him, he leaps into the brush out of sight and is not seen for an hour or two. This born gamester has been found time and again pursuing the ends of surveyors' chains as they were dragged along by the lineman, or, on golf grounds, running down stray balls with the eagerness of a playful dog.

You will never mistake the road runner. The bristle-tipped topknot which he raises and lowers at will, the reptile-like face with its deep-slit mouth, and the long tail which so unmistakably registers his emotions, make him a bird of most singular appearance.

This strange cousin of the cuckoo has earned his name from his habit of sprinting along roadways, especially when pursued by horsemen or moderately slow-going vehicles. In the old days of California, when tourists were frequently driven over country roads in tallyho coaches, it was no uncommon sight to see this bird running a half-mile or so in front of the fast-trotting horses. Another common name, "chaparral cock," is given in allusion to his living in the chaparral or scrub forest of the semideserts; and he is called "ground cuckoo" because of his inability to leave the ground in long-sustained flight.

Formerly the range of the road runner included the grassy plains, chaparral-covered hills, and arid mesas from Kansas to the Pacific Ocean and from central California to Mexico. With the settlement of the land and the increase in the number of gunmen, this unique bird is rapidly becoming rare, and the familiar Maltese-cross footprints which he leaves along dusty roads are now all too seldom seen except in the wildest portions of his former range.

The road runner makes no regular migrations and is seldom seen except when alone. He prefers the protection of thorny, low-growing mesquite and saltbush thickets, and once he chooses a clump of mesquites, he seldom leaves the vicinity and may be found there year after year.

Like a policeman, the road runner apparently has his beats, and anyone who watches him day after day will note how punctual he is in passing certain points at definite times. An invalid on the Colorado Desert recently called my attention to the fact that a road runner passed her porch regularly at 12:25 p.m. every day for over a week, never varying by more than a minute or two. A gentleman who some months ago put up a new board fence tells me that a road runner almost daily jumps on the upper rail and runs at top speed the full length of one side of the fence. He invariably does this at the same time of day—just about noon.

I became acquainted with a young road runner as a pet in the home of O. H. Wickard, at Antelope, California. The bird stayed in the house at night but went out early in the day.

First on its program was generally a sun bath. Mounting one of the granite boulders about the house, he would puff out his feathers until his body looked round as a ball, spread his wings, and lower his tail. In this position, he would sit quietly for some 30 minutes. Sun bath over, he would go into a cactus patch. In a succession of dizzy leaps and jumps and hurried flights and runs, he would go round and round a cactus clump, perhaps as many as 20 times. He always seemed to make an effort to assume as many different clownish attitudes as possible. This over, the road runner might then go to the house and annoy the cat awhile. Dogs he had no use for. Even a very small Pekingese would send the bird fleeing in what appeared to be terror.

Cat-teasing consisted of rushing toward the animal with spread wings, extended neck and head, and wide-open mouth, followed by a snapping of the beak and a strange sound of rattling in the throat. The cat often countered this noisy, showy charge with a quick bat of its paw. Then the bird would deftly retreat and rush at the cat again. Both seemed to enjoy the sport. It generally ended after the cat ran away, with the road runner giving chase for a yard or two.

This road runner was unusually fond of fuzzy objects such as loose wads of cotton and milkweed seeds. He would run round and round the room, holding the object in his beak. Crayons he found in a box on a shelf were picked up one by one and thrown to the floor; flowers in a vase fared likewise.

From time to time his amusements were varied by running from the open door, picking up a leaf in the garden, and then dashing inside with it. Once he picked up a sizable piece of glass, brought it to show to his mistress, and to her amazement, swallowed it without ill effects. As she sprinkled the family wash he hugely enjoyed having her sprinkle water on him. When the neighbor's barefooted children came in, he would rush at them, make a rattling noise in his throat, and then peck at their toes, often frightening them from the house. If they had shoes on he pulled at the buttons or the ends of the shoestrings.

At night the bird slept inside the house on a branch of a tree nailed above the door, or on top of the iron-cased wall clock, his tail pushed flat up against the wall. The striking of the clock he wholly ignored, and he went to sleep even with the lights on; to evening conversations he gave no heed.

One evening a stranger came in and sat down in a chair near the clock. Old Roady jumped from his sleeping perch onto the visitor's head, and from there to his lap, where he made repeated stabs with his beak at the visitor's fingers.

One summer morning one of the boys found the pet caught in a spring trap set out for the rabbits that had been eating the garden vegetables. One foot was so nearly severed from the leg that amputation was necessary. With only a stump left, it was no longer able to leap or run, either in sport or while hunting for food.

But Old Roady was resourceful. For several days he spent most of the time lying in the shade; before the week had ended, however, he was hobbling around, even attempting to run on his stump. On the third day after the accident I saw him with the aid of his wings jump upward and snatch cicadas from the branches of shrubs. He was soon back at most of his old tricks. The end of his leg sometimes got a bit sore from overuse, but the callus was soon thick enough to stand much abuse, and before a month went by he was again visiting at the homes of the farm neighbors. Often he stayed away all morning and traveled several miles. Once he frightened a housewife by bringing her a live snake; he apparently enjoyed her excited screams. He usually stayed out in the brush all morning, seldom coming into the house until noontime. If the boys tried to find him he was very clever at eluding them by crouching low under the bushes.

ANTELOPE VALLEY
CALIFORNIA POPPY
RESERVE

In "Copa De Oro," Ina Coolbrith—inaugural poet laureate of California, one-third of the "Golden Gate Trinity" of literary tastemakers (along with Bret Harte and Charles Warren Stoddard), and mentor to Jack London—praises the beauty of the California poppy above all the ancient splendors of the Western world. "Not all proud Sheba's queenly offerings, / Could match the golden marvel of thy blooms," she writes. One encounter with the orange petals of California's state flower will prove her words true, and a wander through the hillsides of the Antelope Valley California Poppy Reserve, blanketed in orange in springtime, will wholly overwhelm the senses with the splendor of these "kingly cups."

The 1,781-acre Antelope Valley California Poppy Reserve is located in the Mojave Desert, west of Lancaster. A meander along the Antelope Loop Trail between March and the end of May will afford the walker a visual feast of wildflowers: poppies amidst lupine, cream cups, owl's clover, goldfields, and fiddlenecks. A few picnic tables are available on a first-come, first-serve basis—the perfect place for a moment of repose amidst the desert bloom.

INA COOLBRITH
"COPA DE ORO (THE CALIFORNIA POPPY)"

Thy satin vesture richer is than looms
   Of Orient weave for raiment of her kings.
  Not dyes of old Tyre, not precious things
Regathered from the long forgotten tombs
Of buried empires, not the iris plumes
   That wave upon the tropic's myriad wings,
   Not all proud Sheba's queenly offerings,
Could match the golden marvel of thy blooms.
For thou art nurtured from the treasure veins
   Of this fair land; thy golden rootlets sup
      Her sands of gold—of gold thy petals spun.
Her golden glory, thou! on hills and plains
   Lifting, exultant, every kingly cup,
      Brimmed with the golden vintage of the sun.

EL PRESIDIO DE SANTA BÁRBARA STATE HISTORIC PARK

In terms of his upbringing, Richard Henry Dana Jr. was certainly more used to evenings spent on shore dancing among the upper-class than he was to life aboard the hide-trading *Pilgrim*, which took him on a rough-and-tumble tour along the coast of Alta California. Dana was a Massachusetts native, born to a wealthy colonial family and destined to become a lawyer and politician, but when a case of measles impelled him to leave Harvard College for the curative effects of sea air, he headed west. His reminiscences about his time with the *Pilgrim*—including his experience in the thriving Presidio of Santa Barbara of the 1830s—are full and rich and provide a clear-eyed look into a culture and landscape very different from that of Harvard, where he reenrolled promptly upon his return.

Two sections of the original Santa Barbara Royal Presidio remain standing in the state historic park, notable for their characteristic sundried adobe bricks, sandstone foundations, and red-tiled roofs. Later adobes are preserved as well, including an American-era adobe built by José María Rochin in 1856. Outside, a heritage garden created in 2001 by the Presidio Heritage Plant Project flourishes across the seasons with edible offerings including heirloom grapevines, white Sonora wheat (used to make flour tortillas), prickly pear cacti, banana trees, and more. The park hosts many programs throughout the year, among them living history demonstrations, public events, and lectures.

RICHARD HENRY DANA JR.
from TWO YEARS BEFORE THE MAST

Sunday, January 10th. Arrived at Santa Barbara, and on the following Wednesday slipped our cable and went to sea, on account of a southeaster. Returned to our anchorage the next day. We were the only vessel in the port. The Pilgrim had passed through the Canal and hove-to off the town, nearly six weeks before, on her passage down from Monterey, and was now at the leeward. She heard here of our safe arrival at San Francisco.

Great preparations were making on shore for the marriage of our agent, who was to marry Doña Anita de la Guerra de Noriego y Corillo, youngest daughter of Don Antonio Noriego, the grandee of the place, and the head of the first family in California. Our steward was ashore three days, making pastry and cake, and some of the best of our stores were sent off with him. On the day appointed for the wedding, we took the captain ashore in the gig, and had orders to come for him at night, with leave to go up to the house and see the fandango. Returning on board, we found preparations making for a salute. Our guns were loaded and run out, men appointed to each, cartridges served out, matches lighted, and all the flags ready to be run up. I took my place at the starboard after gun, and we all waited for the signal from on shore. At ten o'clock the bride went up with her sister to the confessional, dressed in deep black. Nearly an hour intervened, when the great doors of the Mission church opened, the bells rang out a loud, discordant peal, the private signal for us was run up by the captain ashore, the bride, dressed in complete white, came out of the church with the bridegroom, followed by a long procession. Just as she stepped from the church door, a small white cloud issued from the bows of our ship, which was full in sight, the loud report echoed among the surrounding hills and over the bay, and instantly the ship was dressed in flags and pennants from stem to stern. Twenty-three guns followed in regular succession, with an interval of fifteen seconds between each, when the cloud blew off, and our ship lay dressed in her colors all day. At sundown another salute of the same number of guns was fired, and all the flags run down. This we thought was pretty well—a gun every fifteen seconds—for a merchantman with only four guns and a dozen or twenty men.

After supper, the gig's crew were called, and we rowed ashore, dressed in our uniform, beached the boat, and went up to the fandango. The bride's father's house was the principal one in the place, with a large court in front, upon which a tent was built, capable of containing several hundred people. As we drew near, we heard the accustomed sound of violins and guitars, and saw a great motion of the people within. Going in, we found nearly all the people of the town—men, women, and children—collected and crowded together, leaving barely room for the dancers; for on these occasions no invitations are given, but every one is expected to come, though there is always a private entertainment within the house for particular friends. The old women sat down in rows, clapping their hands to the music, and applauding the young ones. The music was lively, and among the tunes we recognized several of our popular airs, which we, without doubt, have taken from the Spanish. In the dancing I was much disappointed. The women stood upright, with their hands down by their sides, their eyes fixed upon the ground before them, and slided about without any perceptible means of motion; for their feet were invisible, the hem of their dresses forming a circle about them, reaching to the ground. They looked as grave as though they were going through some religious ceremony, their faces as little excited as their limbs; and on the whole, instead of the spirited, fascinating Spanish dances which I had expected, I found the Californian fandango, on the part of the women at least, a lifeless affair. The men did better. They danced with grace and spirit, moving in circles round their nearly stationary partners, and showing their figures to advantage.

A great deal was said about our friend Don Juan Bandini, and when he did appear, which was toward the close of the evening, he certainly gave us the most graceful dancing that I had ever seen. He was dressed in white pantaloons, neatly made, a short jacket of dark silk, gayly figured, white stockings and thin morocco slippers upon his very small feet. His slight and graceful figure was well adapted to dancing, and he moved about with the grace and daintiness of a young fawn. An occasional touch of the toe to the ground seemed all that was necessary to give him a long interval of motion in the air. At the same time he was not fantastic or flourishing, but appeared to be rather repressing a strong tendency to motion. He was loudly applauded, and danced frequently toward the close of the evening. After the supper, the waltzing began, which was confined to a very few of the "gente de razón," and was considered a high accomplishment, and a mark of aristocracy. Here, too, Don Juan figured greatly, waltzing with the sister of the bride (Doña Angustias, a handsome woman and a general favorite) in a variety of beautiful figures, which lasted as much as half an hour, no one else taking the floor. They were repeatedly and loudly applauded, the old men and women jumping out of their seats in admiration, and the young people waving their hats and handkerchiefs. The great amusement of the evening—owing to its being the Carnival—was the breaking of eggs filled with cologne, or other essences, upon the heads of the company. The women bring a great number of these secretly about them, and the amusement is to break one upon the head of a gentleman when his back is turned. He is bound in gallantry to find out the lady and return the compliment, though it must not be done if the person sees you. A tall, stately Don, with immense gray whiskers, and a look of great importance, was standing before me, when I felt a light hand on my shoulder, and, turning round, saw Doña Angustias (whom we all knew, as she had been up to Monterey, and down again, in the Alert), with her finger upon her lip, motioning me gently aside. I stepped back a little, when she went up behind the Don, and with one hand knocked off his huge *sombrero,* and at the same instant, with the other, broke the egg upon his head, and, springing behind me, was out of sight in a moment. The Don turned slowly round, the cologne running down his face and over his clothes, and a loud laugh breaking out from every quarter. He looked round in vain for some time, until the direction of so many laughing eyes showed him the fair offender. She was his niece, and a great favorite with him, so old Don Domingo had to join in the laugh. A great many such tricks were played, and many a war of sharp manoeuvering was carried on between couples of the younger people, and at every successful exploit a general laugh was raised.

Another of their games I was for some time at a loss about. A pretty young girl was dancing, named—after what would appear to us an almost sacrilegious custom of the country— Espíritu Santo, when a young man went behind her and placed his hat directly upon her head, letting it fall down over her eyes, and sprang back among the crowd. She danced for some time with the hat on, when she threw it off, which called forth a general shout, and the young man was obliged to go out upon the floor and pick it up. Some of the ladies, upon whose heads hats had been placed, threw them off at once, and a few kept them on throughout the dance, and took them off at the end, and held them out in their hands, when the owner stepped out, bowed, and took it from them. I soon began to suspect the meaning of the thing, and was afterwards told that it was a compliment, and an offer to become the lady's gallant for the rest of the evening, and to wait upon her home. If the hat was thrown off, the offer was refused, and the gentleman was obliged to pick up his hat amid a general laugh. Much amusement was caused sometimes by gentlemen putting hats on the ladies' heads, without permitting them to see whom it was done by. This obliged them to throw them off, or keep them on at a venture, and when they came to discover the owner the laugh was turned upon one or the other.

The captain sent for us about ten o'clock, and we went aboard in high spirits, having enjoyed the new scene much, and were of great importance among the crew, from having so much to tell, and from the prospect of going every night until it was over; for these fandangos generally last three days. The next day, two of us were sent up to the town, and took care to come back by way of Señor Noriego's, and take a look into the booth. The musicians were again there, upon their platform, scraping and twanging away, and a few people, apparently of the lower classes, were dancing. The dancing is kept up, at intervals, throughout the day, but the crowd, the spirit, and the *élite* come in at night. The next night, which was the last, we went ashore in the same manner, until we got almost tired of the monotonous twang of the instruments, the drawling sounds which the women kept up, as an accompaniment, and the slapping of the hands in time with the music, in place of castanets. We found ourselves as great objects of attention as any persons or anything at the place. Our sailor dresses—and we took great pains to have them neat and ship-shape—were much admired, and we were invited, from every quarter, to give them an American dance; but after the ridiculous figure some of our countrymen cut in dancing after the Mexicans, we thought it best to leave it to their imaginations.

Our agent, with a tight, black, swallow-tailed coat just imported from Boston, a high stiff cravat, looking as if he had been pinned and skewered, with only his feet and hands left free, took the floor just after Bandini, and we thought they had had enough of Yankee grace.

The last night they kept it up in great style, and were getting into a high-go, when the captain called us off to go aboard, for, it being southeaster season, he was afraid to remain on shore long; and it was well he did not, for that night we slipped our cables, as a crowner to our fun ashore, and stood off before a southeaster, which lasted twelve hours, and returned to our anchorage the next day.

LOS ANGELES STATE HISTORIC PARK

For anyone accustomed to the dense, car-thick, palm-lined chaos of present-day LA, scenes from Leo Carrillo's memoir *The California I Love* provide a refreshing window into the more leisurely world of Mexican-era Los Angeles. Here, cows low languidly and wild dogs run freely from street to street while women dress in their best red and green and gold clothing, and peppers roast spicy and sweet as tortillas are made by hand for a festival. Actor and political cartoonist Leo Carrillo's roots stretched back far into California's history (his great-grandfather Carlos Antonio Carillo was the governor of Alta California from 1837 to 1838), and *The California I Love*, published just before Leo Carrillo's death in 1961, is an exploration and celebration of the heritage of which he was so proud.

On thirty-two acres just northeast of Chinatown in the heart of Los Angeles, with the Metro Gold Line whizzing by, the land of Los Angeles State Historic Park was once a rich and fertile river basin where both native Tongva people and Mexican settlers flourished. Today the park features historical buildings, educational displays, and open space for walking and picnicking.

LEO CARRILLO

from *THE CALIFORNIA I LOVE*

It is true, too, that on the day of which I speak El Pueblo de Nuestra Señora la Reina de Los Angeles de Porciuncula—which we have cruelly abbreviated to "Los Angeles"—was animated in all the area of the Plaza with another fervor typically Spanish. It was having a fiesta.

The sun came up with strength that morning, shining down as if in warm benediction upon the adobes it had helped to create. Almost all the houses were built of this adobe. A relatively few modern, baked-brick business buildings stood proudly among the modest adobes. A notable one was the elegant three-story Pico House, a fine hotel which stood just across the roadway to the southwest of the Plaza on the exact site where my great-uncle, the notable military leader, José Antonio Carrillo once had his home.

My family—my father and mother and their four children—lived in what was known as the Bell Block, a long row of adobe dwellings, mostly one-story, running along the east side of Los Angeles Street from Aliso to First. Part of the Bell Block was two-story, with a wide verandah.

Silence had descended upon all the Plaza region just before dawn.

Then scarlet streaks stabbed the sky above the gentle hills to the east, and a warm breeze caressed the large leaves of the young rubber trees planted in a large circle around the Plaza.

A young man's voice, accompanied by the gentle strumming of a guitar, was heard in the strains of *Las Mañanitas—The Little Mornings*—as he serenaded beneath the window of his loved one.

In contrast to this tender scene, three drunks lay on the parched grass of the Plaza snoring gently as the first wandering sunbeams came creeping into the pueblo. The sun shone on the flat roofs of the little adobe houses, all of them covered with brea or tar from the tar pits to the west. Somewhere a cow bawled for the milker and roosters crowed vociferously to welcome the new dawn. The innumerable half-wild dogs of the

Plaza area roused from their torpor long enough to scratch for fleas. The sun was hot even at this early hour. It was going to be a typical August day.

The tinkling of water could be heard where the Zanjero, the keeper of the community's water supply, walked along the Zanja, or Mother Ditch, from which the poor people still scooped their drinking water in these days.

The Zanjero was a very important man in the community; he received more salary than the alcalde or the councilmen because his duties were considered the most important of any. Now he was checking the Zanja to see that everything was all right for the people who soon would be coming with their buckets and jars for water for their homes.

It was the sixth day of August.

A good reason existed for the selection of this particular date for the fiesta. Times had been hard in the pueblo and many had gone to bed suffering the pangs of hunger. Masa, the ground corn for tortillas, was difficult to obtain. Some simply did not have the few centavos necessary to buy the daily supply.

But everyone had joined in the desire for a fiesta. It was decided not to hold it on August fourth, which was St. Dominic Day, but on the sixth, which was the observance of the Day of Transfiguration. St. Dominic was a dour, self-denying saint who did not look with favor upon merry-making, music and eating. It would have been inappropriate to have it on his day. But the Day of Transfiguration was one of extreme holiness in the church and thus a religious note could be added to the celebration. So the fiesta committee had chosen the sixth and the people had joyously begun their preparations.

The señoritas had been busy washing and ironing their best— the bright colored flaring skirts, and the white blouses with the tight bodices, ornamented with crimson, green and gold embroidery—and had been gloating over their treasures, such as the high Spanish combs and the black earrings—the aretes— which they planned to wear during the fiesta and the dancing.

The young cabelleros likewise had been making preparations. Their saddles with the silver ornamentation were polished bright. Their horses had been groomed until they shone with great brilliance. Even the bridles and stirrups had been oiled and polished so that they too were at their peak.

Now as the sun crept higher, casting long shadows from the adobe homes, the whole pueblo seemed to begin to awaken at once. The smells of sausage, fresh roasted peppers and tortillas floated from the windows. From the homes came the sound of tortillas being slapped with the bare hands.

In many homes, too, blown egg shells were being filled with confetti so as to form the cascarónes for breaking on the heads of the merrymakers in traditional Spanish style.

All during the morning the pace of the preparations grew more frenzied. By the time the sun peered straight down on the pueblo, casting no shadows at all, the gathering of the towns-people and country dwellers from miles around was in full swing.

The all-pervading and unmistakable odor of fresh horse manure grew more intense as the mounted visitors arrived and engulfed the whole Plaza region.

One group of guitarreros, having been up all night playing in one of the cantinas, came in tipsy parade down Los Angeles Street, too tired to sound another note, one portly musician dragging his bull fiddle behind him.

Just as the guitarreros were going by in the dust of the street, a young woman far along in pregnancy came out on the verandah of the second-story of the old adobe Bell Block. She walked slowly and carefully and a faint smile appeared on her lips as she watched the weaving figures below.

One of the musicians, carrying his guitar under his arm, looked up and saw the young woman and waved his hand and bowed. She waved in return.

"It is a pity that the Señora Carrillo's husband is so far away at this time," the guitar player said to one of his companions who was carefully carrying a violin.

From the verandah Señora Carrillo could see preparations for the fiesta going on all up and down the street. Down toward the Plaza there was great activity around the kiosco, or band-stand. Seats were being arranged for the officials and the dueñas who would oversee the evening's festivities. Tables were being set up for the feast.

Señora Carrillo gazed wistfully at the scene wishing she might be taking a more active part. She tried to picture where her husband might be on his business trip to Magdalena in Sonora for a group of mining men in Los Angeles. Desperately she wished he would return, because she knew the hour of her delivery was near.

CALIFORNIA CITRUS STATE HISTORIC PARK

The thousands of acres of citrus groves that grow from Pasadena to Redlands have had a mythic appeal since the late nineteenth century, due in no small part to the efforts of citrus producers, whose colorful crate labels portrayed California as a paradise on earth. The boom of lemons, grapefruits, and in particular Washington navel oranges was called a "second gold rush" for the state, and, just like the first bonanza, hundreds of thousands of people poured in to the fabled land of opportunity, seeking their fortune.

Susan Straight, an award-winning author and cofounder of the MFA in Creative Writing program at UC Riverside, was born and raised in California's "Inland Empire," the area just east of Los Angeles. In her introduction to *Inlandia: A Literary Journey Through California's Inland Empire*, she brings to life a childhood among citrus and apricot groves, revealing her passionate loyalty to this place of conflicted histories and fecund fields.

The California Citrus State Historic Park in Riverside boasts a Varietal Collection of over one hundred different species of citrus trees, a visitors' center set up like a packing house, and a collection of antique farm equipment. Much of the land is still a working citrus grove; it's the perfect place to stop in for a cup of orange juice and a trip back in time to when Citrus was King.

SUSAN STRAIGHT

from the introduction to *INLANDIA*

We had forests. As a child, I read of Sherwood Forest in England, where men could be lost to sight for years; of haunted woods in Europe, like those where my mother was born, where wolves and witches and darkness reigned amid the huge firs; of rain forests in South America where birds and monkeys screamed amid the dripping branches; of the chestnut and hickory and dogwood of Appalachia and the wilderness of trees in the great eastern forests of America.

And though no one knew it, in my part of Southern California, the inland reaches of terrain where most of us see only smog-shrouded hills and dried wild oats and mazes of freeway, we had magical, mythical woods as well—thousands and thousands of acres planted in orange and lemon and grapefruit trees that covered much of Riverside and San Bernardino and Redlands. Apricots and olive groves in Hemet, the date palm groves in Mecca and Indio, walnut trees in Elsinore, and cherries and apples in Cherry Valley and Oak Glen. Between them, in the wild San Gorgonio and San Jacinto Mountains, on the rolling hills of Temecula, we had pines and oaks that had lived for centuries. Along the riverbeds were cottonwoods and willows, and in the desert Joshua trees made their own eerie forests, and smoke trees rose from the sand. All my life, here in this place, we have had our own myths and legends and stories, but they were not heard very often outside in the world.

· · · · ·

I live in a house three blocks from Riverside Community Hospital, where I was born, where my brothers, my ex-husband, and his siblings were born, and most of our friends and all of our children.

I have always lived here, except for my college years, and I have seen nearly every mile of land in the region which this new anthology calls "Inlandia." When I was a child and people from elsewhere asked adults about where we lived, I remember hearing again and again that we were an hour from the mountains, an hour from the desert, an hour from the ocean, and an hour from Los Angeles. And I always thought, when I was a child, But why would we want to leave?

We had everything, in my eyes. The endless forests of cultivation, the lush wildflowers of the desert in spring, the date groves and pine forests. Trout from mountain lakes, lemons and oranges and avocados all winter, and as children we didn't care when smog veiled the hills in the summer. We mined the foothills near our house for fool's gold and rose quartz, and then we lay panting in an orange grove, and swam in the swift waters of the canal, where grass waved on the bottom as though in a true stream.

In fact, I realized as I grew older, everyone wanted to come here, to the inland region. Everyone's parents had come from somewhere else. My own mother was from Switzerland; her parents had moved from their small valley to seek their fortunes. They did not find them in Ontario, Canada, or northern Florida, but then they saw the ultimate pictures of prosperity and success, the land of milk and honey as represented in decades past: the postcards of purpled, snow-covered mountains in the distance, and orange trees in the foreground, all golden in the sun.

That is truly what we saw, growing up here, all winter. It was paradise, though I have since learned that the rest of the world might not recognize it.

In elementary school and junior high, I found that nearly everyone's parents had immigrated here—from Louisiana and Oklahoma and Mississippi, from Michoacán and Zacatecas and Guanajuato, from the Philippines and Germany and Japan. I had friends whose fathers were military men and whose mothers were immigrant brides from those countries. I had other friends whose fathers were military men and who'd returned to the South and vowed never to live in poverty and segregation again. All settled in Riverside, in San Bernardino, in Victorville—wherever there were military bases. And their children grew up in the Inland Empire—a new people. They played with the children of the Okies who'd broken down here, with my mother-in-law's people, who'd broken down in Calexico and whose sons became some of the first black Border Patrol agents.

I lived in a neighborhood called Okietown for the first three years of my life, and then my mother married my stepfather, who had also found his promised land here, having left New Brunswick, Canada. We moved to Riverside, and they have never left.

We ran freely as children, to the foothills and groves and river, and my parents, who loved this landscape with the passion of those raised in snow, took us camping everywhere. We knew every mile of Inlandia.

The dinosaurs of Cabazon, where people could eat hamburgers inside the head of a brontosaurus. The date palm groves in Mecca and Oasis and Indio, where even the names were exotic, and where I stood under the gray-green fronds arching above me, touching the etched trunks and the golden sprays of dates cascading overhead, and knew it was really a cathedral. The heat was so intense, and the cicadas' song filled my forehead, and the smell of water in the irrigation furrows was silver. On the way home, we got date shakes in Indio and watched the famous movie—*The Sex Life of the Date*.

I love every mile of my homeland. The fields of watermelon and cantaloupe in Blythe and Ripley, where my foster brothers and sisters came from. The savanna-like golden grasses in the Temecula Valley, with the oaks gathered like black clouds in the distance. The steep entrance of the Cajon Pass, where the mountains are purple in winter dusk and the wind is so fierce it will throw trucks like toys. The dunes outside Palm Springs and Whitewater, where the sand is white and soft as cake flour, and the smoke trees rise like ghosts in the distance. (My ex-husband once worked at a juvenile correction facility in Whitewater, and when Los Angeles boys tried to run away, he followed them in that desert, as they trudged with suitcases and radios through the creosote and rabbitbrush and hot sand, until they gave up in what they considered a particularly impersonal hell.)

I love the tiny communities that only we in this place know— Rubidoux, named for a pioneer of the area, and Belltown, where our cousins live near the Santa Ana River; Agua Mansa and La Placita, where New Mexicans came to grow grapes along that river and build adobe houses, marked now only by a cemetery and a few scattered homes; the old Cucamonga, where vineyards flourished and my parents bought wine; and Muscoy, on the outskirts of San Bernardino, where my brother liked to check out fighting roosters.

For twenty-five years I have written about this region and tried to infuse my work with love and desire and the fierceness we retain in these small places where people loved their own with the vehemence, the stubborn and suspicious and inventive qualities required to survive in this part of Southern California. It was a place where the land and sun and smog and violence and people could be forbidding, but the same land and sun and people offered survival and love and tungsten-hard loyalty to each other.

And for all these years, I have wanted to see my place represented in literature, in a wide-ranging collection of all the communities and voices and landscapes I've known.

Here it is.

BOLSA CHICA STATE BEACH

In the mid-twentieth century, a three-and-a-half-mile strip of Orange County oceanfront known as Tin Can Beach had a bad reputation. Bolsa Chica Beach acquired its nickname from the hundreds of rusting beer cans strewn across the sand among bottles, paper plates, and even makeshift houses built from tarpaper, cardboard, driftwood, and burlap. Some houses were relatively flimsy—it wasn't unheard of for house timbers to be repurposed for fire kindling—while others felt more permanent, boasting oil stoves and iceboxes. The occupants of these dwellings were an assemblage of people from all walks of life, from teenagers to seventy-two-year-old ex-railroaders to vacationing families. Ray Torrey, the self-proclaimed mayor of Tin Can Beach, called it "the last frontier...[where] a man can camp free in these parts." Meanwhile, the *Los Angeles Times* called it "the shame of the Southern California coastline," and the *Orange County Register* described it as "hell's half acre." By 1960, the state had acquired the property from over two hundred individuals and developers, and today the only reminders of Bolsa Chica's Tin Can days are the numerous rings for beach bonfires. Tent camping is not permitted, although RV/trailer camping is available by reservation. Bolsa Chica remains a popular place for fishing, clamming, diving, and surfing.

In an account of his yearlong quest to master a big-hollow wave, adventure writer and novelist Peter Heller leads us out into the waters off Bolsa Chica to overcome kookdom. (A "kook" is a surfing novice so unaware of surfing etiquette that he is a danger to himself and others in the water.) As Heller discovers, learning to surf is about more than mastering technique: it requires humility and a sense of environmental stewardship. A good sense of humor doesn't hurt, either.

PETER HELLER

from *KOOK*

We wrestled with the foam for two hours. I felt less like a surfer than ammo in a human slingshot. I was so tired I couldn't lift my arms to paddle. We'd stood up for a combined cumulative time of four seconds. I thought I'd understood what Andy had said about the peak and the surfer with priority, but when I finally got out past the break I couldn't figure out where the peak was. I didn't know how far away from the other surfers was safe to sit, and I must have gotten it wrong, because another dude collided with me and asked me if I was born on Planet Kook. That really hurt my feelings. Andy and I crawled out onto the sand and went for a late breakfast at the Sugar Shack, a block and a half from the pier on Main. It was always packed. Working people, tourists, surfers. We squeezed into a table against the wall, an arm's-length from the backs of the guys at the counter, and I ordered eggs over easy with bacon and coffee. Andy asked for poached eggs on dry toast. The brisk young gal in a black Shack T-shirt snagged a pen from behind her ear, blew away a wisp of ponytail, and asked us how the waves were. How did she know? The tangled hair? My osprey eyes? I was thrilled. She had broad shoulders and strong forearms.

"Waist-high, kinda mushy," I said, repeating something I'd heard in the parking lot.

The walls were covered in surfing photos. We sat under a framed cover from *Surfer* magazine: a guy standing straight up and relaxed, like he was waiting for a bus, in the middle of a barrel about as big as the Holland Tunnel. Above that was a signed blowup photo of someone riding a giant, and next to it were two local Shack-sponsored kids' surf teams and a framed memorial to a young surfer who had died somehow. He must have been sixteen. Below his head shot, very blond and forth-right, were the words:

> *Whenever you are riding,*
> *We hope the waves are forever*
> *glassy and hollow*

The guy in the tube was Timmy Turner. Timmy was behind the counter punching orders into the register. Timmy was twenty-six, and he'd been surfing for twenty years. He wore a black T, and it hung loosely on his wide shoulders and he seemed thin, almost slight, for being one of the most hard-core surfers around. His mom, Michelle, had bought the Shack twenty-five years before from her own parents and was known for feeding full meals to homeless people, and for sponsoring local school-age surfers. The kids got one free meal a week, salad through milkshake. I loved the place right away. The generosity of spirit, the rock-solid values of decency and civil duty, seemed to permeate the whole restaurant. It was there in the respectful way the young waitresses talked to the broken-down beachcomber at the end of the counter, the way everyone who passed asked if we needed more coffee.

Andy burst the yolk of his egg over his single piece of butterless bread.

"I love surfing," I confided.

Andy sipped his coffee and studied me over his cup, through his round gold wire-rims. "How do you know?" he said.

"Well..."

He smiled. "Maybe tomorrow we should try Bolsa Chica. It'll probably be closed out, but it won't matter. We need some time in the whitewater."

That sounded good. I didn't know what "closed out" meant, but I liked the idea of giving it all another go, maybe miles from any tatted-up dudes who kept saying fuck when talking to me.

Bolsa Chica State Park begins two and a half miles north of the Huntington Beach Pier. It is three miles of wide sand beach along a lightly curving southwest-facing coast. At the southern end, the Bolsa Chica estuary runs out through a cut in the beach. A rich tidal wetland, the estuary is one of the great American success stories of grassroots conservation and surfer activism. Once one of the largest oil-drilling fields in the world, the estuary and much of the beach were slated in the nineties for development as a mega-marina. The critical habitat would have gone the way of the rest of Southern California's 75 to 90 percent of coastal wetlands lost to development. This single lagoon was so important because the Pacific Flyway is one of the largest north-south bird migration routes on the planet, and many species are forced to skip much of Southern California because the tidal marshes where they used to stop over have been destroyed in order to build ports, marinas, and houses. The marina at Bolsa Chica would also have probably wrecked a favorite local surfing spot. A consortium of environmental groups led by the Surfrider Foundation stopped the project, and in 1997 got the state to put up $91 million to restore the marsh and to widen a cut through the beach to increase crucial tidal flow. At 880 acres, it has been one of the biggest and most successful coastal wetland restoration projects in the country, and has reestablished a stepping-stone in the flyway for migrating waterfowl. Now, every day, a few hundred yards from scores of surfers, birdwatchers can be seen walking the wood-plank trails in the marsh with their binoculars. Endangered birds such as the light-footed clapper rail are nesting there again. And outraged surfers led the charge. Go figure. The Surfrider Foundation is mostly made up of surfers, and today it has over fifty thousand members in the U.S. In '91 they won the second largest Clean Water Act lawsuit in American history, against two pulp mills in Humboldt County. More recently, they have worked with Laguna Beach to mitigate coastal water pollution from runoff, and they stopped Orange County from dumping 240 million gallons per day of partially treated sewage into the sea. Why should it surprise me? Surfers are an intense bunch and they love their coast the way they love their mothers.

We pulled up to the beach in a stiff offshore wind. Numbered lifeguard towers sat at two-hundred-yard intervals along the sand; the numbers went up as the towers marched northward. We would find out later that the towers served as landmarks for surfers—a few friends might decide to meet at Tower 21, or if it's too crowded or the waves are dumping, they'd go south to 18.

Bolsa Chica was pretty, but it was no picnic. We trotted out to an empty part of the beach and jogged into the surf. As soon as we stepped off the sand it was like walking into a swift river. We got swept south by the strong riptide. When I did manage to get through the surf to calm water, I was beat, but happy to be way past where any waves were breaking. I looked out to sea and blinked, transfixed like a highway deer. What the hell was *that*? *That* was a set wave. Bigger than anything yet and breaking much farther out. I got squashed.

Having learned my lesson, I paddled way, way out. No set wave would catch me inside again. Out here, it was pretty but it wasn't surfing. I clambered onto my board to sit—which in itself was a tenuous operation. I breathed, gut hollow with exhaustion, arms and back burning with lactic acid, and looked around. Relief to be out of the crashing mayhem. Just easy rolling swell. Phew. Three dolphins swam lazily by, heading north, their backs glossy and dark. Now, this was the life. But no waves broke so far out, so I edged back in. And then another wave, much larger than the others, walled up and broke on my head. It tumbled me back inshore, right into the impact zone, which is where the brunt of the waves collapse. It was also the worst part of the riptide, and I got trundled south, and the first wave's posse clobbered me one after another.

Was this fun? Two-foot waves were turning me into Play Doh. On the fifth wave, I managed to crawl up and stand and just as fast flew through the air like a catapulted cow. I know now that with the waves dumping the way they were, and the length of our boards and our skill level, we didn't stand a chance. Once, in sheer frustration, I rode the egg in on my belly, just to feel some speed. I got off it in ankle-deep water, and turned and lifted the heavy board. I carried it back into the white foam in front of me and across my body and got slammed by the next sweep of whitewater, and the egg leveled me like a snowplow. I unpeeled myself from the sand inch by inch the way Wile E. Coyote detaches himself from the pavement after Road Runner drives over him with a cement mixer.

I took a breather on the beach. Then, on the wet sand, carelessly attaching the Velcro of the leash to my ankle, I let the egg wallow in two inches of wash, and the next surge sent it sideways into me and nearly broke my legs. It could have snapped them like dry sticks had my feet been set.

If two inches of afterthought from a waist-high wave could do that to me, what would a real wave do? The forces a surfer deals with are beyond reckoning.

• • • • •

That night, covered with bruises, aching everywhere, I lay on Andy's fold-out couch in the library. I revisited the last two days and winced. I was such a kook. In surf slang, kook doesn't just mean beginner; it means outrageous, awkward, clueless novice who cuts people off on waves, thrashes around speaking to other surfers like it's a cocktail party, hollers rebel yells when he does manage to stand up for a split second, has no tact, no respect for the finely tuned protocol of surf, and is dangerous to boot, because when he drops in on a wave without looking, boards and bodies collide. That was me. I had called my girlfriend Kim and she was sympathetic to a point. She was getting sick of me being away all the time. She did not demand that I change, but she pointed out that it was hard to stay close. Ouch. It dawned on me that kook also perfectly described my aptitude with women.

I was unwilling to turn out the light and let sleep claim me before I had salvaged something of the day. Andy's old shepherd Cody lay on my legs and watched me with a concerned expression. I had known him for years. Now he seemed to sense that I was wrestling with powerful forces: vanity, pride, surf.

I rubbed his forehead with my fist and slid a notebook off the side table. I glanced up at the bookcase that occupied the entire wall opposite. A thousand spines, a thousand reverberating names, the best efforts of the truest minds. I scanned across the modern canon and their antecedents. Eliot, Coleridge, Proust, Stein, Dickinson, Brecht, W. C. Williams, Plato, Faulkner, Homer, Rilke, Cervantes. Waves of their own, waves that broke over reefs of readers and worked their own geologic power. I felt small. What the hell was I doing here? I had hoped to write some fiction and I was setting that aside for the moment to take up a new sport that everybody said was consuming. Why do that to myself at forty-five? Why take the risk? If I was going to get any good writing done, I needed every minute I could get. I knew myself—the king of distraction.

The last title that popped out made me laugh. When I did, Cody lifted and cocked his head.

"It's nothing," I said. "Don Quixote. I'd read it to you, but it would drive a dog like you nuts."

I opened the notebook and wrote at the top of a page: SURFING, then *What I Learned Today.*

Set waves break farther out than you think and then you're screwed.
Do not get the surfboard between you and the wave. Keep it beside or down-wave from you.
Set waves are not alone. They come in...sets. D'oh!

Now we were getting somewhere. I closed the notebook and went to sleep.

SALTON SEA STATE
RECREATION AREA

When the Colorado River flooded into an ancient seabed called the Salton Sink in 1905, the forty-five-mile-long and twenty-mile-wide inland Salton Sea was born. It hasn't dried up since, being constantly refilled by rain, nearby canals and rivers, and agricultural runoff. This area is a fascinating mix of human- and nature-made ecosystems, and it is now a seasonal home to more than four hundred species of birds, which are drawn to the unusual nexus of desert and saline habitats. This is a very important stop along the Pacific Flyway, which runs from Alaska to the lowest tip of South America. The Salton Sea State Recreation Area in Riverside County encompasses fourteen miles of coastline and offers fishing, boating, beach camping, and, of course, excellent birdwatching.

In Kent Nelson's "Irregular Flight," the Salton Sea is both metaphor and character in the unfolding relationship between two birdwatchers seeking the rare Cook's storm petrel in this basin of salt and flooded canals. Nelson holds a JD in environmental law from Harvard and has published four novels as well as several collections of short fiction.

KENT NELSON
"IRREGULAR FLIGHT"

Claire heard about the vagrant Cook's Petrel at the Salton Sea on a Thursday morning in October on the rare-bird tape in Los Angeles, and she called me right away in Tucson. She had a mandatory lunch meeting at her lab in Pomona, but offered to meet me at five at the post office in Indio. Indio was six hours from Tucson, but how could I refuse? Cook's Petrel was a *Pterodroma* that nested on the islands off New Zealand—thirteen inches from head to tail, black M pattern across its gray wings and back. Except for its breeding period, the Cook's, like other gadfly petrels, spent its life wandering erratically around the Pacific. It fed on the wing and rarely alighted on water. Its status off the California coast was unclear. Over the years, several individuals had been photographed on pelagic trips, but none had ever been seen inland, none ever before at the Salton Sea.

When I arrived at the post office, Claire was sitting on the ground in the parking lot in the shade of her Land Rover, dressed in shorts and a loose khaki shirt and hiking boots, beautiful as ever. Since I'd last seen her months before, she'd cut her hair and had lost weight, but what struck me more than her appearance was that she was older, if thirty could be called old. Something had changed in her life. She tilted her head and shielded her eyes from the sun, then stood up, uncoiling her body from the earth. Her movements suggested patience, even restraint, but they belied the intensity of her personality: She was too smart to be casual or calm.

"Let's take my car," she said. "The light's going fast. We should hurry."

"Is it all right to leave my car here?"

"Park it on the street," Claire said. "No one will notice."

I drove my Corolla to a side road, fetched my scope and overnight bag from the trunk, and loaded what I had into the back of her Land Rover, beside the cooler and campstove and a sack of groceries from Vons. My binoculars were already around my neck.

"Who found the bird?" I asked when I got into the passenger side of the Rover.

"Strachen Donelly."

"You think the sighting is reliable?"

"One hundred percent. You know Strachen. He gave excellent directions on the tape."

"Is it far?"

"North shore, mouth of the White River. There are details. It's maybe twenty miles from here. He saw it late yesterday afternoon."

"So it might be gone already."

"A petrel could be anywhere," Claire said, handing me a piece of paper. "Here, you navigate."

• • • • •

In Tucson Claire was married to a man I had never met. She was a biologist, dark hair to her shoulders, a little overweight. We shared a ride to the research institute on Tanque Verde, thirty-five minutes each way, and spoke mostly about our ongoing projects monitoring the effects of radiation on flora and fauna in the Southwest. Our relationship was professional: she was a biologist, I a chemist. She never asked me a personal question and, though I knew she was married, never confessed anything about herself. Still, I was attuned to her moods. She was cheerful early in the mornings, moody and quieter in the afternoons. I couldn't know whether these differences were derived from what she had left at home or what she was going toward in the evening or whether they were related to what happened during the day at work. Always, though, morning or evening, I was surprised by her observations. She noticed wind directions and cloud formations, whether a street vendor had changed his prices, that a woman's baby carriage was missing a wheel. She paid attention to everything around her, except me.

She knew nothing about me. I lived alone, had never been married, and was at ease in my solitariness. I'd never needed to be with people and had few expectations or desires. My father had died when I was a child, and my mother, sensitive and repressed, lived a recluse's life in Boston. I'd done well at Haverford and earned a PhD in biochemistry from Princeton, after which I'd signed on with the government research program. The work was challenging, but I had little ambition. I spent my free time looking for birds.

I was an insomniac, though, and to appease the darkness, I watched the news on television at all hours of the night. Something was always happening somewhere, in another time zone where it was day—I might see a bomb fall into a building in the Gaza Strip or feel an earthquake shake a town in Indonesia or watch the unearthing of a mass grave in Rwanda. I witnessed not only the aftermath of events but the actual occurrence. Even if what I saw was videoed by a hand-held camera or filmed by a reporter, it was real. I felt as if I knew everything, everywhere all at once.

• • • • •

One day on a fact-finding excursion to a missile range west of Tucson—there were six of us; I was driving—a bird flew low through a tangle of palo verde and mesquite. It was long-tailed, grayish, bigger than a robin. A thrasher, I thought.

"Crissal Thrasher," Claire said.

I reconfigured what I'd seen: yes, larger than a Sage Thrasher, darker, too, not a Curve-billed Thrasher because it had a rusty undertail patch. Its bill was curved more like a California Thrasher, but that bird wasn't in Arizona.

"Do you know birds?" I asked.

"A little," she said. "Do you?"

"A little."

"I like thrashers because they're secretive," Claire said.

"So is the government," someone else said.

And we talked about the high contaminate levels we had found on our core sampling area, the radiation in the groundwater, the two dead lizards. But I was still thinking of how Claire had identified the Crissal Thrasher. How had she observed so much in so brief a moment? And why had she kept such a secret as bird-love from me for so long?

• • • • •

After that, on our daily commute Claire and I talked birds. She knew courtship rituals, food sources, habitat, range overlaps. She had pursued birds with a passion in quest of rarities, to Alaska, South Texas, Maine, Point Pelee and Key West. She had done boat trips off Hatteras and Monterey. What she knew was far beyond my ken. She had spent weeks once on a rocky island in the Bering Sea studying the behavioral relationship between Arctic Foxes and cliffside bird populations. Foxes had been introduced to kill rodents, but once the rodents were hard to find, the foxes preyed on the nests of kittiwakes and puffins. But the birds adapted, too, especially the kittiwakes. When a fox appeared, they flew away in alarm, leaving their nests exposed, and the fox was lured onto the cliff by the cries of abandoned fledglings. When he'd gone too far, the birds swooped back and knocked him from the cliff into the water two hundred feet below.

Compared to Claire, my skills were amateurish. But in all her travels and hours in the field and on the water, she had never seen a Cook's Petrel.

· · · · ·

We drove from Indio to Mecca, passed dozens of migrant workers hoeing lettuce in red and yellow and blue shirts and dresses, slid by the groves of date palms and oranges. To the west were the treeless, sun-weary Santa Rosas, and southeastward, the Orocopia Mountains and the Chocolates, which framed the valley on either side with a receding jagged horizon.

"How is work?" Claire asked.

"I can't complain."

"You never do. No new discoveries?"

"We found radiation at Cabeza Prieta," I said, "but we knew we would."

"The government denies it?"

"You know the story. They pay for the research and then hide the results. What about you? Do you like the new job?"

"Oh, you know." She laughed and didn't elaborate.

I remembered last April when we were driving home—it was a Friday, and Claire was at the wheel. She'd slowed for traffic at a red light. It was hot. Neither of us liked air-conditioning so the windows were open. A Cactus Wren was singing in a gully nearby. My arm was slung out on the window ledge. Her hand was on the stick shift between us. "My husband got promoted," she said. "We're moving to Los Angeles."

The Cactus Wren sang again. The light changed, and the cars ahead of us moved forward. I smelled exhaust. I remember the colors around me faded—green palm trees, red neon, the blue sign of a bar. It was the first mention of her husband. I conjured up questions to ask: What about your job? How can you leave the desert? Is this what you want? But I asked nothing. We passed through the green light and stopped again in the dry heat.

"Where from here?" she asked.

I roused myself from the pointless memory and looked at the directions. "Proceed to Mecca," I said. "Then we turn right."

Mecca was a few rundown pastel buildings—a general store, a gas station, and a café. The houses and trailers had trellises covered with brilliant red bougainvillea, and in the dirt yards were empty fruit crates stacked high.

"Turn on Road 42," I said. "Go a half mile to an adobe house. There'll be a bridge. Turn left toward the sea."

"I told you the directions were clear," Claire said.

"They don't show us the bird," I said. "Where is the water?"

Through the windshield the mountains were visible, sunlit on one side of the valley, shadowed on the other. There was no sea, only the absence of trees where the water must have been, rows of date palms in the fading light, and the enormous, wide sky.

· · · · ·

After Claire left Tucson, I was lonely at the institute, and I focused on my projects with a vengeance. I proved chromatic genes had been altered in rattlesnakes, that the petals of cactus flowers were contaminated, that Verdins were sick, but so what if genetic predispositions had been altered for generations? The government was silent. No accounting would be made, no guilt assigned to responsible parties, nothing would change. I knew my work suffered.

Weekends I went to canyons in the mountains and camped— Cave Creek in the Chiricahuas, Madera in the Santa Ritas, French Joe in the Whetstones. In the mornings I found Sulphur-bellied Flycatcher, Grace's Warbler, and Hepatic Tanager, and in the afternoons I read in the sun and let the heat erode my body. At night I listened to the soft calls of poorwills and the Elf Owl's chattering song.

Always there were other events in the world: a train crash in Rhodesia, the assassination of the prime minister in Norway, a wildfire in the Carpathian Mountains.

And Claire was gone.

•　•　•　•　•

The Land Rover raised dust behind us on the dirt track. Ahead was the adobe house and to our left the steel bridge appeared. We clanked across it and ran a hundred yards or so along a broken fenceline. The smell of orange blossoms was thick on the breeze. A narrow lane opened up. Claire threaded the Land Rover between a tangle of mesquite and a broken-down Ford parked in the weeds by a canal.

"Is this right?" I asked.

"You have the directions."

"They don't say anything about after the bridge."

We proceeded to a nearly dry alkaline pond where four Black-necked Stilts dipped their long bills into the scum. A few peeps flew up and swerved over the canal. We climbed a low rise, maybe ten feet, and there before us was the sea, a great blue-gray sheen without wind or sunlight. High, white cirrus clouds were reflected in the water, and the mountains in the distance on both sides were shrouded in a blue haze.

The sea lay in a sink created eons ago by the uplifting and erosion of the mountains. The original river, now called the Colorado, had silted in and changed its course eastward, leaving the Salton Basin without water. For thousands of years nothing happened. But history proceeded. The West was settled and grew; California had a good climate and became the most populous state. It was also a food producer, and at the turn of the last century, the U.S. Army Corps of Engineers decided to construct an irrigation canal to the Imperial Valley. Typically, the government miscalculated, and during a high spring run-off, the river cut a new channel before the canal was ready. For eighteen months the Colorado River flooded into the Salton Basin, and a new sea was born.

In the winnowing light, this was the place we'd come to, and Claire drove ahead to the collar of gray sand bordered on either side by thick saltillos.

"Strachen saw the bird here," Claire said. "From the beach."

Ducks and grebes floated on the near sheen, and a few gulls whirled in the air above us and out over the water. We got out and scanned the sea with binoculars. The near birds were familiar—wigeons, coots, shovelers, cormorants. A small flock of sandpipers flew eastward through the circle of my glasses.

"Do you see anything farther out? " Claire asked.

"Terns and gulls," I said. "And a Black Skimmer. More gulls. Cormorants."

"Let's set up the scopes."

We set up our tripods and scopes on the rise behind the beach. My Questar gave good resolution to forty power, and through it the indistinguishable birds far out became Common Terns, Black Skimmers, and Cinnamon Teal. Three White-faced Ibises flew as silhouettes against the paling hills.

"Nothing unusual," Claire said. "Do you agree?"

"What was farther out is closer," I said, "but now there are more birds farther still."

"Like stars, when you look through the scope at the night sky," Claire said. "But the petrel has an irregular, bounding flight. We might be able to see that."

"If it's there."

"Yes, if it were there."

The sun vanished from the high clouds, and without the refracted light, the sea diminished to gray. I saw no bounding arcs, no birds I could identify, and while Claire kept looking, I abandoned my scope and walked down to the shore. The smell of acrid, brackish brine rose to my nostrils, but I took off my shoes and socks—I already had shorts on—and waded out around the saltillos at the edge of the beach. The water was as warm as the air. On the other side of the brush, the irrigation canal fed in, and there was a cove filled with drowned trees. Before the sea was filled, before the land had become orange groves, before chemicals had leeched in from irrigation, this must have been a riparian woodland fed by springs. Now it was a wasteland, the bare branches of the trees spidering into the air, with herons and cormorants perched on them like huge, grotesque, faintly colored leaves. I felt as if I had stepped into a world already destroyed.

And why did I perceive it so? Was this dark interpretation the creation of my lonely soul? Had I let myself be affected by tenuous conversations with Claire, reading into her words the meanings I wished them to have and yearning for what was not possible? Or was it purely the moment *now*, being with Claire again, that conjured up these feelings? Her desire to know and see birds was something I had once thought was a bond between us, but I sensed now it was a division.

I imagined an earthquake happening at that moment in Malaysia, or a train wreck in France, children starving in Ethiopia—yes, these may have happened. Something like these events happened all the time. But all I knew, really, was the world before my eyes—the cove, the reflected orange of the clouds, the rim of blue mountains. I saw a few date palms with their spiky fronds silhouetted against the barren hills, the dead trees in front of me with a few herons sitting on the branches, the darkening shore beyond.

"Slater?"

Claire's voice came to me from the other side of the saltillos.

"Right here," I said.

"Look west, flying low."

I raised my glasses. "How far out?"

"Three o'clock, against the hills."

I waded out clear of the brush and lifted my glasses. Dark birds, backlit, winged over the water. I made out gulls and terns and dark birds on the water.

"Do you see the bird I see?"

"The light isn't very good. Are you seeing the petrel?"

I circled the saltillos to where she was, and she raised up from her scope. "I saw a possible possible," she said. "A different pattern of flight…"

"I didn't see what you saw."

"You're right, though. The light isn't good enough to be positive." She collapsed the legs of the tripod and leaned the scope against the fender of the Land Rover. "Are you hungry?" she asked. "I bought ham-and-cheese sandwiches, potato salad, and beer."

It had not occurred to me to be hungry, and I was surprised by her casual tone and the ease with which she let the petrel go.

"I could drink a beer," I said.

She raised the back of the Land Rover and got two Coronas from the cooler. "So there's tomorrow morning," she said, "but I have to leave by nine to be back at the lab."

"I have accumulated leave," I said, "so I took the whole day."

She opened the beers and handed one to me. "But you're going back?"

"Yes."

"I mean, you're staying at the institute. You're frustrated, but you won't quit."

I drank more beer. "It's what I know. What choice do I have?"

"You have infinite choices."

There was a silence, and we stood looking out, sipping our beers. Lights were coming on the shore across from us, tiny points drifting over the water.

"My husband was never promoted," Claire said. "I wanted to quit, so I did."

"Why did you say he was, then?"

She turned toward me, but her expression was unclear.

"I have to pee," she said.

She set her beer on the bumper and walked past the Land Rover and up over the rise.

I climbed onto the hood of the Rover and rested my back against the windshield. The beer was warming, and I drank it quickly and stared out over the paling sea. There was a wisp of orange on the surface, the soft lapping of the waves, insects chirring far away and near. Ducks and coots squawked in the shallows. On the east shore, a train was barely visible, coming toward Mecca. A star or two emerged from the blue that hovered over me.

I waited and closed my eyes, and I must have dozed for a few minutes because when I opened my eyes it was night. Insects were chirring in the saltillos, but the birds were silent. I watched the red blinking light of an airplane cross among the stars. Claire was leaning into the fender of the Land Rover, but in the darkness I couldn't see her well.

"Do you love me?" she asked.

I sat up from the windshield. "You're married."

"Is that an answer?"

"Isn't it?"

"All that time driving together, you never called me."

"You never called me," I said.

"I did today. When I heard about this bird, I thought you might meet me."

"Today there was an earthquake in China," I said. I looked out over the sea to the faraway lights of towns along the black shore.

Claire walked around to the grille and climbed up on her hands and knees onto the hood. "What do you feel, Slater? Do you feel anything?"

I didn't know how to answer.

"Don't turn away. Look at me."

She raised up so she was on her knees and unbuttoned her shirt. Beneath it she was naked, and her skin was pale in the warm air. Her breasts were luminous. I don't know what gave her the courage to risk herself in this way, but I had to look at her.

She took her shirt off and scrabbled toward me. "What do you see?"

Again I didn't answer.

She unsnapped my shorts and pulled them down. "Is this all right?" she asked.

I didn't resist. I felt the warm air slide over my skin.

"Let me," she said.

She touched me. I was afraid of falling and wanted to fall. I was afraid to move. The insects, the lights of towns, the stars dissipated into one sensation, and for the first time in my life I felt the eerie helplessness of desire.

• • • • •

We spent the night on the hood of the Land Rover, and at dawn we dressed and heated water on the campstove and made coffee in a sieve. The air was heavy with dew. The sun threw down its wash of pink into the mountains, and across the water the pale, faraway colors of houses appeared. The sea was flat and windless and reflected the sky.

We took up our vigil on the beach and scanned through our scopes back and forth, back and forth across clouds of gulls and terns already feeding. We were looking for the irregular, bounding flight of the petrel that may never have been there.

ANZA-BORREGO DESERT STATE PARK

All that remains of the adobe cabin called Yaquitepec—where from 1930 to 1947 Marshal South and his wife, Tanya, raised their three children on the windswept peak of Ghost Mountain in the Anza-Borrego area of California's Colorado Desert—is an eerie rusted bedframe, several cisterns once used to catch rainwater, an arched doorframe, and the base of an adobe oven. While he was living there, South wrote monthly columns for *Desert Magazine* chronicling his family's "experiment in primitive living."

Anza-Borrego Desert State Park spans 586,304 acres and is the largest of California's state parks. The bowl of the desert and the surrounding mountains offer a stunning variety of terrain, from wildflower-rich springtime valleys to creosote bush scrub to dry slot canyons in the badlands to palm oases. In Anza-Borrego, the endangered bighorn sheep for which the park is partially named (*borrego*) abound, as do roadrunners, iguanas, red diamond rattlesnakes, and kit foxes. Humans make use of the park's campgrounds and interpretive programs, and some make the mile-long hike to the top of Ghost Mountain to visit the ruins of Yaquitepec, where they can ponder the peace and the hardship of a home made on a desert peak.

MARSHAL SOUTH

from *MARSHAL SOUTH AND THE GHOST MOUNTAIN CHRONICLES*

Desert Diary 2

March 1940, February at Yaquitepec

The clear, metallic calling of quail in the grey dawn. There is something particularly fascinating and "deserty" in the call note of the quail. On Ghost Mountain our quail have confidence. They seem to know well that no gun will ever be raised against them. And they repay our protection with friendliness.

Sometimes in the nesting season they bring their energetic, scurrying broods on exploring expeditions right around the house; the lively youngsters, looking for all the world like diminutive ostriches, padding and pecking everywhere, while the old birds patrol proudly on watchful guard, or dust themselves luxuriously in the dry earth at the base of our garden terrace. There are few birds more handsome and decorative than the quail.

They nest regularly on Ghost Mountain, but not often do we discover where. They are adept at concealment. Once the glint of the sun upon broken eggshells betrayed an old nest that had been made scarcely 18 inches from our foot-trail. Screened by a bush and under the shelter of a granite boulder it had been hidden perfectly. Scores of times we must have tramped past, almost scattering gravel upon the sitting bird. But we had never glimpsed her.

Dawns decked with grey cloud and sometimes rain-streaked are a feature of our season now. There is nothing "regular" about the desert. Uncertainty is its keynote and its eternal fascination. Last night the drumming beat of rain made music on the iron roof of Yaquitepec and this morning we woke to a shower-splashed dawn. The sky to eastward was piled high with scudding mountains of white and grey mist, their summits tinged pink in the rays of the rising sun.

Away out above the lowland desert, sun and cloud-wrack fought a battle for supremacy. About nine a.m. the sun won through to complete victory. Against a backdrop of silver showers that screened the footslopes of the Laguna range the desert flashed up in dazzling brilliance. And over all, like a jeweled scimitar, its hilt in the desert and its point upon the summit of Granite Mountain, a mighty rainbow arched the sky. It will be a warm and brilliant day today. Tomorrow there may be snow. *Quién sabe!* This is the desert.

February touches always a warm spot in our hearts. For it was in a February that we first came to Ghost Mountain and set up the beginning of our desert home. That, too, was a year ordered in the desert's consistently irregular fashion. For spring was exceptionally early. Warm breezes blew through the junipers and the days were hot.

We like often to go back in memory to that day. Tanya carried an axe and a can of pineapple. I carried a rolled seven-by-nine palmetto tent. Already, on exploring ascents, we had made seven previous climbs on as many different days seeking an easy trail to the summit. And we had convinced ourselves that there was no easy trail. On this day of "homefounding" we cast caution to the winds and made a frontal attack, toiling upward through the cholla and the mescal bayonets and the frowning boulders and the slides of loose, broken rock.

It was a savage climb. But at last we reached the east-facing slope of the little sub-ridge that we had named Yaquitepec. We dumped our burdens in the shade of a juniper and dropped breathless beside them. A tiny, jewel-eyed, turquoise-hued lizard, sunning itself on a weathered hunk of granite, cocked its head at us speculatively. Past our feet, through the pattern of shade flung by the branches above us, a huge pinacate beetle, solemn and dignified as an old rabbi in a long frock coat, ambled, wrapped in meditation. Overhead against the dazzling glint of the blue sky a lone buzzard wheeled. All about was the drowsy hush of peace. "It's heaven," Tanya said softly. "Oh, why didn't we come here years and years ago?"

There was work, that first day, as well as climbing. Among the rocks and sagebrush and mescals that crowded around us there was no space even for a tiny tent, there was scarce room to pick wary footsteps. Space had to be made.

Mescals are stubborn things at times. Especially when attacked with such an unsuitable weapon as an axe. And the chollas were frankly hostile and had no intention of being evicted without wreaking vengeance. I chopped and hacked and Tanya carried, lugging the ousted vegetation and heaving it off to one side in a bristling heap. It is astonishing how heavy a swollen-leaved, lusty mescal plant can be. And what a devilish thing it is to carry. Sweat ran down our faces and our bodies. Before beginning we had piled our clothes in the cleft of a great rock. Nevertheless, we were desperately hot. We were glad enough, after a while, to call a halt. We sat down in the thin shade of our friendly juniper and stove in the head of the pineapple can with the axe. We munched the juicy yellow slices and drank the syrup. Ever since that day we have had a particular affection for pineapple.

A space to accommodate a seven-by-nine tent doesn't sound excessive. But by the time we had removed all the rocks and shrubbery we felt as though we had cleared at least an acre. Then we set up the tent. That was triumph. We stored the axe and the empty pineapple can inside it, carefully tied the entrance flap shut, and weary but happy, turned to go back to our base camp at the foot of the mountain.

It was late. The sun had already reached the jagged mountain crests to westward, and across the lowland desert to the east fantastic shadows were gathering about the buttes and washes. We knew we would have to hurry, for we had to run the gantlet of a myriad bristling lances before we reached the mountain foot. It wouldn't be a pleasant thing to attempt in the dark.

Despite wearied muscles, we forced ourselves to speed. At the edge of the cliff, just before we swung over to tackle the long downward trail, we paused to look back. There it stood, the brave little brown tent, amidst a tangled desolation of rock and thorn. The long leagues of desert shadows were chill and purple behind it. It looked very tiny and lonely, standing there where never tent had stood before.

It brought a queer lump to our throats. "It's going to be *home*," Tanya said huskily. "It *is* home, already. I wonder why we didn't come here before?"

Then we scrambled away down the mountain to a campfire and welcome supper and bed. And that night, as we stretched weary limbs in our blankets and watched the march of the desert stars, coyotes sat on the ridges and yammered at us. And the wind came up across the long stretch of yucca-staked wilderness and skirled through the tall, dead mescal poles and through the junipers with eerie whisperings. But our hearts were warm. They were with that brave little tent, keeping guard amidst the mescals and the shadows and the wistful brown ghosts upon the summit, far above us.

That was in a February. Yes, we like February. It is a grand month.

· · · · ·

Desert Diary 7

August 1940, July at Yaquitepec

Heat! And the distant phantoms of mirage. Desert summer is with us now and Yaquitepec shimmers in the heat of a midday glare that is thirstily metallic. Birds cower, droop-winged and panting, in the shelter of the junipers; and upon the dry, scorching earth the snaky wands of the ocotillos throw sharp-edged shadows that are black as jet.

It is hot these days. But not too hot. The human system is adaptive; it adjusts speedily to its environment. The desert dweller becomes used to his summer with its tingling strike of dry sunshine. The heat that really sets him gasping and complaining is the humid choke of supposedly more favored sections.

There is a good deal of myth about the tenors of desert summer. It is born, most of it, from inexperience and from a curious American trait of deliberately refusing to conform to climatic conditions. The "old people" and the early Spaniards were wiser. It was not indolence but sound sense that created the midday siesta habit. With a common-sense adaptation to conditions. The desert in summer is as much a region of enchantment as at any other season, and has charms peculiar to itself.

Nowhere but in the desert, and in summer, can you see such magnificent cloud effects as those which tower into the hard, turquoise sky above the heat-dancing wastelands. These mighty mountains of dazzling white and ominous grey cease to be clouds. Rather they are the Titan sculptures of invisible gods. Sinister they are often. And awe inspiring. Small wonder that you will find no glib atheists among the dwellers of the unspoiled wasteland. Such things belong to the shadows of smoky walls; to the dulling thunder of machinery and the milling of tired crowds.

Out where the little thirsty winds run panting across the shoulders of sun-furnaced buttes there is no room for disbelief. The message is in the sky and in the wide sweep of the glowing earth. To Indian and to white man alike the mighty thunderheads that march across the blue vault, their crests lifting white into staggering immensity, their footsteps tracking league-long blots of indigo upon the panting earth and their voices calling each to each in hollow rumble, speak of the Great Spirit. The arrows of His wrath are in their hands and the rain of His infinite mercy is in their hearts. Atheists do not flourish in desert solitudes.

But the marching cloud giants that come stalking up out of the mystery of the Gulf of Cortez [California] are but one of the attractions of Yaquitepec in summer. There is the heat. Heat is not just "heat." It is something that grows upon one. It is fundamental with life. Desert heat is electric. Scientists, whose mission in life it is to make simple things as confusing as possible, will tell you that it is ultraviolet rays. Possibly! But shorter terms for it are life and health. The Indian knew nothing about ultraviolet rays. But he did know about health; before he was spoiled.

And some still remain unspoiled. The Tarahumara Indians of Mexico belong—or did belong, if they have not been changed within the last few years—to the unspoiled clan. One of the Tarahumara joys was to bask naked in the sun in temperatures that would almost frizzle a white man. And the Tarahumaras were noted for their endurance. One of their sports, indulged in by both men and women, was long distance running.

Perhaps it is another indication of how far and how shamelessly we of Yaquitepec have slipped from the skirts of civilization in that we also like to bask on the rocks in summer. Sometimes the rocks are pretty hot, and they have a damp appearance afterwards as though something had been flying on them. But as you lie there you do not think of these things. All you can feel is the tingle of life and of electricity striking healing rays through every bone of your body. Try it sometime; but little by little and gradually at first.

· · · · ·

Yesterday a whirlwind came and charged down upon the house in an attempt to scatter our shade ramada. These summer whirlwinds are mysterious things. You hear them coming up the mountain, roaring and grumbling. And, because of the absence of light soil among the rocks that would make dust, you can see nothing. It is like listening to the approach of a disembodied spirit; often not until it leaps upon you can you tell just where it is. Yesterday's was a big one. Rider and Rudyard were up on the garden terrace, watching the uncouth antics of Satan, the big black scaly lizard who makes his living up there catching flies. And all at once, from the shoulder of the mountain rim, there was a coughing roar. Rudyard took one peek at emptiness and twinkled brown heels in headlong flight for the house. Rider, with something of the spirit of a scientist, stood his ground, peering and squinting. He at least knew what the roaring invisible thing was. But he could not locate it.

Not until suddenly, a dead bush and a couple of dry mescal poles leaped into the air from just behind him and went sailing a hundred feet into the sky. And the next instant, as he crouched, grabbing at a big boulder for support, the thing yelled past him and fell upon the house. Doors banged and roof iron strained. There was the shrieking hiss of wind through the porch screens, and the tied bundles of mescal poles of the ramada roof surged and rattled as Tanya came darting out, snatching at wildly slamming window shutters, Rudyard yelling lustily at her heels. Then the thing was gone, hurtling away in a wild leap back over the mountain rim. We saw dry bushes, bits of paper, an empty sack and the two mescal poles hung grotesquely in the sky—far up and still spinning. Then the hot stillness flowed in again; the wildly threshing ocotillos quieted. Satan came out of his rock cleft and waddled his fat metallic sheened bulk back onto the terrace, headed for a new fly victim. Rider came down the trail blinking the sand grains out of his eyes. "Phooey!" he said. "That was the biggest one ever. You ought to put some more screws in the roof iron, Daddy."

But it is not often that our desert twisters are so large or hit us so squarely. Usually they are just phantoms, rushing out of nowhere and tearing off into silence along the ridges. We feel rather kindly towards them. Their mood of mystery suits the atmosphere of Ghost Mountain.

Summertime is "bug time," it is true. But really there are worse bugs in other sections than the picturesque crew that inhabit the desert. The scorpions perhaps are the most fearsome. Especially the big ones, four to six inches in length and with a corresponding spread of claw. But these big fellows are in about the same proportion in the scorpion world as are city gangsters in our own social setup. The sting of these magnates we have so far managed to avoid. But the venom of the rank and file—little fellows ranging in size from an inch upward—is no more painful than that of a honey bee.

For a long time, remembering the prowess of the scorpions of Durango, the hot country of Jalisco and of other parts of Mexico, we trod in fear of them. Then one day Tanya, groping for a new typewriter ribbon in the depths of a box filled with old letters, was stung. Her prompt recovery from the pain, with no ill effects, exploded the scorpion myth. Both of us have been stung on several occasions since and we pay little attention to it. This is no attempt to whitewash the scorpion tribe. Some of the Mexican "hot-country" ones, especially where children are concerned, are deadly. The small Ghost Mountain variety is practically harmless.

The centipedes however are not so pleasant; especially when the spirit moves the six and eight inch ones to take tight rope exercises along the roof beams over the beds. The big ones are "bad hombres," to be wary of. But here again the little fellows are in the majority. Their chief sin, as far as we are concerned, is that being flat and slender they can squirm through negligible crevices; and therefore the covers of water cisterns and all other regions barred to bugs must be exceptionally tight fitting.

And this also goes for the ants. Our Ghost Mountain ants are well behaved and seldom drink to excess. Except in the hot reaches of summer. Then they go crazy for moisture. They will go anywhere, and to any lengths, to obtain it. It's not enough to screen a water cistern. It has to be absolutely ant tight or it is likely, at the end of summer, to contain less water than dead ants. In a way they seem a bit confused in their knowledge of water. They will walk down into it and under it until they drown, as humans might walk to destruction under some heavy, invisible gas. Their habits in this respect are annoying. But with food supplies they give us little trouble. We have found a certain defense against them. When we first came to Ghost Mountain we religiously kept the legs of all food cupboards in tin pans filled with either water or kerosene. This was effective if properly attended to. But the pans were always running dry, or grass stems and wind blown twigs would make bridges for the marauders, so one day we shifted to the trick of just painting the legs with ordinary creosote. It worked marvels. It doesn't look particularly handsome, but it is 100 percent effective. And the painting is renewed only at long intervals. Not only ants but all sorts of other bugs give creosoted cupboard legs a wide berth.

The yellow glory of the Ghost Mountain mescal flowers has departed. But the seed pods which have succeeded the flowers are full and plump. They look like elongated green pecan nuts, arranged in bunches somewhat like small upstanding clusters of bananas. The mountain squirrels like them, and many of the mescal heads are already denuded of seed pods by their raidings.

We are watching anxiously for rain. Each day now, when the mighty thunderheads form upon the horizon and march in upon the shimmering glare of the wastelands, we watch them with hopeful eyes. But so far Ghost Mountain is not on their schedule. Their shadows fall black and mysterious over the distant buttes; their cannonading rolls across the wasteland and the black skirts of their local torrential downpours beat dust from a thirsty desert on our very borders. But the crest of Ghost Mountain they ignore. They will come, however, in time. Patience is a virtue that is a desert necessity. Mayhap they will come in August.

OLD TOWN SAN DIEGO STATE HISTORIC PARK

Helen Hunt Jackson's *Ramona* was a huge success when it was first published as a serial in 1884, and to this day it continues to be one of the most enduring romantic depictions of Mexican-era Southern California, as well as an early outcry against the mistreatment of California Indians. Here, drawn in rich, poetic prose, we see the dilapidated chapel of the fiery Father Gaspara—on the site of Junípero Serra's original San Diego Mission—where the Scottish-Native Ramona and her lover, Alessandro, come to be wed.

The popularity of Jackson's novel coincided with the arrival of the railroad in Southern California, and many tourists flocked west to view the sites depicted in the book. San Diego has some of the oldest Spanish-era roots in the state, as it was the site of the first Franciscan mission in California, founded in 1769. Today, Old Town San Diego State Historic Park provides historical presentations, reenactments, and museum displays to transport visitors back in time to the Mexican and early American periods, from 1821 to 1872—the era of *Ramona*. Historical landmarks include five original adobe buildings around the old plaza.

HELEN HUNT JACKSON
from *RAMONA*

The road on which they must go into old San Diego, where
Father Gaspara lived, was the public road from San Diego to
San Luis Rey, and they were almost sure to meet travellers on it.

But their fleet horses bore them so well, that it was not late
when they reached the town. Father Gaspara's house was at
the end of a long, low adobe building, which had served no
mean purpose in the old Presidio days, but was now fallen into
decay; and all its rooms, except those occupied by the Father,
had been long uninhabited. On the opposite side of the way, in
a neglected, weedy open, stood his chapel,—a poverty-stricken
little place, its walls imperfectly whitewashed, decorated by a
few coarse pictures and by broken sconces of looking-glass, res-
cued in their dilapidated condition from the Mission buildings
now gone utterly to ruin. In these had been put candle-holders
of common tin, in which a few cheap candles dimly lighted
the room. Everything about it was in unison with the atmosphere of the place,—the most profoundly melancholy in all
Southern California. Here was the spot where that grand old
Franciscan, Padre Junipero Serra, began his work, full of the
devout and ardent purpose to reclaim the wilderness and its
peoples to his country and his Church; on this very beach he
went up and down for those first terrible weeks, nursing the
sick, praying with the dying, and burying the dead, from the
pestilence-stricken Mexican ships lying in the harbor. Here he
baptized his first Indian converts, and founded his first Mission.
And the only traces now remaining of his heroic labors and
hard-won successes were a pile of crumbling ruins, a few old
olive-trees and palms; in less than another century even these
would be gone; returned into the keeping of that mother, the
earth, who puts no headstones at the sacredest of her graves.

Father Gaspara had been for many years at San Diego.
Although not a Franciscan, having, indeed, no especial love for
the order, he had been from the first deeply impressed by the
holy associations of the place. He had a nature at once fiery
and poetic; there were but three things he could have been,—a

soldier, a poet, or a priest. Circumstances had made him a priest; and the fire and the poetry which would have wielded the sword or kindled the verse, had he found himself set either to fight or to sing, had all gathered into added force in his priestly vocation. The look of a soldier he had never quite lost,—neither the look nor the tread; and his flashing dark eyes, heavy black hair and beard, and quick elastic step, seemed sometimes strangely out of harmony with his priest's gown. And it was the sensitive soul of the poet in him which had made him withdraw within himself more and more, year after year, as he found himself comparatively powerless to do anything for the hundreds of Indians that he would fain have seen gathered once more, as of old, into the keeping of the Church. He had made frequent visits to them in their shifting refuges, following up family after family, band after band, that he knew; he had written bootless letter after letter to the Government officials of one sort and another, at Washington. He had made equally bootless efforts to win some justice, some protection for them, from officials nearer home; he had endeavored to stir the Church itself to greater efficiency in their behalf. Finally, weary, disheartened, and indignant with that intense, suppressed indignation which the poetic temperament alone can feel, he had ceased,—had said, "It is of no use; I will speak no word; I am done; I can bear no more!" and settling down into the routine of his parochial duties to the little Mexican and Irish congregation of his charge in San Diego, he had abandoned all effort to do more for the Indians than visit their chief settlements once or twice a year, to administer the sacraments. When fresh outrages were brought to his notice, he paced his room, plucked fiercely at his black beard, with ejaculations, it is to be feared, savoring more of the camp than the altar; but he made no effort to do anything. Lighting his pipe, he would sit down on the old bench in his tile-paved veranda, and smoke by the hour, gazing out on the placid water of the deserted harbor, brooding, ever brooding, over the wrongs he could not redress.

A few paces off from his door stood the just begun walls of a fine brick church, which it had been the dream and pride of his heart to see builded, and full of worshippers. This, too, had failed. With San Diego's repeatedly vanishing hopes and dreams of prosperity had gone this hope and dream of Father Gaspara's. It looked, now, as if it would be indeed a waste of money to build a costly church on this site. Sentiment, however sacred and loving towards the dead, must yield to the demands of the living. To build a church on the ground where Father Junipero first trod and labored, would be a work to which no Catholic could be indifferent; but there were other and more pressing claims to be met first. This was right. Yet the sight of these silent walls, only a few feet high, was a sore one to Father Gaspara,—a daily cross, which he did not find grow lighter as he paced up and down his veranda, year in and year out, in the balmy winter and cool summer of that magic climate.

"Majella, the chapel is lighted; but that is good!" exclaimed Alessandro, as they rode into the silent plaza. "Father Gaspara must be there;" and jumping off his horse, he peered in at the uncurtained window. "A marriage, Majella,—a marriage!" he cried, hastily returning. "This, too, is good fortune. We need not to wait long."

When the sacristan whispered to Father Gaspara that an Indian couple had just come in, wishing to be married, the Father frowned. His supper was waiting; he had been out all day, over at the old Mission olive-orchard, where he had not found things to his mind; the Indian man and wife whom he hired to take care of the few acres the Church yet owned there had been neglecting the Church lands and trees, to look after their own. The father was vexed, tired, and hungry, and the expression with which he regarded Alessandro and Ramona, as they came towards him, was one of the least prepossessing of which his dark face was capable. Ramona, who had never knelt to any priest save the gentle Father Salvierderra, and who had supposed that all priests must look, at least, friendly, was shocked at the sight of the impatient visage confronting her. But, as his first glance fell on Ramona, Father Gaspara's expression changed.

"What is all this!" he thought; and as quick as he thought it, he exclaimed, in a severe tone, looking at Ramona, "Woman, are you an Indian?"

"Yes, Father," answered Ramona, gently. "My mother was an Indian."

"Ah! half-breed!" thought Father Gaspara. "It is strange how sometimes one of the types will conquer, and sometimes another! But this is no common creature;" and it was with a look of new interest and sympathy on his face that he proceeded with the ceremony,—the other couple, a middle-aged Irishman, with his more than middle-aged bride, standing quietly by, and looking on with a vague sort of wonder in their ugly, impassive faces, as if it struck them oddly that Indians should marry.

The book of the marriage-records was kept in Father Gaspara's own rooms, locked up and hidden even from his old housekeeper. He had had bitter reason to take this precaution. It had been for more than one man's interest to cut leaves out of this old record, which dated back to 1769, and had many pages written full in the hand of Father Junipero himself.

As they came out of the chapel, Father Gaspara leading the way, the Irish couple shambling along shamefacedly apart from each other, Alessandro, still holding Ramona's hand in his, said, "Will you ride, dear? It is but a step."

"No, thanks, dear Alessandro, I would rather walk," she replied; and Alessandro slipping the bridles of the two horses over his left arm, they walked on. Father Gaspara heard the question and answer, and was still more puzzled.

"He speaks as a gentleman speaks to a lady," he mused. "What does it mean? Who are they?"

Father Gaspara was a well-born man, and in his home in Spain had been used to associations far superior to any which he had known in his Californian life. A gentle courtesy of tone and speech, such as that with which Alessandro had addressed Ramona, was not often heard in his parish. When they entered his house, he again regarded them both attentively. Ramona wore on her head the usual black shawl of the Mexican women. There was nothing distinctive, to the Father's eye, in her figure or face. In the dim light of the one candle,—Father Gaspara allowed himself no luxuries,—the exquisite coloring of her skin and the deep blue of her eyes were not to be seen. Alessandro's tall figure and dignified bearing were not uncommon. The Father had seen many as fine-looking Indian men. But his voice was remarkable, and he spoke better Spanish than was wont to be heard from Indians.

"Where are you from?" said the Father, as he held his pen poised in hand, ready to write their names in the old raw-hide-bound book.

"Temecula, Father," replied Alessandro.

Father Gaspara dropped his pen. "The village the Americans drove out the other day?" he cried.

"Yes, Father."

Father Gaspara sprang from his chair, took refuge from his excitement, as usual, in pacing the floor, "Go! go! I'm done with you! It's all over," he said fiercely to the Irish bride and groom, who had given him their names and their fee, but were still hanging about irresolute, not knowing if all were ended or not. "A burning shame! The most dastardly thing I have seen yet in this land forsaken of God!" cried the Father. "I saw the particulars of it in the San Diego paper yesterday." Then, coming to a halt in front of Alessandro, he exclaimed: "The paper said that the Indians were compelled to pay all the costs of the suit; that the sheriff took their cattle to do it. Was that true?"

"Yes, Father," replied Alessandro.

The Father strode up and down again, plucking at his beard. "What are you going to do?" he said. "Where have you all gone? There were two hundred in your village the last time I was there."

"Some have gone over into Pachanga," replied Alessandro, "some to San Pasquale, and the rest to San Bernardino."

"Body of Jesus! man! But you take it with philosophy!" stormed Father Gaspara.

Alessandro did not understand the word "philosophy," but he knew what the Father meant. "Yes, Father," he said doggedly. "It is now twenty-one days ago. I was not so at first. There is nothing to be done."

Ramona held tight to Alessandro's hand. She was afraid of this fierce, black-bearded priest, who dashed back and forth, pouring out angry invectives.

"The United States Government will suffer for it!" he continued. "It is a Government of thieves and robbers! God will punish them. You will see; they will be visited with a curse,—a curse in their borders; their sons and their daughters shall be desolate! But why do I prate in these vain words? My son, tell me your names again;" and he seated himself once more at the table where the ancient marriage-record lay open.

After writing Alessandro's name, he turned to Ramona. "And the woman's?" he said.

Alessandro looked at Ramona. In the chapel he had said simply, "Majella." What name should he give more?

Without a second's hesitation, Ramona answered, "Majella. Majella Phail is my name."

She pronounced the word "Phail," slowly. It was new to her. She had never seen it written; as it lingered on her lips, the Father, to whom also it was a new word, misunderstood it, took it to be in two syllables, and so wrote it.

The last step was taken in the disappearance of Ramona. How should any one, searching in after years, find any trace of Ramona Ortegna, in the woman married under the name of "Majella Fayeel"?

"No, no! Put up your money, son," said Father Gaspara, as Alessandro began to undo the knots of the handkerchief in which his gold was tied. "Put up your money. I'll take no money from a Temecula Indian. I would the Church had money to give you. Where are you going now?"

"To San Pasquale, Father."

"Ah! San Pasquale! The head man there has the old pueblo paper," said Father Gaspara. "He was showing it to me the other day. That will, it may be, save you there. But do not trust to it, son. Buy yourself a piece of land as the white man buys his. Trust to nothing."

Alessandro looked anxiously in the Father's face. "How is that, Father?" he said. "I do not know."

"Well, their rules be thick as the crabs here on the beach," replied Father Gaspara; "and, faith, they appear to me to be backwards of motion also, like the crabs: but the lawyers understand. When you have picked out your land, and have the money, come to me, and I will go with you and see that you are not cheated in the buying, so far as I can tell; but I myself am at my wit's ends with their devices. Farewell, son! Farewell, daughter!" he said, rising from his chair. Hunger was again getting the better of sympathy in Father Gaspara, and as he sat down to his long deferred supper, the Indian couple faded from his mind; but after supper was over, as he sat smoking his pipe on the veranda, they returned again, and lingered in his thoughts,—lingered strangely, it seemed to him; he could not shake off the impression that there was something unusual about the woman. "I shall hear of them again, some day," he thought. And he thought rightly.

PERMISSIONS

Allende, Isabel. Excerpt from *Zorro* by Isabel Allende and transl. by Margaret Sayers Peden. © 2005 by Isabel Allende. English translation © 2005 by HarperCollins Publishers. The use of "Zorro" and other characters created by Johnson McCulley has been licensed and authorized by Zorro Productions, Inc. © 2005 by Zorro Productions, Inc. All rights reserved. Zorro is a trademark owned by Zorro Productions, Inc., Berkeley, CA. Reprinted by permission of HarperCollins Publishers.

Asisara, Lorenzo. "The Assassination of Padre Andrés Quintana by the Indians of Mission Santa Cruz in 1812: The Narrative of Lorenzo Asisara" translated by Edward D. Castillo, from *California History,* Volume 68, Number 3, 1989. © 1989 by the Regents of the University of California. Reprinted by permission of University of California Press.

Atherton, Gertrude. "Natalie Ivanhoff: A Memory of Fort Ross" from *The Splendid Idle Forties: Stories of Old California* by Gertrude Atherton. New York: The Macmillan Company, 1902.

Barbas, Samantha. Excerpt from *The First Lady of Hollywood: A Biography of Louella Parsons* by Samantha Barbas. © 2005 by Samantha Barbas. Reprinted by permission of University of California Press.

Barnes, Lewis. Excerpt from *Take Me to the River: Fishing, Swimming, and Dreaming on the San Joaquin,* edited by Joell Hallowell and Coke Hallowell. © 2010 by Joell Hallowell and Coke Hallowell. Reprinted by permission of Heyday.

Bidwell, John. Excerpt from *Echoes of the Past: An Account of the First Emigrant Train to California, Fremont in the Conquest of California, The Discovery of Gold and Other Reminiscences* by John Bidwell. Chico, CA: Chico Advertiser, 1900.

Brewer, William. Excerpt from *Up and Down California in 1860–1864: The Journal of William H. Brewer* by William H. Brewer. © 2003 by the Regents of the University of California. Reprinted by permission of University of California Press.

Carrillo, Leo. Excerpt from *The California I Love* by Leo Carrillo. © 1961 by Leo Carrillo, renewed 1989 by Marie A. Carrillo Delphy. Reprinted with the permission of Simon and Schuster Publishing Group. All rights reserved.

Cendrars, Blaise. Excerpt from *Gold: The Marvellous History of General John Augustus Sutter* by Blaise Cendrars and translated by Nina Rootes. © 1960 by Editions Denoël. English translation © 1982 by Nina Rootes. Reprinted by permission of Peter Owen, Ltd., London.

Coolbrith, Ina. "Copa De Oro (The California Poppy)" from *Songs from the Golden Gate* by Ina Coolbrith. Boston: Houghton Mifflin, 1895.

Dana, Richard Henry Jr. Excerpt from *Two Years Before the Mast* by Richard Henry Dana Jr. Boston: Houghton Mifflin, 1911.

Dawson, William Leon. "Spotted Owl" from *The Birds of California* by William Leon Dawson. San Diego: South Moulton Co., 1923.

de Angulo, Jaime. Excerpt from "First Seeing the Coast" from *The Lariat and Other Writings* by Jaime de Angulo, edited by David Miller, Counterpoint Press. © 2009 by Gui Mayo. Reprinted by permission of Gui Mayo and David Miller.

Derby, George Horatio. Excerpt from *Phoenixiana; or, Sketches and Burlesques* by George Horatio Derby. New York: D. Appleton and Co., 1855.

Didion, Joan. "Many Mansions" from *The White Album* by Joan Didion. © 1979 by Joan Didion. Reprinted by permission of Farrar, Straus and Giroux, LLC.

Everson, William. "Steelhead" from *The Masks of Drought* by William Everson. © 1980 by William Everson. Santa Barbara, CA: Black Sparrow Press.

Hackett, Josephine, and Henry Singleton. Excerpts from *Allensworth, the Freedom Colony: A California African American Township* by Alice C. Royal with Mickey Ellinger and Scott Braley. © 2008 by Heyday Institute. Reprinted by permission of Heyday.

Heller, Peter. Excerpt from *Kook: What Surfing Taught Me About Love, Life, and Catching the Perfect Wave* by Peter Heller. © 2010 by Peter Heller. Reprinted with the permission of Simon & Schuster Publishing Group from the Free Press edition. All rights reserved.

Hill, Julia Butterfly. Excerpt from *The Legacy of Luna* by Julia Butterfly Hill. © 2000 by Julia Butterfly Hill. Reprinted by permission of HarperCollins Publishers.

Houston, James D. Excerpt from *Snow Mountain Passage* by James D. Houston. © 2001 by James D. Houston. Used by permission of Alfred A. Knopf, an imprint of Knopf Doubleday Publishing Group, a division of Random House LLC. All rights reserved.

Jackson, Helen Hunt. Excerpt from *Ramona* by Helen Hunt Jackson. Boston: Little, Brown and Co., 1884.

Jaeger, Edmund C. Excerpt from "California Road Runner" from *Desert Wildlife* by Edmund C. Jaeger. © 1950, 1961 by the Board of Trustees of the Leland Stanford Jr. University, renewed 1989 by the Executor of the Estate of the Author. All rights reserved. Used with the permission of Stanford University Press, www.sup.org.

Jeffers, Robinson. "Birds" and "The Cycle" from *The Collected Poetry of Robinson Jeffers*, Volume 1, 1920–1928, edited by Tim Hunt. © 1938 Robinson Jeffers, renewed 1966 by Garth and Donnan Jeffers. All rights reserved. Used with the permission of Stanford University Press, www.sup.org.

Kerouac, Jack. Excerpt from *The Dharma Bums* by Jack Kerouac. © 1958 by Jack Kerouac, renewed 1986 by Stella Kerouac and Jan Kerouac. Used by permission of Penguin, a division of Penguin Group (USA) LLC.

Leese, Rosalía Vallejo. "Original Transcript of Interview of Rosalía Vallejo by Henry Cerruti," translated by Rose Marie Beebe and Robert M. Senkewicz, from *Testimonios: Early California through the Eyes of Women, 1815–1848*, edited by Rose Marie Beebe and Robert M. Senkewicz. © 2006 by Rose Marie Beebe and Robert M. Senkewicz. Reprinted by permission of Heyday.

London, Jack. Excerpt from *The Valley of the Moon* by Jack London. New York: The Macmillan Company, 1913.

Margolin, Malcolm. Excerpt from "Building a Roundhouse" by Malcolm Margolin from *News from Native California*, Volume 19, Number 4, Summer 2006. © 2006 by Malcolm Margolin. Reprinted by permission of Heyday.

Marshall, James. "Marshall's Own Account of the Gold Discovery" by James W. Marshall. *Century Magazine*, Volume 41, Number 4, February 1891.

Mayfield, Thomas Jefferson. Excerpt from *Indian Summer: Traditional Life among the Choinumne Indians of California's San Joaquin Valley* by Thomas Jefferson Mayfield. Berkeley, CA: Heyday, 1993. First published in 1929.

Miller, Joaquin. "The Battle of Castle Crags" by Joaquin Miller. San Francisco: The Traveler, 1894.

Muir, John. "The Bee-Pastures" from *The Mountains of California* by John Muir. New York: The Century Co., 1894.

Nelson, Kent. "Irregular Flight" by Kent Nelson from *Getting Over the Color Green: Contemporary Environmental Literature of the Southwest*, edited by Scott Slovic. Tucson, AZ: University of Arizona Press, 2001. Originally published in *Southwestern American Literature*, Volume 21, Number 1, Fall 1995. © 1995 by Kent Nelson. Reprinted by permission of the author.

Preston, Richard. Excerpts from "Nameless" and "The Kingdom" from *The Wild Trees: A Story of Passion and Daring* by Richard Preston. © 2007 by Richard Preston. Used by permission of Random House, an imprint and division of Random House LLC. All rights reserved.

Singleton, Henry, and Josephine Hackett. Excerpts from *Allensworth, the Freedom Colony: A California African American Township* by Alice C. Royal with Mickey Ellinger and Scott Braley. © 2008 by Heyday Institute. Reprinted by permission of Heyday.

South, Marshal. "Desert Diary 2" and "Desert Diary 7" from *Marshal South and the Ghost Mountain Chronicles: An Experiment in Primitive Living.* © 2005 by Marshal South. Used with permission of Sunbelt Publications, Inc.

Steinbeck, John. Excerpt from *Travels with Charley* by John Steinbeck. © 1961, 1962 by The Curtis Publishing Co., © 1962 by John Steinbeck, renewed 1990 by Elaine Steinbeck, Thom Steinbeck, and John Steinbeck IV. Used by permission of Viking Penguin, a division of Penguin Group (USA) LLC.

Straight, Susan. Excerpt from the introduction to *Inlandia: A Literary Journey through California's Inland Empire,* edited by Gayle Wattawa. © 2006 by Susan Straight. Reprinted by permission of The Richard Parks Agency.

Torrey, Bradford. Excerpt from *Field-Days in California* by Bradford Torrey. Boston: Houghton Mifflin Co., 1913.

Twain, Mark. Excerpts from *Roughing It* by Mark Twain. Hartford, CT: American Publishing Co., 1872.

Various. Poems numbered 1, 13, 21, 23, 25, and 27 from *Island: Poetry and History of Chinese Immigrants on Angel Island, 1910–1940,* edited and translated by Him Mark Lai, Genny Lim, and Judy Yung. © 1980 by the HOC DOI (History of Chinese Detained on Island) Project. Reprinted by permission of University of Washington Press.

Wilson, Darryl Babe. "Elam'ji" from *The Morning the Sun Went Down* by Darryl Babe Wilson. © 1998 by Darryl Babe Wilson. Reprinted by permission of Heyday.

ABOUT THE EDITORS

Malcolm Margolin is the founder and executive director of Heyday and the author/editor of several books, including *The Ohlone Way, The East Bay Out,* and *The Way We Lived: California Indian Stories, Songs, and Reminiscences.* He has received dozens of honors, including lifetime achievement awards from the San Francisco Bay Area Book Reviewers Association and the California Studies Association, a Community Leadership Award from the San Francisco Foundation, and a Cultural Freedom Award from the Lannan Foundation. In 2012 he received the Chairman's Commendation from the National Endowment for the Humanities, becoming the second person in the United States to receive the award.

Mariko Conner made her way back to her hometown of Berkeley after attending Carleton College in Minnesota. She has worked for Heyday since 2012. Her favorite state park is Montgomery Woods.

ABOUT THE CALIFORNIA
STATE PARKS FOUNDATION

The California State Parks Foundation (CSPF) was founded in 1969 by William Penn Mott, Jr., former director of both California's Department of Parks and Recreation and the National Park Service. With our 130,000 members, CSPF is the only statewide independent nonprofit organization dedicated to protecting, enhancing, and advocating for California's magnificent state parks. Since 1969, CSPF has raised more than $223 million to benefit state parks. CSPF is committed to improving the quality of life for all Californians by expanding access to the natural beauty, rich culture and history, and recreational and educational opportunities offered by California's 280 state parks—one of the largest state parks systems in the United States. To learn more, become a member, or make a donation, visit calparks.org.

CALIFORNIA
STATE PARKS
FOUNDATION

HEYDAY
into California

ABOUT HEYDAY

Heyday is an independent, nonprofit publisher and unique cultural institution. We promote widespread awareness and celebration of California's many cultures, landscapes, and boundary-breaking ideas. Through our well-crafted books, public events, and innovative outreach programs we are building a vibrant community of readers, writers, and thinkers.

THANK YOU

It takes the collective effort of many to create a thriving literary culture. We are thankful to all the thoughtful people we have the privilege to engage with. Cheers to our writers, artists, editors, storytellers, designers, printers, bookstores, critics, cultural organizations, readers, and book lovers everywhere!

We are especially grateful for the generous funding we've received for our publications and programs during the past year from foundations and hundreds of individual donors. Major supporters include:

Anonymous (6); Alliance for California Traditional Arts; Arkay Foundation; Judy Avery; Paul Bancroft III; Richard and Rickie Ann Baum; BayTree Fund; S. D. Bechtel, Jr. Foundation; Jean and Fred Berensmeier; Berkeley Civic Arts Program and Civic Arts Commission; Joan Berman; Nancy Bertelsen; John Briscoe; Lewis and Sheana Butler; Cahill Contractors, Inc.; California Civil Liberties Public Education Program; Cal Humanities; California Indian Heritage Center Foundation; California State Parks Foundation; Keith Campbell Foundation; Candelaria Fund; John and Nancy Cassidy Family Foundation, through Silicon Valley Community Foundation; Charles Edwin Chase; Graham Chisholm; The Christensen Fund; Jon Christensen; Community Futures Collective; Compton Foundation; Creative Work Fund; Lawrence Crooks; Nik Dehejia; Chris Desser and Kirk Marckwald;

Frances Dinkelspiel and Gary Wayne; The Durfee Foundation; Earth Island Institute; The Fred Gellert Family Foundation; Megan Fletcher and J.K. Dineen; Flow Fund Circle; Fulfillco; Furthur Foundation; The Wallace Alexander Gerbode Foundation; Nicola W. Gordon; Wanda Lee Graves and Stephen Duscha; David Guy; The Walter and Elise Haas Fund; Coke and James Hallowell; Steve Hearst; Cindy Heitzman; Historic Resources Group; Sandra and Charles Hobson; Donna Ewald Huggins; JiJi Foundation; Claudia Jurmain; Kalliopeia Foundation; Marty and Pamela Krasney; Robert and Karen Kustel; Guy Lampard and Suzanne Badenhoop; Christine Leefeldt, in celebration of Ernest Callenbach and Malcolm Margolin's friendship; Thomas Lockard; Thomas J. Long Foundation; Michael McCone; Giles W. and Elise G. Mead Foundation; Moore Family Foundation; Michael J. Moratto, in memory of Berta Cassel; Karen and Thomas Mulvaney; The MSB Charitable Fund; Richard Nagler; National Wildlife Federation; Humboldt Area Foundation, Native Cultures Fund; The Nature Conservancy; Nightingale Family Foundation; Northern California Water Association; Ohlone-Costanoan Esselen Nation; The David and Lucile Packard Foundation; Panta Rhea Foundation; David Plant; Alan Rosenus; The San Francisco Foundation; Greg Sarris; Sierra College; William Somerville; Martha Stanley; Radha Stern, in honor of Malcolm Margolin and Diane Lee; Roselyne Chroman Swig; Tides Foundation; Sedge Thomson and Sylvia Brownrigg; TomKat Charitable Trust; Sonia Torres; Michael and Shirley Traynor; The Roger J. and Madeleine Traynor Foundation; Lisa Van Cleef and Mark Gunson; John Wiley & Sons, Inc.; Peter Booth Wiley and Valerie Barth; Bobby Winston; Dean Witter Foundation; and Yocha Dehe Wintun Nation.

BOARD OF DIRECTORS

GETTING INVOLVED

To learn more about our publications, events, membership club, and other ways you can participate, please visit www.heydaybooks.com.

From top: *Prairie Creek Redwoods SP*, Dave Struthers. *Castle Crags SP*, Mike Shoys.

Clockwise from top: *McArthur-Burney Falls Memorial SP*, Hema Sukumar. Inset: *Flower, McArthur-Burney Falls Memorial SP*, David Jennings. *Grizzly Creek Redwoods SP*, Mike Shoys. *Grizzly Creek Redwoods SP*, Greg Hudson.

Clockwise from top: *Giant Bull Creek Redwood, Humboldt Redwoods SP*, Ivan Sohrakoff. *Eel Rock Overlook, Humboldt Redwoods SP*, Mike Shoys. *Bidwell Mansion SHP*, David Leeth.

Clockwise from top: *Donner Lake, Donner Memorial SP,* Kathy Yates. *Kokonee Salmon, Emerald Bay SP,* Sally Cullen. *Emerald Bay SP,* Gary Philbin. *Eagle Falls, Emerald Bay SP,* Steve Castro.

Clockwise from top: *Schooner Gulch SB*, Mike Ryan. *Marshall Gold Discovery SHP*, Kathleen Young. *Marshall Gold Discovery SHP*, Kathleen Young. *Governor's Mansion SHP*, Steve Wilson.

Clockwise from top: *Sutter's Fort SHP*, Claire Toney. *Fort Ross SHP*, John Pusey. *Meadow, Fort Ross SHP*, Dave Struthers.

Clockwise from top: *Indian Grinding Rock SHP*, Michael Hanrahan. *Indian Grinding Rock SHP*, Stephanie Gabler. *Jack London SHP*, Charles Tu. *Salamander, Jack London SHP*, Cyndy Shafer.

Clockwise from top: *Sonoma SHP*, Wayne Hsieh. *Sonoma SHP*, Michael Keiser. *Interior, Benicia Capitol SHP*, Richard Zimmerman. *Exterior, Benicia Capitol SHP*, Richard Zimmerman.

From top: *Mono Lake Tufa SNR*, Steve Albano. *Mono Lake Tufa SNR*, Bill Wight.

Clockwise from top: *East Peak, Mount Tamalpais SP*, Vincent James. *Angel Island SP*, Gary Philbin. *Angel Island SP*, Michael Hanrahan. *Mount Tamalpais SP*, Della Huff.

Clockwise from top: *Mount Diablo SP*, Michelle Smith. *Mount Diablo SP*, Vincent James. *Mount Diablo SP*, Vincent James. *Great Valley Grasslands SP*, Jay Cossey. *Jumping Spider, Great Valley Grasslands SP*, Jay Cossey. *Mount Diablo SP*, Scott Schmolke.

From top: *Pescadero SB*, Mike Shoys. *Millerton Lake SRA*, Kevin Moore. *Millerton Lake SRA*, Rennett Stowe.

From top: *Pacheco SP*, Miroslaw Wierzbicki. *Pacheco SP*, Keary Ingrum Jr.

From top: *Santa Cruz Mission SHP*, Richard Zimmerman. *Fremont Peak SP*, Jerry Ting.

Clockwise from top: *Monterey SHP*, Sara Skinner. *Bird, Point Lobos SNR*, Pat Ulrich. *Point Lobos SNR*, Kathy Yates. *Point Lobos SRN*, Kathy Barnhart.

From top: *Wild Iris Sunset, Pfeiffer Big Sur SP*, Greg Clure. *Beaming, Pfeiffer Beach Arch, Pfeiffer Big Sur SP*, Greg Clure.

Clockwise from top: *Cemetery in 1999, Colonel Allensworth SHP, Scott Braley. Docent John Chew at the forge, Colonel Allensworth SHP, Scott Braley. Photo of Black chaplains in the restored Allensworth home, Colonel Allensworth SHP, Scott Braley. Quilt made by Myrtle Hackett Tibbs on a bed in the restored Hackett home, Colonel Allensworth SHP, Scott Braley.*

Clockwise from top: *Hearst Castle, Hearst San Simeon SHM*, Hema Sukumar. *Hearst Castle, Hearst San Simeon SHM*, Sara Skinner. *Hearst Castle, Hearst San Simeon SHM*, Nick Angelis.

Clockwise from top: *Arthur B. Ripley Desert Woodland SP*, Howard W. Morris. Inset: *Antelope Valley California Poppy Preserve*, Kelly Kuntz. *Antelope Valley California Poppy Preserve*, Esther Corley.

Clockwise from top: *El Presidio de Santa Bárbara SHP*, Michael Imwalle. *El Presidio de Santa Barbára SHP*, Michael Imwalle. *El Presidio de Santa Bárbara SHP*, David McSpadden.

From top: *Los Angeles SHP*, Peter Bennett/Ambient Images. *California Citrus SHP*, Sharon Lee Koch.

Clockwise from top: *Boardwalk, Bolsa Chica SB*, Jason Larsen. *Bolsa Chica SB*, Julianne Bradford. *Surfer, Bolsa Chica SB*, Sean Scanlon.

Clockwise from top: *Salton Sea SRA*, David Herholz. *Salton Sea SRA*, David Herholz. *Salton Sea SRA*, David Herholz.

Clockwise from top: *Anza-Borrego Desert SP*, Ernie Cowan. *Old Town San Diego SHP*, Julianne Bradford. *Anza-Borrego Desert SP*, John Dotta.